THE AMBIVALENT ART OF KATHERINE ANNE PORTER

THE AMBIVALENT ART OF
KATHERINE ANNE PORTER

MARY TITUS

THE UNIVERSITY OF GEORGIA PRESS ATHENS AND LONDON

© 2005 by The University of Georgia Press
Athens, Georgia 30602
All rights reserved
Designed by Mindy Basinger Hill
Set in 10/13.5 Electra
Printed and bound by Maple-Vail
The paper in this book meets the guidelines for
permanence and durability of the Committee on
Production Guidelines for Book Longevity of the
Council on Library Resources.

Printed in the United States of America

09 08 07 06 05 C 5 4 3 2 1

Library of Congress Cataloging-in-Publication Data

Titus, Mary, 1956–
The ambivalent art of Katherine Anne Porter / Mary Titus.
    p. cm.
Includes bibliographical references and index.
ISBN-13: 978-0-8203-2756-3 (hardcover : alk. paper)
ISBN-10: 0-8203-2756-5 (hardcover : alk. paper)
1. Porter, Katherine Anne, 1890–1980—Criticism and
interpretation. 2. Women and literature—United States—
History—20th century. 3. Ambivalence in literature. I. Title.
PS3531.0752Z826 2005
  813'.52—dc22   2005017312

British Library Cataloging-in-Publication Data available

A thinking woman sleeps with monsters.
The beak that grips her, she becomes.

Adrienne Rich

TO MY MOTHER, JILL TITUS, IN GRATITUDE FOR A LIFETIME OF BOOKS

CONTENTS

ACKNOWLEDGMENTS

Katherine Anne Porter has been on my mind for many, many years, and she has been good company. I want to thank the many colleagues, friends, and fellow scholars who have provided invaluable support for this project. A special thank you to the members of the Katherine Anne Porter Society for years of rewarding conversation. I am grateful to St. Olaf College for sabbatical leave time and for funding travel to conferences and library collections. The National Endowment for the Humanities also provided financial support for travel to University of Maryland Libraries. Like all scholars, I can never sufficiently thank the many outstanding librarians who have helped me over the years, including those at Harry Ransom Humanities Research Center, University of Texas; the Library of Congress; and here at St. Olaf and Carleton Colleges. But I must especially acknowledge the generous, indefatigable support of Beth (Ruth M.) Alvarez, curator of literary manuscripts at University of Maryland Libraries. Thank you as well to Barbara Thompson Davis, trustee for the literary estate of Katherine Anne Porter, for permission to quote from Porter's extensive unpublished papers, and to George Platt Lynes II for allowing me to include some of his uncle's fascinating portraits of Porter. I also want to thank the Porter scholars who shared unpublished work with me, including Joan Givner and Anne Goodwyn Jones. Several of my colleagues read portions of this manuscript or provided expertise in special areas; thank you one and all, including Carol Holly, Judy Kutulas, Diana Postlethwaite, and Colin Wells. I also want to thank the people at the University of Georgia Press who have guided this book through the publication process. Last of all, a special and loving thank you to Chris, Ellen, and Laura.

Portions of chapter 3 appeared in "The Booby Trap of Love: Artist and Sadist in Katherine Anne Porter's Mexico Fiction," *Journal of Modern Literature*

16, no. 4. Reprinted by permission of Indiana University Press. Portions of chapter 4 appeared in "'Mingled Sweetness and Corruption': Katherine Anne Porter's 'The Fig Tree' and 'The Grave,'" *South Atlantic Review* 53, no. 2. Reprinted by permission of the South Atlantic Modern Language Association. Drafts of the story "Holiday" by Katherine Anne Porter quoted in chapter 5 courtesy of Harry Ransom Humanities Research Center, The University of Texas at Austin. Portions of chapter 5 copyright 1995 from "A Little Stolen Holiday" by Mary Titus, *Women's Studies* 25. Reproduced by permission of Taylor & Francis, Inc., http://www.taylorandfrancis.com. Portions of chapter 9 copyright 1991 from "Katherine Anne Porter's Miranda: The Agrarian Myth and Southern Womanhood" by Mary Titus in *Redefining Autobiography in Twentieth-Century Women's Fiction: An Essay Collection*, edited by Janice Morgan and Colette T. Hall. Garland Publishing Company. Reproduced by permission of Taylor & Francis, Inc., http://www.taylorandfrancis.com.

INTRODUCTION

"I will make beauty after my own secret thought," said

the Princess, "and I will also devise my own cruelties,

rejecting utterly the banal sufferings imposed by nature."

In a story composed during the 1920s but unpublished in her lifetime, Katherine Anne Porter created a brilliant and masochistic young woman who dedicates her life to art. The Princess glories publicly in her choice but weeps privately at its price—social alienation and childlessness. "Nature is abhorrent, a vulgarity," the Princess proclaims; she celebrates an eccentric creativity expressed in elaborate costume and stages a personal rebellion against proscribed gender roles.[1] Family and social law mass against Porter's Princess, and she dies, literally drowning beneath the weight of her dedication. The oppositions created in this early story, and the tensions they generate, are painful and absolute. On one side is life as an artist, a choice demanding all of body and mind; on the other side are social norms, in particular traditional gender roles. Porter's "The Princess" belongs in the company of other remarkable tales of female sexuality and art, such as Isak Dinesen's "The Blank Page."[2] Like Dinesen, Porter creates an imaginary world to make visible some of the underlying cultural assumptions of her own. This story (which is discussed in far greater detail in chapter 1) provides a standpoint for viewing Porter's literary achievement; evidence of its tensions appears everywhere in her work, from her earliest tales for children to her final opus, *Ship of Fools*.

"The Princess" is an early and extraordinarily important example of Porter's thinking about gender and identity. The story's complex and ambivalent contents merit summary. Society in "The Princess" defines female identity through the physical body; biological materiality determines role and ritual. Yet through her art, which takes the form of elaborate costume, the Princess makes it clear that the body can provide a stage for the imagination. When these two ideological positions meet, tensions arise. The Princess's sartorial art suggests that female identity is endlessly manipulable, performative. Yet, as the

1

story repeatedly reminds the reader, beneath its glittering surfaces the Princess's body remains simple female flesh, compressed and bruised by its elaborate encasements. In death the layers flow away and she lies naked, exposed and unadorned. The tensions evident in Porter's early-twentieth-century tale call to mind key debates in feminist theory between, as one theorist summarizes, "a desire for a materialist articulation of bodies and their liberation in indeterminate or multiple resignifications."[3] There is a real body in "The Princess," and there is great liberation through the "resignification" that occurs when that body becomes the vehicle of the artist's work. The tale also contains mixed emotion. The princess is an admirable artist and a tragic madwoman; her art looks gorgeous, but it hurts to wear it. The combination of her gleeful creativity and gruesome end, drowned and naked, corroborates Elizabeth Wingrove's wry response to poststructuralist efforts to shed biology entirely: "Gender identity is complexly coded through social roles and expressive practices, but its referential sine qua non is biological materiality: the drag show would come to a screeching halt—or at least it would become something else entirely—if the performers took off their clothes."[4]

That Porter should be so attentive to and deeply aware of the complexity of female sexuality and gender identity can be explained, in part, by the coming together of her ambitions, her cultural background, and her historical moment. Born in 1890 and living until 1980, Katherine Anne Porter witnessed almost a century of dramatic changes in the lives of American women. An acute observer, immersed in the cultural and social currents of her historic moment, Porter responded to these changes in her published and unpublished writings: fiction, essays, poetry, extensive private notes, and lively correspondence. Through all the years, from Texas to Paris, from one husband to the next, from poverty to relative affluence, Porter never relinquished her dominant ambition. At the age of seventy-three she told an interviewer, "I started out with nothing in the world but a kind of passion, driving desire. I don't know where it came from, and I do not know why—or why I have been so stubborn about it that nothing could deflect me. But this thing between me and my writing is the strongest bond I have ever had—stronger than any bond or engagement with any human being."[5] Her first biographer, Joan Givner, acknowledges this drive: "Her emotional center, the one continuing thread of her life, was her work as an artist."[6] Yet for Porter, being both a woman and an artist proved challenging, and the interrelations of these two roles became a fundamental subject of her work.

Porter's recurring and intense concern with the relations between "woman" and "artist" emerged, in part, as a response to her conservative nineteenth-century upbringing. Her childhood environment provided limited images of female creativity beyond self-beautification, pursuit of a marriage partner, childbearing, and domestic labor. Although later in life she liked to describe the worn literary classics that filled the family bookshelves, in unpublished notes titled "Reading Matter," she lists as early reading "Beauty and the Beast" and "Cinderella" as well as "a writer named 'The Duchess' whose heroines were made of alabaster and snow . . . [and] Ouida . . . I read at least half a dozen of her novels."[7] Stories of girls whose linked beauty and sweetness bring them wealth and happiness reinforced the childhood lessons that communicated the culturally endorsed belief that appearance and sexual status were of vital importance to a woman's value. In an unpublished autobiographical essay titled "Pull Dick—Pull Devil," Porter recalls that her father "liked vanity and decorative qualities in women" and "shamelessly favored the prettiest [daughter] in turn."[8] For Porter, as well as Willa Cather and other American women writers raised in rural communities, the most evident alternative to marital success through beauty and charm was the theater, in the form of the traveling companies with female performers that visited their areas. Although her grandmother considered the stage an indecent place for any proper young woman, Porter found it a resource for much-needed money. Porter's sister Gay recalled that their grandmother once whipped Katherine Anne ceremoniously and strenuously when she informed a visiting clergyman that she aspired to a career as an actress.

Porter resorted to the stage when she desperately needed money and had only her beauty and natural talent to rely on. In 1905 she and her sister offered lessons for women, listing themselves as "Misses Porter, studio of music, physical culture and dramatic reading."[9] She also briefly pursued a film career, and in 1914 she worked on the Lyceum Circuit, singing sentimental ballads in a beautiful red gown.[10] Certainly among members of "good" society in Porter's youth, public performance was socially unacceptable. Just as in later life she confronted issues of gender and performance with a divided mind, so too, given her sensitivity to her grandmother's (and dead mother's) nineteenth-century standards of female decorum, Porter must have felt both excitement and discomfort about these early forays onto the stage.

Porter's concern with questions of gender and creativity was also intensified and enriched by her cultural moment. Her generation witnessed some of the most dramatic and richly debated changes in female gender roles. Raised by her grandmother, Porter grew up listening to the edicts that controlled the private and public behavior of conservative white nineteenth-century women. In her fictional portrayal of her grandmother's power, Porter examines both the creativity and limitations arising from what we now call the nineteenth-century "cult of domesticity."[11] Porter's mother, although she died young, belonged to the generation of the New Woman, those intrepid pioneers who filled the settlement houses of the burgeoning cities and attended some of the first women's colleges. The New Woman appears in Porter's marvelous portrait of Cousin Eva in *Old Mortality*. Here Miranda—Porter's fictional self-representative—listens to her fierce older cousin's battle for women's suffrage and thinks, "it seemed heroic and worth suffering for, but discouraging too, to those who came after: Cousin Eva so plainly had swept the field clear of opportunity."[12] Like Cousin Eva, the New Woman of the late nineteenth century often rejected marriage for a career and political action. As Carroll Smith-Rosenberg notes, "From the 1870's through the 1920's, between 40 and 60 percent of women college graduates did not marry at a time when only 10 percent of all American women did not."[13] In the portrait of independent Cousin Eva, one can trace not only Porter's admiration for the generation of women that preceded her but also the influence of the social arguments that gradually discredited their story. The women of Katherine Anne Porter's generation, who followed in the footsteps of the New Woman, found their sexuality the subject of public debate and scholarly, scientific study by the sexologists. They witnessed popular culture's adaptation to and ultimate appropriation of women's revisionary struggles, including the transformation of the New Woman from self-made heroine to "invert" and old maid. Thus, although Porter's Eva is clearly admirable, she is also notably "chinless," "withered," and bitter.

This attention to female sexuality, with its accompanying social scrutiny of marriage and career options for women, impelled Porter's thinking about gender identity. As the historian of sexuality Christina Simmons attests, "The years 1900 to 1930 were a period of dramatic and self-conscious cultural, political, and intellectual change in the United States, the beginning of a shift from a Victorian to a modern mentality in which feminism and female public roles, the emergence of sexological science and modern psychology, and the effects of an ethnically diverse urban culture conjoined to undermine Victorian marriage and sexual codes. This change occurred especially among sophisticated and educated urbanites, artists, and intellectuals and most publicly and intensively in major cities like New York and Chicago."[14] These changes encouraged sexual radicalism in many forms, to which Porter responded both directly and indirectly in her writing. Certainly the changes fed anxiety about her vocational choice, for, ironically, sexual liberation brought with it other forms of sexual control that questioned female independence. Although the lightweight, liberated "flapper" replaced the sterner and more serious New Woman, with the flapper came the ideology of companionate marriage, which sought to channel women's increasing autonomy and newly recognized capacity for sexual desire. "Companionate marriage represented the attempt of mainstream marriage ideology to adapt to women's perceived new social and sexual power. . . . [It] directed female energies toward men and marriage."[15] The acknowledgment of female sexual desire as equal to male, promoted by the sexologists and their popularizers, brought with it a new perspective on gender roles. The nineteenth-century concept of a separate women's sphere became potentially divisive and threatening to heterosexual hegemony, for it directed women's sexual and economic power away from the heterosexual establishment.

As a result of these cultural shifts in the ideology surrounding women's sexuality, Porter and her contemporaries, particularly other women artists and professionals, experienced powerful social pressures not to make choices that could potentially separate them from the heterosexual path of marriage and childbearing. Frequently this pressure came in the form of accusations of sexual deviance. "By the 1920s charges of lesbianism had become a common way to discredit women professionals, reformers, and educators."[16] As early as 1910 Havelock Ellis had correlated female success with inversion, noting that many of the "distinguished women in all ages and in all fields of activity . . . have frequently displayed some masculine traits."[17] For lesbian women, the acknowledgment of "inversion" as an identifiable and inborn quality was somewhat liberating, for it named and thus acknowledged them, and the association of lesbianism with "masculine traits" influenced women like Radclyffe Hall to associate lesbianism with masculine attire as well as "physiologically and psychologically masculine traits in women."[18] However, for a heterosexual and often heterosexist woman such as Porter, the suggestions that her ambitious career manifested sexual difference were deeply disturbing. Despite her personal unease, Porter was intrigued by her homosexual compatriots and found their playful experimentation with gender performance and cross-dressing both attractive and repellent. This interest, supported no doubt by her early experiences with theater and time spent watching Sergei Eisenstein filming, generated her attention to gesture and costume, the awareness we see in her fiction that "gender is instituted through the stylization of the body . . . the mundane way in which bodily gestures, movements, and enactments of various kinds constitute the illusion of an abiding gendered self."[19] Witness her depiction of Adam checking his wristwatch in "Pale Horse, Pale Rider."

The rich turmoil of the 1920s, with its radical questioning of sexual and social order, inspired some of Porter's finest fiction, but ultimately she found the decade's disorders threatening. In the 1930s, as she drew increasingly near to members of the Agrarian writers community, she turned to the South and her own past, part memory, part legend, to craft both an ambitious family history and a new public presence. The conservative politics of the Agrarians included a narrow view of women's place and potential, which Porter increasingly seemed to embrace, particularly in public or in the more casual places of publication, such as the pages of women's magazines. As Lewis P. Simpson notes in *The Fable of the Southern Writer*, the Agrarians were particularly self-conscious about their role as public southerners: "writers like Tate and Porter might at times specifically identify themselves as personal representations of the southern experience of defeat."[20] Porter's stories of the South, especially those in *The Old Order* and *Old Mortality*, offer complex and critical views of southern womanhood, but as Porter herself took on the role of southern lady of letters, she increasingly performed a class-bound, highly feminized version of female identity. In her final years of productivity, her intense questioning of gender ideology in her fiction slowly changed into anger and bitterness, and the female characters of her 1962 novel *Ship of Fools* appear trapped in narrow lives filled with romantic disappointment and sexual betrayal.

Katherine Anne Porter certainly rebelled against her upbringing, seeking far more expansive and varied opportunities for creative expression as well as intellectual, cultural, and sexual freedom. No doubt her unhappy early marriage at age sixteen, the changes in women's lives that mark her historical moment, her restless and imaginative character, and countless other influences provided impetus for breaking from the narrowly defined roles for women provided by her early environment. Yet her rebellion was characterized, in Givner's words, by "a complicated ambivalence" due to the influence of her childhood and the pressures on female independence that characterized the 1920s.[21] Raised to admire women—and herself—for decorative beauty, Porter resembles other women writers in the close connections she both creates and questions between the female body and art. At the same time, she never relinquished a belief that domesticity, marriage, and childbearing denote female success; as Givner states, it is notable "how closely linked her idea of femininity was with fertility."[22] A turn away from women's traditional roles toward the independent creativity of an artistic career represented, Porter feared, a turn away from what she had learned was natural to female identity. To become an artist was to deny her sexuality; it was to become, in Porter's own words, "monstrous." Among her papers are notes for a review of Marian Storm's 1937 biography *The Life of Saint Rose* that struggle with questions of gender and vocation:

> The body of woman is the repository of life, and when she destroys herself it is important. It is important because it is not natural, and woman is natural or she is a failure. . . . Therefore women saints, like women artists are monstrosities. . . . You might say that if they are saints or artists they are not women.[23]

Porter rewrote these words, eliminating the link she had made between the woman saint and the woman artist. Her final version is as follows: "Saints create themselves as works of art; their lives are among the most mysterious manifestations of genius. As in all great works of art, there are terrible and even monstrous elements in the beauty of these lives."[24] Both versions are of interest. Explicit in Porter's notes is the belief that a woman is defined by her biological capabilities; her body "is the repository of life," and if she denies this she "destroys herself": women artists are "monstrosities" and are "not women." "If we define the monster as a bodily entity that is anomalous and deviant vis-à-vis the norm," as Rosi Braidotti argues in her essay, "Mothers, Monsters, Machines," then the woman intentionally choosing an "unnatural" vocation is indeed monstrous.[25] Although Porter erased both the terms "woman" and "artist" in her published version, her language retains the intense unease with difference. Hopeful here, however, is the recognition of genius and beauty, compensations for the "mysterious" and "terrible" intentional life.

Overall, the influences of her family upbringing and early experiences created in Katherine Anne Porter what Sandra Gilbert and Susan Gubar in the 1980s usefully termed the woman writer's "anxiety of authorship," a fear that her vocation is unnatural for a woman, that her artistic labors leave her "unsexed," that her gender and her art cannot be reconciled.[26] In this anxiety, Porter joins company with many other women writers from the late nineteenth and early twentieth centuries. In her study of several American women writers concerned about their vocational aspirations, Deborah Barker insightfully argues, "these writers were in many ways very conventional in their attitudes toward gender and aesthetics, yet it was their very desire to be identified as artists that instigated their investigations into the complex gender assumptions" about art and the artist. Like Porter, these women feared, in Barker's apt phrasing, that "the female artist was not simply an anomaly but an oxymoron."[27]

Throughout her long career, Porter repeatedly probed cultural arguments about female creativity, a woman's maternal legacy, romantic love, and sexual identity, always with startling acuity, and often with painful ambivalence. As a result, much of Porter's writing, perhaps all of her best known work, serves as a medium for what this study terms her gender-thinking: her serious and sustained examination of the interrelated issues of art, gender, and identity.[28] This gender-thinking always remained at the heart of her creative work, from her earliest tales for children to her last and longest work, the novel *Ship of Fools*. For many reasons, Porter's ongoing gender-thinking did not yield single, definitive answers. Rather, her fictional processing tended to open up contradiction and complexity. As Janis Stout observes in her intellectual biography of Porter, "her thought and her sensibility . . . were structured not by a single meta-belief or truth-statement but by variance and tension. . . . she responded to and reflected her time, in all its countercurrents and bewilderments, with extraordinary sensitivity."[29] In his work on the relations between Porter's intellectual contexts and her writing, Robert Brinkmeyer fruitfully employs Bakhtin's concept of dialogism to highlight Porter's "inquiring and dissenting sensibility," the source of her fiction's fascinating tangles and tensions.[30] Early in her career, Porter herself made light of her intellectual impressibility, identifying it as a trait of her sex: "Being feminine, our mind makes itself up brand-new every hour or so, and though it keeps life from being dull, it also complicates things a trifle now and again."[31] Rather than set her words aside as a bit of tongue-in-cheek sexism, which is a temptation, it is more interesting to note that they predicate a view of women's thinking that much more recently has been used to characterize female modernist narrative strategies. In their groundbreaking work on women writers in the 1980s, theorists from Marianne Hirsch to Sandra Gilbert and Susan Gubar have identified "oscillation and contradiction," Hirsch's terms, or "double consciousness," Gilbert and Gubar's, as "paradigm[s] for the discussion of women's writing within feminist criticism."[32]

In her fiction exploring questions of gender and sexuality, Porter does oscillate and contradict; her texts are often comic, contentious, and conflicted. Like her contemporaries, she found gender issues front and center during her cultural moment and, again, like many of them, she was not of one mind about new ideas of identity and sexuality. Attracted and repelled, insecure yet often judgmental, she attempted, with fascinating results, to encapsulate it all in her fiction. In this writing, Porter repeatedly confronted interpretations of female experience and representations of female identity in her culture, at times acknowledging their appeal to her, at times attempting alternative formulations. Occasionally, as in "Holiday" and "Pale Horse, Pale Rider," she not only critiques the gender configurations of her cultural moment but also attempts visionary and revisionary reconfigurations. Because she witnessed a remarkable range of female gender roles and ideological takes on female sexuality—from those of her grandmother to those of revolutionary Mexico, 1920s New York, and 1930s Paris—she was keenly aware of the socially constructed quality of female identity. From her own lived experience, she knew firsthand how "sex/gender systems," in the language of contemporary theory, "are transformed—contingently, contextually—as a function of the transformations of political, economic, and religious ideologies."[33] Each and every such transformation, Porter knew, has implications for a woman choosing to be an artist. In her own life, she chose, increasingly, to play a highly feminized public role of southern lady, emphasizing certain portions of her own and her family's past while repressing others. But where her public appearance became increasingly performative, her writing never relinquished its intense drive for truth in all of its complexity: "Only there," in her fiction, as her biographer Joan Givner affirms, "did the austere truth-teller in Katherine Anne Porter consistently triumph over the theatrical public performer."[34]

During her life and even more so after her death, Porter has benefited from the attention of biographers and critics, some already mentioned, whose work has contextualized and enriched her achievement. Joan Givner's authorized biography in 1982 (revised in 1991) was followed in 1995 by Janis Stout's intellectual biography, *Katherine Anne Porter: A Sense of the Times.* At the same time two ambitious overviews of her work identified core sociopolitical contexts for her work: Thomas Walsh's 1992 *Katherine Anne Porter and Mexico* and Robert Brinkmeyer's 1993 *Katherine Anne Porter's Artistic Development: Primitivism, Traditionalism, and Totalitarianism.* Both draw on newly available biographical materials, published and unpublished. Accompanying book-length studies of Porter have been collections of hitherto scattered or archived writings. In 1990 Isabel Bayley brought out a selection from Porter's letters; in 1991 Darlene Harbour Unrue published Porter's book reviews and in 1994 Porter's poetry; and in 1996 Ruth Alvarez and Thomas Walsh brought together a rich assortment of Porter's early prose. Over the years many excellent essays have provided feminist readings of Porter's work, and Janis Stout includes a provocative chapter titled "The Issue of Gender" in her biography; however, since Jane Krause DeMouy's 1983 *Katherine Anne Porter's Women,* no book-length study has focused on gender questions in the work of this important modernist woman writer. The biographical materials accumulated since Porter's death and the now available unpublished or out-of-print writings offer a rich lode of hitherto unmined material. *The Ambivalent Art of Katherine Anne Porter* draws on these newly available materials as well as Porter's extensive unpublished papers collected at the University of Maryland, bringing to them current insights from cultural studies and feminist and gender theory in order to illuminate her brilliant and complex gender-thinking and thereby place her creative achievement in a new light.

Like all creative work, Porter's fiction emerges from and is in complex relation to a network of influences, central among them her moment in cultural history, her biographical experience, and both the possibilities and limitations of her medium, language. Although all these influences are necessarily interrelated, *Ambivalent Art* often chooses to focus on one or another, seeking the richest context or most trenchant view. At the same time, this study also draws on a range of theoretical approaches, changing critical perspectives as one or another becomes more appropriate or productive. The chapters that follow do not offer an all-inclusive reading of Porter's achievement; instead, they illuminate aspects of her gender-thinking, bringing together interrelated stories, poems, essays, and unpublished materials, selecting what seems, to this reader, most intriguing and instructive. Because *Ambivalent Art* is in no way meant to be an exhaustive analysis of Porter's work, readers may miss discussion of a favorite story. I encourage them to extend approaches to Porter's gender-thinking on their own. Porter herself never remained fixed in her thinking; she was complex, contradictory, and ambivalent. I see no need for any one of us to limit our reading of her work to one lens when she was such a marvelous shape shifter.

Following Porter's career for the most part in chronological order, *Ambivalent Art* begins with a discussion of an extraordinary and provocative unfinished story, "The Princess" (newly available in print), in which Porter, near the start of her career, took on directly the complex interrelations of "woman" and "artist." "The Princess," already briefly discussed above, presents a young woman resisting her culture's control of female sexuality by inventing art. Through this brilliant, creative, isolated, mad, and ultimately punished heroine, Porter explores multiple aspects of gender proscription and female creativity. Because "The Princess" articulates concerns that recur throughout the rest of Porter's writing career, the story is a touchstone for this study, and each chapter that follows the first opens with an allusion to its complex and ambivalent contents.

Chapter 2 moves back approximately a decade to look at Porter's earliest published fiction, magical and exotic tales that first appeared anonymously.

These "retold" tales all demonstrate Porter's concern for women's power; comparison with their originals reveals how thoroughly and carefully she sought to highlight female capability as she revised. "The Shattered Star," "The Faithful Princess," "The Magic Ear Ring," and "The Adventures of Hadji" explore aspects of female identity and begin addressing questions of female authority and creative power. They also present her early romantic view of the woman artist as an alienated visionary. Her first acknowledged published fictional work, "María Concepción," continues this exploration of female power while addressing the fashionable fascination with primitivism.

Chapter 3 looks at a related group of early stories in which Porter explores women's simultaneous attraction to and rejection of the culturally available roles of beautiful object and muse/inspiration for the creative labor of the male artist. Portraying sadomasochistic pleasures connected to female objectification, these stories, including "Flowering Judas," "Virgin Violeta," "The Martyr," and "The Lovely Legend," address with unflinching honesty women's symbolic role within patriarchal culture.

Reflecting the wide and diverse range of Porter's gender-thinking, chapter 4 examines fiction concerned with an entirely different subject, a woman writer's relation to her mother and maternity. Like Virginia Woolf and other female modernist writers, Porter was interested in questions of the woman artist's maternal legacy. In several stories, including "The Fig Tree" and "The Grave," and in related poetry, she addresses with some ambivalence the ties between mothers and daughters, language and memory, seeking answers to crucial questions for a creative woman: what is the source of language for a woman writer? Is it connected to the mother's absence? Is there a mother-tongue? Does reconnection with her maternal legacy nourish or stifle the woman artist?

If a woman artist is a monster or a madwoman, as Porter seems to have anxiously considered her at times, what happens if she embraces these roles with laughter? Chapter 5 employs Bakhtin's theories of carnival and cultural release to illuminate the comic and radical content of "Holiday," a story in which an isolated and alienated woman writer accepts her otherness and rides far away from the world of patriarchy on a road less taken.

Chapter 6 attempts to shed light on the mysterious connections Porter created between the gestation of "Holiday" and intimate events in her own life. In 1924 Porter completed the story while awaiting the birth of a child, who was stillborn just over two weeks later. Her letters to Genevieve Taggard connect this child's conception to the composition of "Holiday," and the legacy of these events reverberates through "Pale Horse, Pale Rider" and two unfinished stories,

"A Season of Fear" and "A Vision of Heaven" and intensifies the connections she recurrently makes between the woman artist's body and her art.

Chapters 7 and 8 address ways in which Porter responded to the radical rethinking of gender roles and changing social practices of the twenties. Romantic love and traditional marriage both came under scrutiny in that decade as women claimed new independence and sexual freedom. Porter viewed both traditional and modern views of heterosexual relations with suspicion and wrote several stories in which women find that either independence diminishes their lives or commitment constrains their creativity. Three very different stories, "Theft," "The Cracked Looking Glass," and "The Spivvelton Mystery," all examine female independence, economics, and heterosexual relationships. Homosexual relationships also interested Porter, as they did her contemporaries, and she responded to the new awareness and visibility of the gay community. Like other modernist writers, Porter employed costume as a metaphor for gender roles and sexual identity. In letters and both published and unpublished essays, she expressed strong homophobia, yet in fiction she used costume, especially cross-dressing, to expose and undermine patriarchal control of gender roles. She also enjoyed a long, personally sustaining relationship with a close-knit gay community, including the photographer George Platt Lynes, for whom she enjoyed posing in elaborate gowns. Concepts of camp and cross-dressing illuminate the complexity of her response to the changing gender roles and new sexual liberations of the twenties, especially in two of her finest fictional works, "Hacienda" and "Pale Horse, Pale Rider."

Friendships with members of the Agrarian writing community and her own longing to revise and thereby order the painful disorders of her childhood encouraged Porter to increasingly describe herself as a sympathetic member of the southern gentility. Chapter 9 looks at Porter's increasingly strong self-identification as a "Southerner by tradition and inheritance."[35] This chapter also compares Porter's southern identification to that of a younger, but equally ambitious, woman writing about the South, Flannery O'Connor, and examines the complex gender-thinking about southern womanhood in Porter's fiction, most notably in the short novel *Old Mortality*. The conservatism nascent in Porter's attraction to the Agrarian cause strengthened through the 1940s and 1950s and was accompanied by a narrowing of thinking about gender and identity. Anger tended to replace ambivalence, and comedy became bitter edged. Jenny Brown, the young woman artist of *Ship of Fools*, suffers all the personal anxiety and social adversity that Porter herself endured. To the complex and contradictory gender-thinking about all the changes Porter witnessed in women's lives from the late nineteenth to the mid-twentieth century, *Ship of Fools* offers a final scathing portrayal of sexual relationships, of unhappy men and women seemingly unable to change.

Ambivalent Art establishes Porter's significance as a *woman* writer, in whose beautifully crafted fiction we can trace a brilliant artist's shifting and complex response to the changing discourses on sexuality and gender in American culture during the first half of the twentieth century. In the end, an understanding of the ways in which gender shaped Porter's achievement illuminates that of her contemporaries. The tensions and ambivalence inscribed in her fiction as well as the vocational anxiety and gender performance of her life tell us much about what happens when an ambitious young woman resolves to bring together in her own life those two never simple roles: woman and artist.

CHAPTER ONE

THE PRINCESS OF ART

Sometime around 1927, Katherine Anne Porter struggled to complete a strange and bitter tale about a young woman who has dedicated her life to creating art. The result, although unfinished, represents an extraordinary document in Porter's exploration of gender roles and sexuality and, indeed, in the history of women's writing. "The Princess" creates a symbolic world that serves to define the cultural conflicts surrounding a woman artist. For Porter, the intellectual freedom allowed in an invented world was clearly libratory, providing a landscape in which she could explore dangerously charged materials with less risk because she made no claims for representational veracity.[1] The story presents with mingled irony and bitter humor the generational replication of a gender system, the social control of female sexuality, and a young woman's attempt to escape cultural conscription through the invention of art. "The Princess" is a remarkable and disturbing tale. Much revised, and incomplete, especially near its close, it yet represents a crucial document in Porter's gender-thinking, raising key questions that she continued to explore throughout her career.[2]

In the imaginary kingdom of "The Princess," daily life is dominated by a religious ideology "dedicated to the love and worship of nature."[3] The kingdom's inhabitants live naked and unshorn for most of their lives, rejecting anything that would alter what they view as their natural state. Technological developments, they believe, could lead their nation in the disastrous way of their neighbors, "the Ruzanites who put their food in the fire before eating it, so that their stomachs rotted while they yet lived" (232). Women's lives are strictly regulated in this kingdom, and marriage and childbearing are viewed as their natural goals. Under the authority of a powerful High Priestess, rituals are built around the stages of female physical development; the clothing allowed women functions solely to identify the reproductive status of its wearer's body. Prepubescent girls and women past the age of childbearing cover their bodies, wearing white or plain gray shifts respectively. When they reach puberty, girls undergo a springtime ritual at the temple in which a male acolyte takes their virginity. During this "feast of marriage with the god" (230), they discard their white shifts; from then on they remain naked until menopause.

Into this rigid "natural" order Porter sets a rebel. At the proper age of thirteen, her Princess, sole child of the kingdom's current rulers, refuses to participate in the "rites of the spring sowing" (230). In response to demands that she "cast her shift upon the fire" (228) and undertake the ceremony, she dons first one more shift and then many heavy, colorful layers. As her protest builds and solidifies, she invents and then perfects the decorative arts, training her handmaidens in weaving, dyeing, silkworm cultivation, and increasingly sophisticated metal work. Porter's Princess and her maiden attendants become marvelously skilled, "beating heated metal into divers shapes, and fashioning splendid ornaments of brightly coloured stones" (231). All of their art is dedicated to one purpose— covering the Princess's body in increasingly elaborate materials.

From the moment she refuses to participate in the temple ceremony, Porter's Princess endures intense pressure to reverse her decision and conform to cultural dictates. For five years she ignores the prayers and threats of the High Priestess and her parents, the King and Queen. Although she attends the temple ceremonies each spring, she remains "by the side of her mother" (230). Finally, despite the Princess's odd appearance and demeanor, a young acolyte at the temple falls in love with her: "he felt a strangeness about her, and a terrible fated loneliness, and afterward he could not forget her" (230–31). When the Princess is eighteen, this acolyte asks the King for her hand, and he quickly consents, telling the Queen, "whoever wants this mad girl may have her and welcome" (231). But the Princess has other plans. When the marriage ceremony occurs at the temple, she wears so many heavy, ornate layers that she can barely walk. Rejecting the High Priestess's final command to "disrobe and cast upon the fire your heretical garments" (232), she walks out of the temple with her lover. The two dedicate themselves to "the beauty [the Princess] created out of a dream and a vision" rather than the beliefs and symbols of their culture (233).

Although the Princess has agreed to marry the acolyte, she rejects all sexual contact. In response to her lover's amorous pleas, she increases her ornate armor until she is entirely encased in her art: "an image in stiff woven robes of gold, with corselet and girdle of jewels, and a tall crown of pointed crystals, and the face of the image was a golden mask, with eyes of amethyst" (234). Along with the decorative arts, the Princess develops a philosophy that exalts artifice over nature. "Nature is abhorrent," she professes, "a vulgarity perpetually to be denied by the soul of man" (234). Her philosophy, her art, and her elaborate, disturbing presence all begin to threaten the religious order that regulates her kingdom. The women in particular fear her, calling her "mad" and a "heretic" and asking each other, "Since when has she become a god, to create with her hands?" (237). Of all the kingdom's women, the High Priestess most fears and hates the Princess and repeatedly commands her to strip off her decorative armor and participate in the rituals of sexual initiation. In her anger, the Priestess foretells the Princess's fate with an oracular proclamation: "Remember that the holy river shall wash away all that is dust." She decrees that "the fruitless woman may not inherit the throne" (233, 235), thereby cutting the Princess off from her inheritance.

Finally the Princess must face a sacred tribunal. While the judges interrogate and sentence her, she laughs, mocking them behind her golden mask. However, when she hears their "sentence of death"—"escort [the Princess] down to the river's edge at sunrise of tomorrow and with due and appropriate ceremonies . . . drown her as a heretic"—she weeps, "the tears rolling down the mask to her jewelled hands" (238). Porter worked through several possible scenes depicting the death of her heretical artist-Princess; as a result, the ending of her manuscript is particularly fragmented. However, all of her drafts show the High Priestess's prophecy coming true. In the most fully developed draft, the one chosen by the editors of *The Uncollected Early Prose*, the Princess flees at night from her prison tower accompanied by her devoted acolyte, who is now called the Poet. They pass under "a great scared faced moon" to a lake where the Princess refuses one last time to unmask herself for her lover (239). Instead, "she leaned straight over the brink of the lake, and slipped into the water like a falling stone" (239). Deep under the clear water she undergoes a sea-change, the water gently washing away her jewels and heavy robes until she lies "naked and glistening" in the transparent depths: "the crown slipped away and released the long red hair that streamed out like a soft flame, the mask slipped and fell aside" (239). Depending on different fragments among Porter's papers, the acolyte suffers several fates after the Princess's death. In two very brief fragments he joins her, slipping "quietly into the water." In a much more lengthy version, again the version chosen by Porter's editors, the acolyte, or Poet, lives on to create songs about the Princess and his love for her.

"The Princess" is an extraordinary and provocative text, and it is intriguing to speculate about Porter's sources. Ruth Alvarez suggests that the story may be indebted to T. A. Willard's account of the legend of the Mayan princess Ix-Lol-Nicte in *The City of the Sacred Well*,[4] which Porter reviewed for the *New York Herald Tribune* on February 6, 1927. However, another source may lie in James George Frazer's extraordinarily influential *The Golden Bough: A*

Study in Magic and Religion.[5] In his discussion of South American religions, Frazer describes vestal virgins who serve a temple, guarding the sacred flame. In Peru, he says, these "virgins were of the royal family. . . . Besides tending the holy fire, they had to weave and make all the clothes worn by the Inca and his legitimate wife." The virgins lived in a convent where "all the furniture . . . down to the pots, pans, and jars, were of gold and silver" (244). Frazer then points to a similar arrangement in Mexico (which would certainly have been of great interest to Porter), where girls "offered incense to the idols, wove cloths for the service of the temple. . . . They were clad all in white, without any ornament" (245).

Images similar to Frazer's do appear in Porter's text, especially the royal descent of the temple virgins, weaving and precious metals, and the plain white shifts. But Porter may also have gathered inspiration from the host of other texts surrounding and springing from Frazer's. Late-nineteenth and early-twentieth-century culture was fascinated with sexuality, and studies of the sexual practices of cultures past and present were commonplace. In his study *The Literary Impact of the Golden Bough*, John Vickery quotes one of Porter's peers who expresses fascination with issues similar to those addressed in "The Princess," in particular ways in which "the sexual instinct has moulded the religious consciousness of our race."[6] Chapter 2 of this study will probe Porter's initial attraction to but final disenchantment with primitivism, an attraction that may have led her to Frazer and his associates.

Overall, "The Princess" is remarkable for the complexity of its gender-thinking. In this text, Porter sought to represent and scrutinize the several institutions that together work to direct women toward marriage and childbearing, exploring the ways in which these interrelated social systems work to control female sexuality and define women's choices. The Princess's kingdom bases gender/sexual identity fully on an ideology of biologism: "social and cultural factors are regarded as the effects of biologically given causes. In particular biologism usually ties women closely to the functions of reproduction and nurturance."[7] One's biological status is marked on the body by regulated costume and in the life span by custom and ritual. What is institutionalized finds its verification and justification through invocation of the natural; custom, being grounded in the body, is termed natural and hence not open to question or change. Porter's view of a rigid biologism comes through in the edicts against haircuts and cooking in "The Princess." There is clear irony in her comic images and parodic language when she describes how no man "hindered his beard" and "food must be eaten without the pollution of fire."

The definition, boundaries, and articulations of the natural are all cultural constructs at the service of ideology, and "The Princess" delineates strikingly how claims for gender roles based in nature may serve patriarchal social control. The kingdom's purported obedience to natural orders overlays its actual, active construction of gender identity. The exaltation of nature and debasement of culture in this imaginary kingdom work to control women. Most clearly in the ritual Porter calls "the rites of the spring sowing," in which maidens go "in a procession to the inner temple to bid farewell to their virginity," and in the associated sign system of shifts and nakedness, one can see how reverence for nature simultaneously masks and supports a cultural order whose central goal is regulation of the processes of female sexuality (230). Once it is named natural, Porter's text teaches, the cultural becomes inevitable and unquestioned.

In "The Princess" Porter's gender-thinking highlights ways in which patriarchal social systems collaborate in perpetuating and enforcing what they have defined as nature. From its legal system to its religious rituals and forms of dress, all the practices of the story's imaginary kingdom seek to confine women to a biological destiny. In the kingdom, for example, inheritance is limited to women who are both married and fertile. As the High Priestess warns the King and Queen, "Tell the Princess . . . that if she scorns and rejects the natural office of motherhood it is written that she will never rule over this kingdom" (235). Religion and law work together to encourage all women, including the Princess, to pursue heterosexual relations and childbearing. Religious sanctions are not only supported but also enforced by laws and courts. Thus the High Priestess's oracular condemnation of the Princess finds more secular expression in a legal sentence; while the High Priestess names the Princess a heretic, it is the court that condemns her to death. It is interesting to note that both here and in "The Adventures of Hadji," another early story discussed in chapter 2 of this study, Porter sets her heroine's climactic confrontation with cultural authority in a courtroom. But where in "Hadji" the female protagonist overwhelms authority with her verbal skill, proving herself master of the law's own terms, here the Princess, enraged and deeply alienated, entirely refuses to participate in her culture's rituals. She remains masked and contemptuous, responding to the law with mocking laughter. To even recognize her culture's governing authorities is to give them some validation. Any such validation would compromise the absolute freedom of her vision.

In its representation of the relations between women's traditional roles and their creativity, "The Princess" demonstrates particularly complex and brilliant gender-thinking. Like the majority of Porter's other explorations of sexuality and art, the tale does not embrace a single stance, but rather provides a complex and conflicted view. On one level, the story opens up gender identity itself, hazarding questions about its substantiality, whether female gender is solely a product of costume and performance or rooted in something essential, if not biology then some sort of natural and fulfilling urge to nurture, some characteristic of femaleness. The Princess's choice of costume as her medium points to gender as something entirely fabricated. In the words of Judith Butler, "The gendered body is performative": "acts, gestures, enactments, generally construed, are *performative* in the sense that the essence or identity that they otherwise purport to express are *fabrications* manufactured and sustained through corporeal signs and other discursive means."[8] The Princess's costuming is ongoing, endless; she is constantly "devising new ways of covering herself" (231) and staging her glittering presence before her people. She is repeatedly described with language that emphasizes this constructedness: "an image with the voice of a woman," for example, or "an image wearing a mask" (234, 239). At the end she is not one, but many: "Every one remembered her in a different guise, so that at last there were so many legends, no one knew which was the truth" (237). If a woman is white-shifted until puberty, naked until menopause, and grey-shifted thereon until death—what is the Princess? She is clearly disturbing: "maidens blushed for shame of her strangeness"; "not even the gods know what manner of woman is concealed in that robe!" (231). Through costume, the Princess destabilizes her culture's gender system, calling into question the signification of a woman. Law, religion, family—all unite to control or destroy her.

The forms the Princess's art takes, decorative cloth and jewelry, also call attention to Porter's interest in the female body as the medium of art, a practice deeply embedded in Western culture. As Bloch and Ferguson note at the start of their history of misogyny, "the linking of the feminine with the aesthetic, the decorative, the ornamental, and the materially contingent . . . as one of the deep-seated mental structures of the west . . . has served historically to define women as being outside of history."[9] In a richly suggestive essay from the early 1980s, "The Blank Page and the Issues of Female Creativity," Susan Gubar explored the possible meanings and consequences of linking women's art with women's bodies. Because male texts often employ women as art objects, on whose bodies they inscribe their creative vision, and because women for generations were denied opportunities to create art of their own, Gubar argued, many women experience their bodies as "the only accessible medium for self-expression": "the woman who cannot become an artist can nevertheless turn herself into an artistic object."[10] This is precisely what Porter's Princess does, and it is an act both painful and powerful. Obsessed with her appearance, the

Princess is a monster, and her "creativity has been deformed by being channeled into self-destructive narcissism." She finds it difficult to see outside herself or to love anything but her own objectification.[11] The Princess makes herself into a spectacle, her life and her body her text.

Porter's fairy tale princess has real-life counterparts in women artists of the late nineteenth or early twentieth century who used costume to stage their difference—Emily Dickinson forever in white, Edna St. Vincent Millay gamine among the apple trees; Willa Cather in her splendid hats. The lives and work of women like these raise important questions. Where does a woman artist's art begin and end? Is becoming oneself an object of art self-creative or self-destructive? With her bejeweled Princess, Porter joined her contemporaries, the "many female modernists [who] have studied the deflection of female creativity from the production of art to the re-creation of the body."[12]

Costume in "The Princess" raises some of the most radical aspects of Porter's gender-thinking. But the story remains deeply ambivalent. The Princess's splendid performances thrill, she glitters and declaims, but the personal cost is devastating. When, shut behind her hard gold mask, the Princess laughs at her death sentence and then weeps, it is unclear whether she is an entirely admirable revolutionary deserving uncritical sympathy, or if, in fact, she has become what her father calls her, a "mad girl." Not just in the depiction of her final grief before the tribunal or in the suggestion that she commits suicide at the close, but throughout this tale's portrayal of an artist-heroine, the reader can sense Porter's refusal to simplify the issues she saw surrounding gender identity and women artists. Although brave and talented, the Princess is also isolated, too different; she has been set apart since early childhood. At the age of five, according to the Queen, the Princess "read the magic runes on her father's sword . . . and that without instruction!" The image suggests that early on the Princess could penetrate the codes that mask and mystify the proscriptions of patriarchal authority. This knowledge of the texts that inscribe her father's power disturbs those around her, suggesting that she is unnatural, even insane. According to the High Priestess, it is "a certain sign of holy madness. . . . That is too great wisdom for a natural infant" (229).

Focusing on costume in "The Princess" highlights Porter's awareness that gender may be fabrication and performance and reveals a freethinking, heroic Princess; however, focusing on physical and emotional pain offers an entirely different reading. "Insane" and "unnatural," the Princess is a beautiful figure in Porter's story and also a terrible one—a monster in her gold mask with glittering eyes. Identified early by the power and difference of her vision, the Princess steps fully onto a different path at puberty. From then on she moves further and further from common humanity as she embraces her vocation. The more elaborate and skillful her art becomes, the less she resembles a human being. In her madness—or "too great wisdom"—in her monstrosity, and in the violence that surrounds her portrayal, Porter's Princess invites comparison with the mad-women inhabiting nineteenth-century women's fiction as they were viewed by Sandra Gilbert and Susan Gubar in their classic study *The Madwoman in the Attic*. According to Gilbert and Gubar's approach, the Princess represents an aspect of Porter herself: "In projecting their anger and dis-ease into dreadful figures, creating dark doubles for themselves and their heroines, women writers are both identifying with and revising the self-definitions patriarchal culture has imposed on them."[13] Identification with, exposure of, and even revision of the proscriptions of patriarchy all can be found in Porter's acute analysis of social institutions in "The Princess" and in her heroine's creative and theoretical la-bors. And it is not difficult to see in the Princess the freakish, sexually unnatural "monster" Gilbert and Gubar identified as representative of a woman writer's anxiety about her vocation: "If becoming an *author* meant mistaking one's 'sex and way,' if it meant becoming an 'unsexed' or perversely sexed female, then it meant becoming a monster or freak."[14] Again Rosi Braidotti's definition of the monster as "the bodily incarnation of difference from the basic human norm" reflects Porter's discomfort with her independent heroine.[15]

Yet normalcy fares no better. Not only the Princess but all the women in this early fairy tale are imprisoned and diminished by the gender identity avail-able to them, and they have no fully positive alternative roles. The story treats those who reverence their culture's edicts for women with irony and scorn. The Queen mother, for example, is a figure of ridicule. Cheerful and foolish, she is sure that "a husband will cure her [the Princess] of all these fancies and we shall have twenty grandchildren and a happy succession to the throne" (232). By contrast, the kingdom's other powerful woman, the High Priestess, is ambi-tious, plotting, and bad tempered. Because she frequently eases women's pain in childbirth by drinking a "sacrificial potion, compounded of bitter herbs" that causes "contortions . . . dreadful to endure and behold," the High Priestess finds that "her exalted station [is] gradually souring her temper" (235). The two women compete in petty ways, each trying to bow lower than the other, each striving to win the King's sympathetic ear. For the Queen, the High Priestess's childlessness provides an opportunity for scorn, and she cheers herself with the reassuring thought that she is a married woman and a mother, whereas the High Priestess, a "childless virgin," "is merely a cross old maid" (236). Although the Queen is simple and a bit silly, her view of the High Priestess is supported by the text. The uncomfortable rituals of vicarious childbirth are presented in such a way that they mock the Priestess's dignity, and endorsing the natural is exposed as the High Priestess's means to power over other women in her society. There seems no way out for women in Porter's "The Princess." The Queen, a woman fulfilled through maternity, is merely a fool. The High Priestess, an ambitious unmarried woman, is sour tempered, "merely a cross old maid." And the Princess, a woman artist, is viewed by her society as a madwoman and a monster.

Although Porter dissects patriarchal institutions with an accurate and ironic eye, her portrait of the rebellious Princess raises questions about a young woman's choice of art over motherhood. The Princess is both an admirable heroine and a monster, a brave individualist and an isolated madwoman, simultaneously rejecting and being rejected by her society. Throughout the story, Porter structures absolute oppositions between her heroine's choices. The Princess's art is her own chosen alternative to cultural conformity, in particular sexuality and motherhood. Her decision to be an artist and to determine her own actions stands in opposition to and thus seemingly cannot be reconciled with the traditional female roles available to her. Most potent of all these ideologies is the belief that a woman is ideally fulfilled through motherhood. Porter forcefully juxtaposed fertility and artistic creation, portraying art as armor, a literal wall between a woman and sexuality. It is intriguing that the tribunal, summing up the Princess's crimes, condemns her in part for "offenses against . . . the Woman God." Porter's story links women's artistic creativity to physical sterility: the Princess invents art to escape the ceremony of "spring sowing." Throughout she appears cut off from a fertile natural world associated with the feminine. She cannot join the processions of singing and dancing brides, or the naked maidens who "kicked up their rosy heels" (234). At one point, the acolyte tries to bring her to acknowledge natural beauty, but she cannot see beyond her mask:

> "There's a moon over your shoulder, Princess, a gauze-silver moon, turned askew to spill kisses on lovers—a very antic and young moon, Princess!"
> When the Princess turned her head slowly, her long earrings clashed and tinkled softly against the golden cheek of her mask.
> "Gauze-silver, my love? The moon I see is a sickle-shaped emerald!"[16]

Inviting the Princess to admire the moon, the acolyte is encouraging her to see the beauty of cycles in the world and changes in her own body, but she can only see a "sickle-shaped emerald" through her mask. The image suggests a deathliness about her art, as if it is her grim reaper. The Princess may reject "abhorrent," "vulgar" nature for created beauty and attempt to transform her body into an artifice of eternity, but the beauty she achieves resembles a living death.

The sadomasochism everywhere evident in the Princess's art is likewise complex and disturbing. Her exaltation of culture over nature is accompanied by physical pain. The heavy robes are laborious to wear; the jewels are razor-sharp. This physical oppression seemed particularly important to Porter, and she drafted several dialogues in which the acolyte urges the Princess to free her body from its glittering prison. In one, for example, he pleads, "Oh Princess, what a cruel thing that your tender breast, the little shy breasts of a young maid, should be crushed under such a corselet . . . let me heal your bruised breasts with kisses!" (239). The story suggests that a woman's art requires, even originates in, the repression of her body. It is her triumph and at the same time her punishment. Art literally hurts. Creation is both vision and masochism, self-fulfilling and self-punishing.

However, at the same time that the Princess's glittering corselets and crowns punish her body, they also serve as weapons; she creates increasingly ornate armor to defend herself against human contact. When the acolyte asks to kiss her hand, she creates "a glove of woven silver . . . set with thorny jewels, so that his lips bled at the touch." And when he pleads to kiss her "soft woven hair," she dons "a tall crown of white jewels . . . and the braids of her hair were woven with these same stones, all sharpened like little daggers. And the lover could not touch them without cutting his hands cruelly" (233–34). A woman's art can be both terrible to its creator and terrifying to others, Porter's story also suggests. At the same time that a woman pursues power and independence through her creative genius, she is isolated and punished by the very thing she creates. And her creation—literally her powerful and beautiful (albeit monstrous and sterile) self—wounds those who seek to know and love her.

At this point, it is crucial to acknowledge that in her gender-thinking Porter does not present the expression of female creativity through the medium of the body as entirely negative. Such self-transformation brings power as well as pain and can even initiate social change. Despite the emotional and physical suffering her art requires, the Princess finds liberation through her glittering confines. "I will make beauty after my own secret thought," she tells the Chief of the Royal Council, "and I will also devise my own cruelties, rejecting utterly the banal sufferings imposed by nature" (235). Art represents a choice for the Princess; she has her own self-made cruelties, rather than those imposed on her from without. Until her death sentence she remains triumphant, not remorseful, telling the gathered lawgivers at the tribunal, "This is the beauty I have dreamed and made" (237). In the Princess's proud claims one can find hope for the ability of art to effect cultural change, perhaps even to liberate women. Despite the social institutions that surround and seek to define her, the Princess possesses real power because she is an artist. Choosing to create art rather than children, she attempts to claim her body as her own, wresting it away from cultural dictates, rejecting the roles offered to women in "her father's kingdom." If her art is deflected creativity, it is also self-inscription, a choice rather than passive acceptance of the cultural inscription signified by the white and gray shifts that mark women by their biological status. The young women who work for the Princess as weavers and metalworkers are both ashamed by her difference and attracted to her vision; they secretively try the decorative jewels "on their wrists, and about their bodies for a moment, blushing at their own reflections in the oval pool of green water." Like a good feminist mentor, the Princess encourages their actions, telling her handmaidens, "Some day you will wear these things without blushing. And at last you will wear them with pride" (231). As a visionary and revisionary woman artist, the Princess represents a great threat to her culture, so great that despite the fact that her death leaves the kingdom without an heir, this risk is preferable to the disorder potential in her rebellion.

One of the several conclusions Porter drafted for "The Princess" directly depicts another way in which women's creative power has been controlled or appropriated by men. This version (which was selected by Walsh and Alvarez) describes the acolyte-become-poet and his final song about the Princess's life. The narrator informs the reader that the Poet's song is in fact the origin for this story of the Princess:

> So sitting there waiting for his death, he made his last song about the Princess. In it he told of his faithful love, and her unrelenting cruelty, and how now at last she had brought him to the dark grave. Indeed, the song was not at all about the Princess, but about himself. . . . And it was from this song of his that I learned about the Princess, about how cruel she really was; and of how the Poet loved her, and of what a faithful lover he was, and how fine a poet. (240)

Despite her effort to control her experience by constructing art and transforming her sexual status, at the last the Princess is recontained by a man's text, and her life and art are reduced to an occasion for the male poet. From him will come the words that record and thereby create her history. Now silent, she is transformed by his language and becomes the subject matter of his own art.[17]

Depicting the commandeering of a woman artist's work, Porter follows a pattern that shapes some of the most influential accounts of female creativity. According to Karen E. Rowe, in her study, "To Spin a Yarn: The Female Voice in Folklore and Fairy Tale," a similar kind of appropriation occurs in two paradigmatic narratives of women's creative labor, *The Arabian Nights* and Ovid's account of Philomela in the *Metamorphoses*. Both narratives may be fruitfully related to Porter's gender-thinking in "The Princess." In *The Arabian Knights*, Sheherazade tells innumerable tales to postpone the consummation of her marriage; her artistry, like the Princess's robes and jewels, defends her from sexual contact. But Sheherazade's oral art is transformed into a written text by the king, who commands "chroniclers and copyists and bade them write all that had betided him with his wife, first and last; so they wrote this and named it *The Stories of the Thousand Nights and a Night.*"[18] Thus, Sheherazade's tales become a man's text, his voice now the substance and vehicle of her vision.

In Ovid's text, Philomela, raped and then mutilated by Tereus, who cuts out her tongue to silence her, turns to weaving to tell her story. In her analysis of Philomela's plight, Rowe examines the legacy of weaving as a representation of female creative labor. As a weaver/storyteller, Philomela has endured as a representative of the woman artist, Rowe notes: "Philomela as a woman who weaves tales and sings songs becomes the prototype for the female storytellers of later tradition."[19] It is notable that Porter has her artist-princess begin as a weaver. After rejecting the ceremony at the temple, she directs her maids to weave lengths of cloth for new garments:

> The simple looms which served to weave the scant garments of the little girls, and of the women past the time of bearing were not enough, and she devised new ones. Soon three maidens were employed in the sole task of pressing out the juices from berries and leaves wherewith to dye these robes, and the Princess walked abroad wearing them, vari-coloured and the number of five, one over the other, and when she stirred her knees she rustled like a tree in full leaf. (230)

The Princess's woven garments speak her protest visibly and audibly, rustling and "crackl[ing] like flame" (230). She trains young women in her subversive arts and thus not only tells her story but also passes on the arts by which it is told. Likewise, the wise woman, teller of fairy tales, weaves forbidden messages in an ostensibly innocent, domestic female form. As Rowe suggests, "In the history of folktale and fairy tale, women as storytellers have woven or spun their yarns, speaking at one level to a total culture, but at another to a sisterhood of readers who will understand the hidden language, the secret revelations of the tale."[20] In a letter to her sister Gay, Porter described herself as a spinner and used the powerful corollary image of the female spider to describe her own creative labor: "working as I do in art, spinning it out of my substance like a spider its web."[21]

Like the king textualizing Sheherazade's oral tales in his printed tome, Ovid appropriates Philomela's visual art for his text. According to Rowe, Ovid lays claim to Philomela's tapestry by placing her voiceless creativity in his text. "Through his appropriation, he lays claim to or attempts to imitate the semiotic activity of women par excellence—weaving, by making his linguistic recounting an equivalent, or perhaps implicitly superior version of the original graphic tapestry."[22] Here we can recall Porter's description of the Poet's version of the Princess's story: "Indeed the song was not at all about the Princess, but about himself. . . . And it was from this song of his that I learned about the Princess, about how cruel she really was; and of how the Poet loved her, and of what a faithful lover he was, and how fine a poet" (240). The close of Porter's "The Princess," where the Poet becomes the weaver-teller, raises the astonishing possibility that the entire narrative of a woman inventing art to escape nature is in part, or whole, the product of the male imagination. It suggests Porter's own awareness at the start of her career that whether she rejects or accepts her culture's gender proscriptions in her labor to construct an identity as a female artist, she is inescapably bound by the images available to her.

Much revised but never completed, "The Princess" remains an extraordinarily rich and thought-provoking narrative about female sexuality, gender identity, and art. In its complex and conflicted pages lie questions Katherine Anne Porter continued to ask throughout her career. Before turning to the published stories from approximately the same time period as "The Princess," this study will move back about a decade to look at the story's predecessors, some of Porter's earliest fiction, much of it published anonymously. Here, too, we find women who are creative, independent, and resourceful: mothers, daughters, and, again, princesses with special powers.

FAIRY TALES AND FOREIGNERS

When the young acolyte looks at the Princess, he sees her alienation and dif-ference. An artist, she is set apart from common women by her creativity and dedication to her craft: "with her red hair braided, her grey eyes wide and cold; he felt a strangeness about her, and a terrible fated loneliness."[1] Similar isolation and extraordinary skill characterize most of the women in Katherine Anne Porter's earliest fiction, including her first published stories, three "retold" tales of magic and transformation: "The Faithful Princess," "The Magic Ear Ring," and "The Shattered Star." All appeared in 1920 in the children's maga-zine *Everyland*.[2] These stories of other women and other worlds mark Porter's entrance into the tradition of women storytellers, weaving new cloth from old threads, reshaping old tales to express new and personal concerns. Her beau-tiful and distinctive heroines—alienated, intrepid, resourceful—acquire the skills and visions of those who wield power over them, and eventually become more powerful than their masters, gain love, or create works as astonishing and beautiful as the Northern Lights or the Princess's bejeweled gowns. In these first heroines, we can find Porter's own desire for self-determination, her ambi-tion and powerful sense of personal potential. Yet in their physical suffering and psychological sense of difference are apparent her fear of alienation as she gains power and independence, and her deeply conflicted response to the union of those two identities "woman" and "artist." Overall, these stories mark the beginning of a long career of rich, complex, and productive gender-thinking that fueled some of Porter's finest fiction.

From the start, Porter's stories reveal her concern for women's choices, the freedom they can achieve, the ways their creative powers are constrained or distorted. Although Porter later "disowned" these stories, saying they were de-rivative, "that there was nothing of hers in them,"[3] in fact, when compared to the available originals, they reveal that she made significant changes, making them very much her own. All three tales address questions of female authority and creative power, subjects that remain central to Porter's art; all three present a brave young female heroine whose distinctive abilities set her apart from family and community. Porter's biographer Joan Givner suggests that these young heroines reflect Porter's own feelings of difference, both promising and painful. Says Givner, "She had fantasized from childhood that she was a changeling."[4] It is not difficult to see in Porter's fairy tale heroines her own romantic image of the woman artist: alienated, visionary, possessing extraordinary creative, even magical, abilities. As she revised these tales of magic and transformation, Porter raised crucial questions for a woman writer: How do women gain the knowledge and expertise to become powerful in their own right? How can ambitious women either employ or avoid traditional gender roles in their quest? Can they combine success with traditional heterosexual relationships? Once they have left home, studied, and gained the skills of the masters, can they go home again?

In her stories for children, Porter followed in the footsteps of the large company of nineteenth-century women who retold old stories for new purposes. Marina Warner's *From the Beast to the Blonde: On Fairy Tales and Their Tellers* establishes well the genre's subversive history: "Once this imagined voice was established as legitimate for certain purposes—the instruction of the young— writer's co-opted it as their own, using it as a mask for their own thoughts, their own mocking games and even sedition."[5] Tales of magic and transformation, often termed fairy tales, were, for several reasons, a suitable form for a beginning woman writer. Such tales belong to an ancient tradition of women's narrative, as Nina Auerbach points out in her collection of tales by nineteenth-century women: "Fairy tales and romances were grounded in an oral narrative tradition that may well have been initiated by women. The antiquity of fairy tales, their anonymous origins, had the feel (and perhaps the fact) of a lost, distinctively female tradition."[6] Although of ancient origin, such tales are continually updated, retold in ways that reflect the teller's cultural moment. "Their different versions have authors who, in their turn, have created in response to social, political and cultural values of their context."[7] Presented as fantasy, most often anonymous, tales of this genre serve as ideal vehicles for safely addressing prescriptive social values. In the late nineteenth century, they often provided imaginary counternarratives, their content "related to a longing by adult writers to open up and subvert traditional socialization by posing infinite textual possibilities for the subjects/readers to define themselves against the background of finite choices proposed by society."[8] Retelling allowed women writers to explore visions that might be deemed unacceptable if they claimed full responsibility for their texts; however, "by posing as mere translators or adapters [women writers] can activate the traditional materials they appropriate without having to risk being accused of indulging in child-like fantasies."[9] Of the three *Everyland* tales Porter created, "The Faithful Princess" and "The Magic Ear Ring" are the least complex. Within the wider context of tales of magic and transformation, they belong both to the general category of "fairy tales," narratives "dominated by fantasy" that "involve significant interaction with the magical and the marvelous,"[10] and more specifically to the Oriental tale, a discourse as popular as the fairy tale in nineteenth-century literature. Both tale forms originate in and express the Romantic fascination with imagination, exoticism, or otherness.[11]

"The Faithful Princess" is based on the first of the tales of Nala and Damayanti published by Donald A. MacKenzie in 1913 in a collection titled *Indian Myth and Legend*. In this story, Damayanti, the daughter of a great king, loves and is loved by Nala, a young and powerful rajah. Various gods, hearing of Damayanti's purity and beauty, take on Nala's appearance, and soon all the lovers together—disguised gods and the true young rajah—present themselves at her father's court, demanding that Damayanti choose among them. Weeping that she has faithfully pledged herself only to the real Nala, Damayanti awakens the gods' sympathy, "so in pity they made her eyes to see clearly the signs that mark the deities from men."[12] She and Nala are then happily united with blessings from the gods. In her adaptation of this tale, Porter significantly streamlined the original so that the focus is far more on princess Damayanti's beauty and wisdom. Where, in the original, Damayanti pines for Nala, cries easily, and trembles when he appears, in Porter's revision she is smiling and decisive, quick to formulate a plan. Even more significantly, after Damayanti penetrates the disguises of the gods in Porter's version, the entire court shouts "well done, brave daughter!" far different from the original, where all the praise goes to Nala. To Nala too, in the original, the gods bestow gifts; Porter divides them more equitably, having both the Princess and her paramour receive "power over the mountains and fire and water and darkness" (18). From a tale about a wealthy and powerful rajah named Nala, who impresses the gods and wins the beautiful maiden, Porter extracts the story of a smart and resourceful Princess named Damayanti, who wins not only a handsome rajah but also special powers from the gods. The title of her version reflects her intentions. Where in the original "Nala and Damayanti," the princess took second place, in Porter's "The Faithful Princess," she receives the lead role.

The heroine of "The Magic Ear Ring" also must penetrate spells to win her beloved prince, who is stolen shortly after their marriage. And in this "retold" tale, Porter again focused her version on a young woman and her powers. As she revised, Porter thoroughly transformed the original tale from a lengthy and somewhat clumsy translation by the Reverend J. Hinton Knowles in his collection *Folk-Tales of Kashmir*, adding colorful details and patterning events while streamlining the overall adventure.[13] In the original, "two great and wealthy kings" and their messengers arrange the marriage of the resourceful princess and her handsome prince, who is subsequently kidnapped by a group of admiring fairies. In Porter's version powerful women abound: an "old woman made the match" and a "Fairy Queen" steals the young man from his betrothed. Porter names her princess and prince, Saila and Tasar, respectively, and, as in "The Faithful Princess," makes her heroine both able and decisive. The original unnamed princess wanders about weeping "day and night" in "anxious search" after her husband is abducted, and finds him only when an old man shows her the way. Saila, by contrast, pursues his abductors immediately and, after awakening him from a spell and learning he is under the magic powers of the Fairy Queen, briskly and optimistically resolves, "Then I will learn magic. . . . Farewell for a little while" (19). In both versions, the princess poses as the long lost daughter of the Dev, or powerful magician in whose castle the fairies hide the bewitched prince. In the original, the Dev welcomes back his ostensible daughter with the words, "My darling! My darling!" Porter's Dev, however, already has plans for his recovered offspring: "Welcome, a hundred welcomes, beloved daughter! What a wonderful Fairy Queen you will be when the present one retires!" Both the original princess and Saila undergo training in magic from the Dev, Saila to become the Fairy Queen's successor. Under the tutelage of this deceived father, she soon becomes invincible. In Porter's words, Saila is "wiser than the Fairy Queen and as wise as the Dev himself" (20). Although both princesses eventually discover their lost prince hidden in an earring, the original princess simply asks for the jewel and receives it on loan; Porter's Saila, espying her beloved "made small as a gnat," is far more forceful: "Give me your ear rings quickly," she tells the Fairy Queen, and "stepped forward boldly and loosed the ear rings from the Queen's ears." More examples abound, and in each we see Porter strengthening the original heroine. Consider the effect her changes make to a single sentence. When, after the rescue, the lovers wish to leave the Dev's palace, Hinton's version states, "the prince quite naturally expressed a great wish to visit his home, and the princess wanted to go with him." Porter revises as follows: "In a few days the Prince and Princess wished to return to their home" (21). Her prose neatly condenses the original and places the young couple on an equal footing.

Extricated from collections that as whole might have provided some sense of their cultural contexts, "The Faithful Princess" and "The Magic Ear Ring" bear only faint ties to their origins; references to lotus flowers and leopards serve only to locate the heroines' tales in the realm of the exotic. Both tales may be identified with the common fairy tale type "The Search for the Lost Husband." According to Swann Jones, in tales of this type, "the heroine must employ magic to reclaim the husband. . . . [she] engages in a quest that brings her into close contact with the magical realm, and she learns to appreciate it and use the magic for her own advantage."[14] Such tales emphasize the resource-fulness of their heroine and show her learning the scope of her own powers before marriage. It is intriguing to speculate why such a tale appealed to Porter in 1920. Besides the mere presence of determined, intrepid heroines, who prove themselves at least as capable as their betrotheds, both tales show young women gaining special vision and power before marriage. Damayanti penetrates the spells of the male gods to achieve her own desire; likewise, Saila studies under the Dev until she possesses knowledge equal to the father figure. With this knowledge she can then pierce all deceptive and dangerous illusions. Perhaps these stories suggest anxiety about marriage, or intimate that women should not enter into relationships until they are well armed, able to see through false-hoods and fabrications and exercise their own powerful skills. Certainly both tales demonstrate that young women are not only capable of special vision but also able to obtain that vision from the powerful men who possess it, and then use it to gain their own desires.

The most interesting of Porter's three earliest stories is "The Shattered Star." The tale falls more readily under the heading of myth than fairy tale, for it provides an explanatory narrative for a natural phenomenon, here the Northern Lights, and does so by demonstrating that the "numinous or divine realm is in some way manifested in the mundane realm of quotidian life."[15] So far, no source has been located for this "retold" tale; however, certain of its elements— the Moon-man, the mother's simple song, the heroine's magic flight—do show up in Eskimo folk narratives. A survey of available far northern folktales from this period suggests that this tale may be more a product of Porter's imagina-tion than her other *Everyland* narratives.[16]

"The Shattered Star" presents the story of Nayagta, an Eskimo girl who bears a moon mark at birth and thus is "claimed . . . for the people of the Moon" (12). In fact, while she is yet an infant, Nayagta is taken by a deity and carried away to the spirit world "beyond the spaces of the Moon" (13). Even before her abduction, however, the girl is distinguished not just by her moon mark but by her attraction to beauty, color, and light. She loves to lie peacefully, gazing at an oil lamp "shining blue and green and silver light" on the icy wall of her igloo. From the start, the story suggests that the cold but beautiful visions Nayagta loves pull her away from her mother's comforting body. Lines are faintly drawn here between the artist and other people and between the world of home, which includes the mother's body, and the world of imagination or art. These lines will be drawn again, far more darkly, in Porter's later work.[17]

"The Shattered Star" carefully contrasts Nayagta's home culture with that of the Moon-demons. The Eskimos fear change and the unknown. They live secure, repeating ancient patterns, loving "the blue ice and the heavy sea, and the slow-moving bergs. . . . They sleep warmly in huts of ice, and cook their food of fish and oil" (14–15). The simplicity and security of repetition shape their muted creativity. Nayagta's mother comforts her with a song, but it is "the same song always, that had only three notes in it" (13). Unlike this unchanging world with its simple, repetitive rituals, the world of the Moon-demons is full of change and conflict. They are creative, magical; at one point Porter describes them as busy "making their world anew, having tired of the old one" (13).

Nayagta's experiences among the Moon-demons resemble Saila's in the castle of the Dev. Both women—Nayagta marked from birth, Saila impersonating a lost daughter—join an alternative, supernatural family. In "The Magic Ear Ring" and "The Shattered Star," magic belongs to powerful males—Dev the demon father or the Moon-man and his spirit demons—but both young women are determined and successful students. After the Dev has taught the princess Saila "all the enchantments of the fairy world . . . the Princess became wiser than the Fairy Queen and as wise as the Dev himself" (20). Likewise, Nayagta soon surpasses the Moon-demons: "They taught her all they knew of magic, until at last she had more power than they, and they no longer had their will over her" (13).

Biographer Joan Givner finds in the heroines of these early tales portrayals of Porter's own self-education: "She was often drawn to talented people and absorbed their skills and knowledge until her expertise exceeded theirs."[18] In this light, it is interesting to compare Nayagta and Princess Saila to the heroine of "The Evening," an unfinished story among Porter's papers. Composed approximately four years after the *Everyland* tales, "The Evening" relates a young woman's ambitious thoughts as she sits, silently, in the midst of a group of Mexican artists, all male. Surrounded by these creative men, the woman is an outsider, excluded from their shared masculinity, struggling to understand both their language and their culture. In one drafted paragraph, Porter describes in detail the woman's determination to acquire their knowledge: "She feared them a little: their solidarity of interest, of race, of sex. They were familiars to one another, but mysterious to her. . . . She was unread, inexperienced in ideas. . . . Their derived theories came to her as from a clear fountain of original thought. But pure feminine mind is a caterpillar, and she absorbed voraciously all tints and dyes against the final spreading of her bright wings."[19] Like Nayagta, who learns from the demons "all they knew of magic, until at last she had more power than they," the young woman in "The Evening" fills her mind with the knowledge of the male artists and thinkers who surround her: a painter, a songwriter, a philosopher of aesthetic theory. She listens in silence, hiding her ambitions yet feeding her creative self.

All three portraits of women's education are somewhat disturbing. Both Nayagta and Princess Saila must undertake a journey, overcome enormous cultural differences, and dwell among demons to learn. Saila impersonates a daughter. In "The Evening," the young woman is also an outsider who masks her fears and desires, careful to appear passive, in Porter's words "serpent-feminine enough to know that her attitude of calm pleased them" (281). "The Evening" suggests furthermore that women possess a special ability to observe and absorb, perhaps even seduce and deceive. "Pure feminine mind is a caterpillar," Porter concludes in a draft of "The Evening" (281). The image—recalling the phrase "serpent-feminine" quoted above—suggests ambivalence about some of the paths women may take to acquire knowledge. Using deception, impersonating the good daughter, or playing the role of silent seductress, these young women manipulate gender relations to achieve their own ambitious ends. Their work is dangerous, and the men they seek to learn from are controlling, even evil—Nayagta and Saila labor in the land of the demons. The male artists who surround the silent woman in "The Evening" possess a "natural hardness of heart" and treat their female companion with condescension: "They talked to her and for her among themselves with the indulgent tenderness one gives to a darling child, with always the subtle inference of . . . her value as a beautiful woman" (281). Manipulating power from her less powerful position, the young woman endures the bondage of apprenticeship until at last she has attained enough skill to break free, spreading "her bright wings." Once she has "more power than they . . . they no longer had their will over her" (13).

Knowledge means freedom from daughterhood for Princess Saila, from the demons for Nayagta, and from men's sexual designs for the unnamed woman in "The Evening." Yet that freedom comes at a cost. In these early tales, Porter looks carefully at the price of power for women. True to the wish fulfillment of many fairy tales, love and power come together in "The Magic Ear Ring" and "The Faithful Princess." Princess Saila and Dayanti use special powers to free their princes, and in the end both contentedly settle down. But "The Shattered Star" presents a less traditional fate. Nayagta gains skill sufficient not only to break the hold of the Moon-man and his demons but also to seize their best treasures when she flees, taking them to her own people. But she has been so transformed by her long years among the demons that she is a stranger in her former home, "changed beyond the knowledge of all those who saw her" (13). Even worse, the Eskimo people, stolidly content in their unchanging, icy world, reject her gifts—a star full of colors, a garden, a castle—beautiful treasures crafted by the Moon-demons. "We do not know these things!" they cry to her in fear. "They are evil!" (14).

Alienated and angered by her people's rejection, Nayagta resolves to leave and gathers up her gifts. But as she departs, Merah, an "Eskimo boy," implores her not to "go away again to the Far Off places," but instead to marry him: "Abide here in our igloo; my mother shall call you daughter and I will call you wife" (14). His proposal, offering her two new names, suggests the re-definition that would accompany her marriage. Rather than being a powerful magician, inhabiting the "Far Off places," Nayagta would become a daughter and wife, a traditional Eskimo woman. But Nayagta refuses to settle down. She rejects the proposal, telling the young lover, "You and your people have not wanted . . . any of the magic I brought you from the spaces of the moon. So I go again" (14).

Although Nayagta rejects Merah's marriage offer and turns away from her people, she can never become entirely free of the past. As she leaves, Merah says to her, "Take with you your memory of us." Nayagta refuses, claiming she will only take the spurned gifts. However, the narrator tells us that "her heart grieved and remembered" (14). For this alienated woman, memory proves inescapable. In her anger and sorrow Nayagta casts away her gifts, and the star shatters in the sky, becoming the Northern Lights. The story closes with Nayagta forever in exile, "screaming her homesickness in the storm rack" or "watching her shattered star as it . . . ripples like the light of the whale oil lamp on the walls of the igloo where Nayagta's mother used to sing three little notes as she swayed in her hood. And Nayagta remembers forever" (15). In the end, Nayagta has become a powerful, legendary creator. Her creation—the Northern lights—sweeps across the sky, forever expressing the anguish of memory and exile.

The editors of *The Uncollected Early Prose of Katherine Anne Porter* suggest that Nayagta's alienation from her people may reflect Porter's own "early suspicion that her family would never truly appreciate her talent" (12). It is not difficult to see Nayagta as Porter's first figure of a woman artist. A wanderer, set apart from birth, gaining knowledge and formidable skill from the powerful, unable to reconcile love and home with her acquired magical gifts and the larger world she comes to know, she reappears throughout Porter's fiction. The suggestion that art, like Nayagta's aurora borealis, emerges from memories, in particular a longing for home and mother, will also reappear in Porter's fiction, essays, and poetry. Its presence here establishes from the beginning the centrality of memory to Porter's view of the creative process. As well, Nayagta's transformation into a figure of legend in her story anticipates Porter's later exploration of women, like Amy in *Old Mortality*, who become a romantic symbol in family cultural memory.[20]

The editors of *The Uncollected Early Prose* also find in "The Shattered Star" evidence of Porter's ambitions, suggesting that "Nayagta's place in the firmament expresses Porter's desire for artistic immortality" (12). Certainly both Nayagta's transformation into legend and her perpetual wandering may express Porter's ambitions and her fears. However, it is intriguing to note that the heroine's immortality is oddly compromised in this tale. Although "The Shattered Star" closes with the words "Nayagta remembers forever," claiming the Northern Lights as eternal expression of the heroine's exile, the first time the lights flash in the sky, the Eskimo people give Merah, "the Eskimo boy," as much or more credit for their appearance, crying out, "Nayagta is remembering. Merah can also make magic!" (14). Their words suggest that in the minds of Nayagta's people, the young man equally or surpassingly represents the creative force: Nayagta remembers, but he is the magic maker. The comment would be too slight for so much attention if we had not already seen how a similar deflection of the heroine's achievement to a male character strongly marks the close of Porter's most complex and significant fairy tale, "The Princess." Both moments suggest Porter's awareness of the ways in which female creative power may be reframed within cultural narratives that control that power or even appropriate it for men.

After the three *Everyland* stories, Porter continued her exploration of female creative power in another retold tale, "The Adventures of Hadji: A Tale of a Turkish Coffee House," which appeared in *Asia* magazine in 1920. Porter's narrative is based on "What Happened to Hadji, a Merchant of the Bezestan," translated by Cyrus Adler and Allan Ramsay for a collection titled *Told in the Coffee House: Turkish Tales*. Again Porter's revisions are extensive. Unlike the *Everyland* stories, which mixed elements of fairy and Oriental tale in narratives designed for young readers, "Hadji" relies more on its "foreign" setting and is directed toward an adult audience. Employing the stereotypes, parodic language and superficial cultural decorations that are staples of Western versions of Eastern narratives, "The Tale of Hadji" tells the story of two familiar folktale figures: the foolish husband and the clever wife.

Retelling an Oriental tale to stage questions of sex roles and power, Porter was again following in the footsteps of nineteenth-century female predecessors who used other worlds and other women to address issues quite close to home. During the nineteenth century, particular features of Asian culture, most notably the harem, became metaphors for women's condition in Western culture (memorably, in Charlotte Brontë's *Jane Eyre*). Like the fairy tale, the Eastern or Oriental tale could provide a safe vehicle for social criticism. Joyce Zonana terms these popular narratives "feminist orientalist discourse" and argues that through them a Western woman writer "displaces the source of oppression onto an 'Oriental,' 'Mahometan' society, [thereby] enabling readers to contemplate local problems without questioning their own self-definition as Westerners and Christians."[21] Like women writing before her, Porter drew on the well-established trope of Oriental misogyny in "The Adventures of Hadji" as she revised the original tale to address her own concerns about women's power. Porter's revision significantly transforms her source text; unlike her "retellings" for *Everyland*, "The Adventures of Hadji" is longer and far more complex than its original. The material Porter added focuses on the tradition of verbal authority, both male control of speech and the misogynist tradition that negates the authority and value of women's voices. She also explores the relationship between male fantasies of women and the repression of women's voices.

To the original "What Happened to Hadji," Porter added an opening frame that establishes male control over the production of narrative and evokes the long tradition of the misogynist proverb. She was clearly inspired by other tales in *Told in the Coffee House*, in particular one titled "Better Is the Folly of Woman Than the Wisdom of Man," in which a young scribe who maligns female wisdom learns the error of his ways. In the frame Porter added to "Hadji," a male speaker addresses a group of listeners, his speech a collection of pithy misogynist maxims. Porter calls her speaker a "medak," providing the parenthetical gloss "(storyteller)" and gives this medak the aphorism-laden speech common in Western stereotypes of Asian speakers. Although indebted to familiar stereotypes, however, the medak's proverbial style also represents a powerful linguistic strategy. Ostensibly communicating practical wisdom gained through common experience, he uses proverbial phrasing to create a neat, closed, seemingly inarguable verbal package. In form and content proverbs belong to a powerful and established tradition of verbal authority.[22]

In Porter's "The Adventures of Hadji," the medak's maxims focus on women's voices; he tells his male audience, "take no heed of the words of women. . . . from a woman nothing is to be had but foolishness and vexation. . . . Once in forty years is it given to a woman to speak with wisdom. . . . once in many centuries, likewise, does there arise among us a woman of understanding" (23). The medak urges the listening men to disregard women's wisdom, "for even when she speaks with knowledge, it is all folly. She sets her words as stones in our paths for our undoing" (23). Deny women voices, the medak urges. Irritating, empty, dangerous—women's words must be ignored, even suppressed. The medak addresses his audience as "effendi," a Turkish term meaning "master," or "man of property, authority, or education in an eastern Mediterranean country."[23] Likely the medak's use of "effendi" represents another convention; certainly it flatters his listeners and thereby gains their approving attention. But the term "effendi" also establishes the medak's audience as men of power, men able to transform his proverbial teachings into social practice and law.

Porter's adaptation of the original tale now follows after the medak's warnings and provides an ironic counterpart to the opening frame. Although the storyteller seems to intend the tale to be illustrative, it contradicts all that he professes; for in "The Adventures of Hadji," a woman demonstrates wisdom, speaks with authority, and saves and educates a foolish man. Porter wove through the original tale a new narrative layer that focuses on foolish male fantasy, female speech, and silence, building on slight references in the original to create entirely new themes. To briefly summarize her version, following the thematic lines stitched in by her additions: Hadji, the hapless male hero, chafes in his marriage, for his hanoum, or wife, "was a woman of energy and much speech" (23). At the "Great Bazar" [sic] he becomes enamoured of another woman, whose veiled lower face ensures her silence: "He thought of his faithful hanoum who talked, and his vitals were bitten with longing for other things" (23). The veiled woman, somewhat to the reader's surprise, desires a liaison with the foolish Hadji and communicates her wishes through a series of symbolic objects and gestures—these Porter drew from the original narrative. A "man of little wit," in his wife's words, Hadji cannot decipher her mysterious signs and must ask his wife to aid him. She finds them easily interpretable and assists her husband in his quest to meet alone with "that veiled and beautiful creature" (24). However, Hadji's wife also arranges for the city guards to attend her husband's liaison. As a result Hadji and his silent paramour are thrown into prison.

To his dismay, while locked in his cell Hadji overhears the voice of his now unveiled beloved. No longer mysterious and silent, she is vigorously "complaining in tones more loud and shrill than the tones of his hanoum" (25). Soon his intelligent and resourceful wife gains access to the prison and switches clothing with her rival. She then unveils herself at Hadji's trial and, claiming to have been the veiled paramour all along, delivers a speech so lengthy and eloquent that the judge finally implores her and Hadji to leave so that "his ears" may "be free from the sound of her voice" (26). Throughout the trial Hadji says nothing. In fact, the narrator tells us, "Wisdom bade him keep silence" (26). Until the story's end he remains "speechless," only bursting forth at the close in excessive praise of his wife. She has the final words:

> The wife of Hadji wept for joy, and fell upon his neck and said, "O Hadji, Hadji, thy wit is small and thy understanding is mean, and thou speakest untruths, but my heart rejoices at thy words!"
> And Hadji said nothing.

With the addition of these closing words, Porter has Hadji's wife reverse the misogynist proverbs of the medak. Men, not women, lack wisdom and speak without truth. Faced with the irrefutable demonstration of his wife's verbal skill, Hadji is rendered speechless. Interestingly enough, the medak seems silenced as well; the story ends without a return to the frame.

Despite the misogynist proverbs of its opening frame, "The Adventures of Hadji" effectively demonstrates throughout the intelligence and verbal authority of its heroine. Using the narrative mask of feminist orientalist discourse, Porter confronted several issues central to her own creative ambitions. Her revision of the original story, emphasizing the mysterious woman's initial silence and Hadji's consequent infatuation, suggests, for example, that men can be caught up in self-deluding fantasies, and lacking true understanding of women, in fact misperceive them. Hadji develops a romantic desire for the woman in the marketplace only because, veiled and silent, she offers a blank surface on which he can impose his fantasy. He is astonished to discover that when the real woman emerges in jail, unveiled and freely speaking her mind, she is as determined and voluble as his own wife. In Porter's version of "The Tale of Hadji," women speak with eloquence and anger; they are verbal forces, the power and sheer volume of their speech overwhelming listening men. Furthermore, women are simply smarter than men, the story suggests. They not only work ably with speech but also communicate through symbolic mediums and are skilled interpreters: it is Hadji's hanoum who can interpret the messages of the paramour. Porter greatly developed the scene before the judge in her revision, highlighting the hanoum's verbal prowess. When she wins in the courtroom, her eloquence overwhelming the judge and gathered officials, and when, at the close, she renders both her husband and the medak silent, the hanoum defeats traditional verbal authority, defeats at least momentarily the misogyny inscribed in law or literature.

The hanoum wins in "The Tale of Hadji," but hers is a comic triumph. Although Porter stages a clever woman winning with words, she does so through the well-worn material of the Eastern folktale. Like her tales of magic and transformation, "The Tale of Hadji" employs a narrative mask, its generic qualities evidence of Porter's hesitancy to directly confront crucial questions of gender and verbal authority. Her next work of fiction shares much with this earlier Eastern tale.[24] In "María Concepción" we again find the foolish husband, the determined wife, and adultery. Unlike the exotic tales that precede it, however, "María Concepción" is set in a country and culture Porter experienced directly—her "familiar country," Mexico.[25]

The first story Porter acknowledged as her own, "María Concepción" bridges the completely imaginary tales of her earliest work and the later Mexico fiction. In this tale, Porter recants the conflict between hardworking, devout María Concepción and her unfaithful husband, Juan, who leaves her for adventures with María Rosa, a beautiful young beekeeper. Abandoned, María Concepción becomes emotionally hardened and socially isolated. In the end, however, she triumphs by murdering her rival and regaining both her husband and the support of the community. Where the earlier tales employed the freedom of fairy tale or drew on the formulaic Eastern tale to indirectly address issues of female creativity and authority, here Porter turns to another increasingly available discourse for staging and critiquing gender identity—primitivism. Despite its ostensibly factual basis in ethnographic observation, anthropological commentary on so-called primitive peoples offers as rich a medium for staging alternative versions of human identity or critiquing present social practices as do tales of magic and transformation. In fact, scholars often group primitivist discourse with other Romantic discourses exploring the exotic, otherworldly, or simply "other," from fairy and Oriental tales to the worlds of dreams and the unconscious.[26]

The modernists' attraction to concepts of the primitive, exemplified in the work of D. H. Lawrence (about whom Porter had much to say at points in her career)[27] or the writings of the influential ethnographers of the late nineteenth and early twentieth century, tells us a great deal about Porter's contemporaries but little about the peoples reconfigured in their texts. In short, the primitive in twentieth-century culture is itself a creative discourse with its own identifiable tropes. As Marianna Torgovnick argues in her influential study *Gone Primitive: Savage Intellects, Modern Lives*, "Primitives are like children, the tropes say. Primitives are our untamed selves. . . . Primitives are mystics in tune with nature, part of its harmonies. Primitives are free." She concludes, "The ensemble of these tropes—however miscellaneous and contradictory—forms the basic grammar and vocabulary of what I call primitivist discourse, a discourse fundamental to the Western sense of self and Other."[28] Porter's contemporaries employed this discourse for many reasons, often drawing on its powerful associations of primitive cultures with the natural to shape their arguments about art, sexuality, or essential human qualities. Porter employed it in her own gender-thinking to continue her persistent examination of female creative power. As Torgovnick observes, "How we conceive of the primitive helps form our conception of ourselves as sexual, gendered beings."[29] Like many of her contemporaries, Porter viewed primitive cultures as alike and fundamentally transparent, their arts or social practices all expressing essential forms discernable to the educated observer. For evidence we might consider her musings about the canoes of the Xochimilcho Indians of central Mexico: "There is something Egyptian, we decide, about this long, narrow barge of hand sawed wood, with legends carved along the sides. There is something darkly African about it, too."[30]

Although her uncritical embrace of the primitive was brief, for a time Porter, like many of her contemporaries, imagined primitive societies could offer curatives for modern malaise.[31] She focused primarily on the potential for primitive cultures to provide alternative visions of female authority and creative power. She was especially attentive to representations of female power as generative, rooted in nature, worshipped in goddess figures such as the Mexican Xochitl. Her unpublished essay, "Children of Xochitl," composed approximately a year before "María Concepción," celebrates "the legendary Aztec goddess of the earth, of fruit, of abundance." Porter sets Xochitl against a panoply of female goddesses, claiming her as the most positive figure of female power: "Of all the great women deities from Mary to Diana, Dana of the Druids to Kwanyin of the Buddhists, this Xochitl has been endowed with the most cleanly, the most beneficent attributes. In a race where the women sowed and reaped, wove and span and cooked and brewed, it was natural that a goddess should be fruitful and strong."[32] For Porter, Xochitl's strength and fecundity, originating in her tie to the natural world and its cycles, shape the lives of the Indian people, the "children of Xochitl." She sees in them instinctive, purely natural human existence; they are childlike rather than adult, their creativity untainted by modern technology, their minds simple and untroubled, free from modern self-consciousness and neuroses. In her portrayal of their daily labors, Porter embodies numerous tropes of primitivist discourse: children play "without toys or invention, as instinctively as little animals"; an elderly man "lives as a tree lives, rightly a part of the earth." She claims that "there are no neurotics among them. . . . No strained lines of sleeplessness or worry mar their faces" (81, 82).

In this Eden of primitive culture, women exist in simple, sated peace, "smooth and untroubled," their state akin, Porter suggests, to a kind of preconsciousness, as if living at one with nature under the rule of the goddess keeps them eternally united with and soothed by a maternal presence. Porter provides a vision of women in this primitive world suffused with the comfort of Xochitl, the fertile mother goddess. Describing a girl washing clothes in the river, she comments, "There is a trance like quality in her motions, an unconsciousness in her sharpened profile, as if she had never awakened from the prenatal dream" (83). Rarely speaking, contented, Porter's primitive women embody a peace that is both alluring and disturbing, the disturbance arising from the implications of their placid silence for a woman writer committed to language and personal freedom.

It is crucial to note, however, that when Porter revised "The Children of Xochitl" for publication in *The Christian Science Monitor*, she made extensive, significant cuts in the original essay. The editors of her *Uncollected Prose* suggest "she eliminated all references to the pagan goddess, apparently so as not to offend [the *Monitor's*] readers with her anti-Christian bias" (73). It is true she eliminated the celebratory passages on Xochitl; however, her cuts were more extensive, carefully pruning away passages that idealized the primitive or claimed neuroses for the modern. Characteristically, Porter's gender-thinking led her quickly to question primitivism as a cultural ideal, particularly the ways in which, concretely enacted in social structure rather than merely serving as a vehicle of expressive art, it defined and limited women's freedom. The complex and ambivalent treatment of primitivism that followed shortly in "María Concepción" suggests that more than the audience of *The Christian Science Monitor* led to such thorough and specific revision.

Appearing a year and a half after "The Children of Xochitl," "María Concepción" continues Porter's exploratory staging of female power and authority in other worlds, imaginary or exotic. Consistently readers have identified primitivism as a key context for interpreting the story's women. As William Nance observed in 1963, "In this first of her published stories Katherine Anne Porter confronts the mysterious forces of nature through the transparency of primitive society and finds that these forces act most strongly through a woman."[33] When the reader first meets María Concepción, she, like the entranced women of "The Children of Xochitl," is more body than mind, drifting in an essentialist dream: "Instinctive serenity softened her black eyes. . . . She walked with the free, natural, guarded ease of the primitive woman carrying an unborn child. The shape of her body was easy, the swelling life was not a distortion, but the right inevitable proportions of a woman."[34] Not surprisingly, most readers argue that "María Concepción" continues Porter's idealization of women's lives within a primitive, pre-Christian social order infused with the presence of the mother goddess. In her myth-based study of Porter's women, Jane Krause De-Mouy draws on Erich Neumann's encyclopedic *The Great Mother* to support this reading, identifying in Porter's title character "the most ancient archetype in human experience: the eternal feminine or the Great Mother, whose office is the continuation of life. . . . María Concepción manifests the character and attributes of the archetypal mother goddess."[35] Others, who note that María Concepción sweats "ichor," or who dwell on her final peaceful pose, baby on lap, breathing at one with "the earth under her," identify her as "an avatar of a fertility goddess."[36] All find María Concepción's condition at the story's close ideal. For some she has reclaimed an essential primitive identity, shedding the false veneer of Catholicism. Thus she articulates Porter's argument against the Christianizing of Mexico's Indian population. For others, María Concepción's claim of María Rosa's baby bespeaks a kind of self-completion.[37] Yet few readers feel entirely satisfied with the story. Allen Tate, one of its first critical reviewers, suggested that "María Concepción" suffers from "an uncertainty of purpose," and his criticism has been recently restated by Janis Stout, who concludes that "it is not a fully controlled work, and its theme is not fully worked out."[38]

The "uncertainty" or lack of control readers experience with "María Concepción" may be attributed, at least in part, to the contradictions sustained in the text right up to the final affirming image of the close. At the same time that the heroine María Concepción moves steadily toward triumph over her rival, María Rosa, winning back her husband and defeating the gendarmes, she moves equally steadily toward silence and loss of power. Before the mystic harmonies of mother, child, and earth weave the beautiful closing passages, "María Concepción" stages Porter's ambivalent, critical vision of primitivism as a resource for reimagining female identity. The story, in short, presents a complex and unresolved enactment of her gender-thinking.

Exploring possibilities for female identity, Porter works with well-drawn dichotomies in "María Concepción": order versus disorder, lawful versus unlawful, civilized versus primitive. Despite her "ease of the primitive woman," María Concepción is strongly associated with the first term in each dichotomy (3). She possesses clear social power that originates in her ability to earn and control her own money. Because she has been "an energetic religious woman who could drive a bargain to the end," María Concepción can pay for a marriage license, "that potent bit of stamped paper which permits people to be married in the church" (4). Active, not passive, self-assured and successful, María Concepción enjoys her proud social status and can bring out a "sack of hard silver coins" to purchase goods for herself or her childish husband whenever necessary. Walking carefully in "the middle of the road," her strong back straight, her mission clear, the María Concepción of the story's first half is a figure of female strength and self-direction, legally married, civilized.

Conflict begins when this lawful, self-determining woman strays from her straight and narrow path to follow her body's urgings. "The delicious aroma of bees, their slow thrilling hum awakened a pleasant desire for a flake of sweetness in her mouth." Seeking honey at the hives of María Rosa, María Concepción encounters a scene of disorder and lust: her husband, Juan, "laughing strangely," and María Rosa, clothes torn, braids "half-raveled." Soon Juan and María Rosa run off into that greatest disorder of all, war. María Rosa's fragrant home suggests Porter's view of women's lives within a primitive culture—sensual, woman-centered, achieving power through nonlegal or precivilized resources. Here we find not only the disheveled young beekeeper but also her "old godmother, Lupe the medicine woman." It is this ancient Lupe, and her fellow older women of the village, who finally claim María Concepción at the story's close. Representing a primitive female community, they possess ancient knowledge of healing or ritual. However, Porter makes clear that they are also united by their shared experience in the suffering of women who have no externally recognized social power. Thus old Soledad urges María Concepción to relinquish her anger and accept her female lot: "All women have these troubles. Well, we should suffer together" (9).

In the world of María Rosa and the other village women, men have authority. María Concepción, with her shrewd skills and hard coins, has managed, up until now, to hold her own in her marriage. Consider her husband Juan's thoughts on his relations with his wife versus his relations with María Rosa: "Sometimes I looked at her and thought, Now I am married to that woman in the church, and I felt a sinking inside, as if something were lying heavy on my stomach. With María Rosa it is all different. She is not silent; she talks. When she talks too much, I slap her and say, Silence, thou simpleton! and she weeps. She is just a girl with whom I do what I please" (11–12). After Juan and María Rosa run off together, María Concepción entirely represses her body, becoming hard and thin, dedicating herself to her work. "María Concepción lived alone. She was gaunt, as if something were gnawing away inside. . . . her butchering knife was scarcely ever out of her hand" (10). María Concepción's gauntness tells us how she is eaten up by her rage and denies her sexual, female self. Like a contemporary sufferer of anorexia nervosa, María Concepción "disciplines [her] body's hungers"; nothing must sway her from her hard purpose. Like the Princess, she has undertaken a "disciplinary project" over her own flesh. In her quest for absolute self-control and invulnerability, "the body becomes [her] enemy."[39] María Concepción's quick and able knife is her means of income, and thus of independence. Her skill at slaughter—at cutting and reshaping flesh—expresses both her rage and her power. This linking of instruments of violence with images of bodily deprivation recalls Porter's Princess, whose razor-edged jewels, glittering corselets, and crowns are simultaneously armor and weapons. The woman who binds her sexuality to her purpose gains a terrible kind of power.

Before Juan's betrayal, María Concepción's social power, achieved through her public, legal status, gave her voice and authority in her marriage. After he runs off she sharpens that power, but without a male counterpart it becomes both admirable and destructive. Her fearsome independence is short lived, however; for when the runaway couple comes back home, María Concepción murders María Rosa. With this act she assumes her rival's place in the traditional women's community. Returning home after the crime, María Concepción crawls toward her new authority, her husband, "down on her knees . . . as he had seen her crawl many times toward the shrine at Guadalupe Villa" (14). At the close, holding the sleeping baby, united with the natural order both in the world around her and within her own body, María Concepción is as imprisoned as she is elevated. Juan's plan to save her restructures the power relations in their marriage; she must now depend on her husband to protect her, relinquishing her own authority and accepting the coverture of his status. Thus this new private maternal role comes at the cost of María Concepción's hard-won economic and social status. Her final peace carries a high price.

It is important to recognize here that Porter's description of this power shift carefully counters María Concepción's loss of personal agency and voice with her assumption of mysterious maternal power. To quote from the passage:

> Juan's voice barely disturbed the silence: "Listen to me carefully, and tell me the truth, and when the gendarmes come here for us, thou shalt have nothing to fear. But there will be something for us to settle between us afterward. . . ." "For me everything is settled now," she answered, in a tone so tender, so grave, so heavy with suffering, that Juan felt his vitals contract. . . . He could not fathom her. . . . He felt too that she had become invaluable, a woman without equal among a million women, and he could not tell why. (15)

Much indeed is settled. As María Concepción moves toward her final transcendence, she also moves out of independence. Conversation between husband and wife is now a sequence of commands: Juan speaking, María Concepción silently obeying. When she faces the gendarmes, María Concepción simply repeats words her husband taught her: "It was true she was troubled when her husband went away, but after that she had not worried about him. It was the way of men she believed. She was a church married woman and knew her place. . . . She had gone to market, but had come back early, because now she had her man to cook for. That was all" (19). In this new lesson, learned from a husband who has assumed authority, spoken to the male authorities of her community, and approved by the listening old women, María Concepción puts traditional women's duties first; the church no longer gives her pride, but instead now endorses her obedience to her husband; the joys of driving a hard bargain in the market yield to her husband's dinner.

As is characteristic of her gender-thinking, Porter sustains complex, even conflicting visions of female power in a single text. In "María Concepción" she draws from a tradition that exalts women's procreative powers in figures like Xochitl to depict a "primitive" woman finding community, union with nature and peace as she breathes at one with the natural world. Yet at the same time Porter recognizes that this vision of female power does not offer women social authority, economic independence, or voice. María Concepción gains her child and breathes in easy harmony with the breathing world, but she also testifies to the authorities that this now obedient woman "[knows] her place" and will not criticize "the way of men."

In her journeys to Mexico, and her initial, albeit brief, idealization of the "children of Xochitl," Katherine Anne Porter joined other twentieth-century women who sought alternative social orders.[40] But as "María Concepción" so clearly communicates, the gender relations Porter encountered in Mexico's "primitive" cultures were solidly patriarchal, despite the celebration of women as fertile goddesses, both representing and nurturing a rich, cyclical natural world. "María Concepción" moves on two levels. On one, it shows a woman fulfilled through union with an archaic, essentialist life force, but on the other, it shows her giving up public power and authority for this new peace. Porter could not see how these two roads for women could come together, how a woman could be socially successful and self-determining while performing traditional, ostensibly natural, female gender roles. She continued to work with these two poles of female experience in much of her later writing, in stories of romantic love and of motherhood. Conflicts that continue to divide American feminism come to mind here, as we see Porter questioning essentialist or biologically based arguments for women's power and vision, revealing her growing recognition that exaltation of women in these terms can exist within patriarchal social orders without any diminishment of male authority. The next chapter analyzes in depth a group of stories from the 1920s, a decade in which Porter's gender-thinking addressed the relations between male and female artists, exploring the seductive power of men's images of women and suggesting that within women there lies a conflict between becoming the creator or the object of art.

CHAPTER THREE

BEAUTIFUL OBJECTS

When Porter's Princess walked the streets of her father's kingdom, fascinated male onlookers "searched the folds of her robes with cautious stares, wishing their eyes were hands; and turned away, saying each one to himself, 'Not even the gods know what manner of woman is concealed in that robe!'"[1] Curiosity, fear, and desire draw these male spectators to the Princess's armored body. Because she has rejected the simple shifts that would have coded her physical state for her culture, her body becomes undefined, potentially a threat, for if a different "manner of woman" is hidden under the thick robes, what then of the cultural order that hitherto had determined gender identity? Seizing control of her own body, the Princess seizes control of the central medium on which her culture institutionalizes its gender codes. The cautious and curious gaze of these male spectators reveals their need to know whether those codes yet remain intact, whether they, as men in a patriarchal order, yet retain their power. As in so many other fictional moments in Porter's work, the depiction of the Princess and her anxious audience raises questions crucial to a woman artist: Whose cultural and aesthetic resource is the female body? Who controls that body's meanings? For whom does the female body perform those meanings? How does a woman transform herself from an object in someone else's discourse to a self-creator, a professional artist?

In the world of Porter's Princess, the female body traditionally served as medium for male cultural scripts. So too in the Western art world Porter sought to enter. In the high form of painting, for example, "the traditional image of the female nude in fine art not only reinforces a view of women as erotic objects, it also helps maintain an ideological fiction in which men are always seen as creative artists and women as their passive models."[2] As we have already seen, Porter was keenly attentive to the ways in which her own move into the position of creative artist threatened her identity as a woman. In a group of stories written early in her career, she turned her gender-thinking to the relationship of male artist and female subject, exploring how women respond to being models, muses, or erotic objects. At the same time, she is attentive to the men's experience within this traditional relation, for the female body not only serves as inspiration and subject matter for male artists, but in the representations they create, men inscribe their fears and desires. Why have women participated in this relationship for centuries, Porter asks. Where do women find pleasure and reward sufficient to sustain and justify their continued role as the medium through which men represent their dominance?

On July 5, 1925, at the near-center of the twenties, Porter reviewed at length the published proceedings of a national symposium: "Sex and Civilization: Our Changing Morality."[3] "Sex and Civilization" collects statements by notable contemporary thinkers, male and female, on the striking changes in sexual behavior and gender roles witnessed since the turn of the century. Porter's review not only summarizes and analyzes the symposium but also contains significant personal responses; she used the symposium as a way to question her own position on the relations between the sexes and to address the connections between art and gender that were much on her mind throughout the decade.

The most personal and significant section of Porter's review brings together three different essays, each addressing the relations between women, men, and the arts. She begins with Sylvia Kopald's query, "Where Are the Women Geniuses?" Kopald argues that genius springs from freedom; once women are free "from the petty personal demands of others, [they] will also do great work in the arts." Kopald's argument undoubtedly appealed to Porter, but in her review, she juxtaposes Kopald's thesis with another by the anthropologist Alexander Goldenweiser, who argues that "woman's greatest work of art is the child . . . and her creativeness expresses itself best in domestic craftsmanship." "This is as it should be," Goldenweiser affirms. The "capacity for self-liberation is a male characteristic." Porter then adds to these seemingly contradictory arguments a third posited by Beatrice M. Hinkle, a well-known New York psychoanalyst. In her essay, "Women and the New Morality," Hinkle argues that women serve as a symbolic medium for men. Through the images they create of women, and cultural meanings they assign to the feminine, men express ideals they cannot meet on their own. Says Hinkle, "Woman was made a symbol or personification of man's morality." Thus men's need to control women's sexual status originates in their need to protect their symbolic order. In a remarkable passage, Porter combines Goldenweiser's argument for female creativity with Hinkle's, transforming Goldenweiser's physical creation—childbirth—into a metaphor for other kinds of generation. Women do create, Porter argues, but what they give birth to are implanted male ideas. Women's art is essentially unfree, imitative, an enactment of another's vision. Thus women take the "first rank in the art of acting" she states, picking up another point from Goldenweiser, and acting is "two-thirds interpreting and one-third dissembling." To quote her conclusion, in full:

> The actress is a plastic medium for the expression of some one else's idea. She is creative only in so far as she can conceive this idea, add to it her own essential quality and bring forth from the thought germ a full born interpretation. Why did woman allow herself to be used as a symbol by man? If this difference is biological, then it may be said that nature is the implacable enemy of woman, and it is the duty of intelligence to combat this destructive law. Nature can be conquered by persuasion, by patience. It is a long process of tree grafting, of seed mixing. (23)

Bringing together, restating, and even altering the arguments of these three social analysts, Porter builds her own conclusions, using the symposium to express her concern, in the twenties, that women are the media but not the makers of art. As the passage above reveals, she fears that woman's function as a passive medium for the male imagination may be natural, even biologically determined. Men carry the "thought germ" from which women "conceive" and then "bring forth . . . a full born interpretation." How then can an autonomous woman artist generate works of her own? Perhaps hers is a sterile creation?

Most of the time Porter treats the several contributions to "Sex and Civilization" somewhat tongue-in-cheek, finding more material for wit than for serious concern. There seems to be little she can wholeheartedly endorse in the social science theorizing of her contemporaries on the topic of gender roles and sexuality. Only Beatrice Hinkle's delineation of woman's role as "symbol or personification of man's morality" retains a hold on her and is actually assigned the word "truth." Hinkle argues that women not only serve as the symbolic medium for men's moral ideals but are punished for any action that threatens that symbolic order. Explains Hinkle, "That was the reason for his indignation at moral transgressions on her part. She had injured the symbol and revealed his weakness to him" (23). A half-century later, arguments like Beatrice Hinkle's have become fundamental to feminist theory. Culturally reproduced and endorsed images of women have historically served to justify and maintain patriarchal social order. Essential to that social order is the control of female sexuality; hence the centrality and power of images and discourses attending to her sexual status, summed up in the timeworn dichotomy, the virgin and the whore. Addressing specifically the place of women in Western art, in particular the female nude, Griselda Pollock attests, "Representing creativity as masculine and Woman as the beautiful image for the desiring masculine gaze, High Culture systematically denies knowledge of women as producers of culture and meanings." Rather than women as artists, we have women as media—the material from which meaning is made; in Pollock's words, "High Culture . . . works in a phallocentric signifying system in which woman is a sign within discourses on masculinity."[4]

The interrelations between creativity, gender, and power that Porter addressed in her review of "Sex and Civilization" concerned many women writers at the turn of the century. In her study *Aesthetics and Gender in American Literature: Portraits of the Woman as Artist*, Deborah Barker looks at the representations of the woman artist in the work of women writers, noting that for many of them, as for Porter, there is a fear that "the female artist was not simply an anomaly but an oxymoron." Like Porter, these women struggled with cultural assumptions about gender and power, as Barker argues, among these "the idea of the Romantic artist as male . . . and of the gaze as a masculine prerogative of artistic and sexual mastery."[5] In the fiction she wrote during the 1920s, Porter looks explicitly at this male prerogative, in particular the male artist's symbolic control of female sexuality. Five narratives evidence Porter's complex gender-thinking: "The Evening" (manuscript dated 1924), "Flowering Judas" (1930), "Virgin Violeta" (1924), "The Martyr" (1923), and its unpublished counterpart, "The Lovely Legend" (manuscript dated 1925). Each originates in her experiences within the Mexican artist community, and all focus directly on the subject of men, women, and art through depictions of the male as spectator and the female as spectacle, or the male artist and his female model/muse. In all of these stories, sadomasochism fuels the gendered relation.

The violence Porter perceived behind the cultural objectification of women is made manifest in tense yet erotic struggles for power and shifting postures of dominance and submission. The male characters share the same sadistic goals: to subject the women to their will, use them in the service of some creative act, and consume them as sexual objects. Yet although threatening, even monstrous, these powerful men are also dangerously attractive, Porter intimates. Confronted with the physical and emotional threat implicit in the presence of the male artists, her passive women respond complexly. They do not imagine a different, active existence; rather, their desires are for safety, escape from or protection against the controlling male gaze, and, at the same time, for the masochistic pleasure that Porter suggests women find in self-objectification. Except for "The Evening," these stories adopt either the woman's point of view, exploring the mingling of desire and terror aroused by the attention of a powerful man, or the man's point of view, exposing his combined obsession with and exploitation of the woman. All share an atmosphere of erotic tension and employ images of gluttony, suffocation, and entrapment. These biographically related stories expose the sadomasochism Porter saw fueling the transformation of women into symbolic and erotic objects. Read together and then set in the context of essays and unpublished journals, they reveal that during the 1920s, Porter's gender-thinking focused intently on both the intimate bonds between women's bodies and art and the issues of power that have shaped gender relations within the world of art.

The least coherent of the unpublished stories forming this group is "The Evening."[6] The manuscript consists of several developed but unconnected scenes, the most complete a café scene describing a long evening of sophisticated argument underlain with sexual speculation and desire. Seated in the Mexican café are an American woman and a group of Mexican artists, aesthetes, and revolutionaries, central among them Gordito, who has just returned from a mission for the revolution, which he privately wishes were more heroic. The woman, Alma (Porter also tried the names Elinor and Miranda), sits in silence, in part because her Spanish is poor, but primarily because she enjoys playing the role of beautiful, mysterious woman—she knows her silence is conducive to fantasy. Although inscrutable without, she is turbulent within: "Her eagerness to be beautiful in their eyes, to draw them to her, made her ache. Her nerve-ends boiled and bubbled. But she kept her face calm as she watched them, serpent-feminine enough to know that her attitude of calm pleased them."[7] The silent, erotic center of Porter's story, Alma cultivates being a spectacle. She is a dancer by profession, performing her art, like an actress, with her body as the medium. In fact, her body is what identifies her for the onlooker; she hides her face beneath a big hat, but her "long shoulder line and lank thigh identified [her] as the American dancer" (219).

Porter's suggestion in "The Evening" and later in "Flowering Judas" that women can experience pleasure in objectification has been a central subject of feminist scholarship on the visual arts. The influential work of critics such as Laura Mulvey, John Berger, and Griselda Pollock in both film and painting probes the historical assumption of a male spectator/artist whose primary subject matter is the female body. Berger argues that one consequence of women's continual representation as objects of the gaze is that women themselves learn this perspective. A woman is "split in two . . . she comes to consider the *surveyor* and the *surveyed* within her as the two constituent yet always distinct elements of her identity as a woman."[8] Film theory has extended this analysis into the realm of sexuality. A woman watching a film in which a female subject is sexually displayed can find pleasure either by identifying herself with the male onlooker or by identifying with the objectified woman. In other words, "Given the structures of cinematic narrative, the woman who identifies with a female character must adopt a passive or masochistic position."[9] Whether she joins in the desires of the spectator or unites with the passive object, she endorses her own objectification. What women learn from men's art is that their objectification is erotic. As E. Ann Kaplan argues in her analysis of the female spectator watching an erotic film, "Assigned the place of object (lack), she is the recipient of male desire. . . . Her sexual pleasure in this position can thus be constructed only around her own objectification.[10]

If we turn back to "The Evening," we find Porter's gender-thinking addressing similar disturbing connections between eroticism and objectification. Porter describes the silent Alma longing to be the central object of passionate male desire, yet to remain entirely passive. As she sits among the men in the café, she fantasizes: "She wished only to be loved, to be loved in an atmosphere of jealousy, of intrigue, of art, of music and gay conversation. She wished to inspire love, not to love. . . . to dance with one man while another stared in another direction with murder in his heart . . . added another fillip of pleasure to the dance" (281). The hints of violence in Alma's fantasy suggest the masochism at the heart of her longing for objectification. At one point Porter lets us into the mind of Alma's lover, Gordito. His fleeting thought: "Why had he not killed Alma?" A man with "murder in his heart" brings Alma to the dangerous but seductive edge of ultimate objectification—dead victim.

Perhaps Porter never finished "The Evening" because she was unable to settle on a point of view for the text. Passages, like the one quoted above, follow Alma's thoughts as her nerves "boil and bubble" in her violent desire to arouse violent desire. Other passages move into the minds of the men surrounding her, and in these Porter reveals how they, either artists or parasitical aesthetes, use women as the passive medium out of which they shape their aesthetic formulae. The men are engaged in a debate about whether beauty requires the presence of ugliness. Alma's body is their text. Declaims Ciro, "'The beauty must labour to be born out of the ugliness. . . . The line of a woman's cheek a little wrong, the pose of her head almost in complete harmony with her neck as it slides down to the exquisite line of her too-thin shoulder. . . .' He did not glance at the girl, but the others did. Her vanity trembled under the regard" (223). Porter punctuates the men's spoken discourse with their unspoken thoughts of desire for or hostility toward Alma. They all think of the silent woman as an object to be exchanged among them and use the traditional dualistic imagery character-istic of all the men in Porter's artist stories. In one draft, for example, Gordito muses, "She would not go back to Ciro or to Roberto—no she would not go back, she would go on to Vicente . . . little whore, adorable angel."[11] Whore and angel—Alma's symbolic significance swings from end to end of the moral spectrum as the men form and reform their fantasies of power and desire using the silent but willing woman as their game piece. Sheila Ruth aptly terms such a sudden shift in naming the "misogynist flip" and suggests that it occurs in relation to a woman's willingness or unwillingness to serve as passive medium for male signification. "The major factor in the flip from good to bad (that is, serviceable to not serviceable) is the matter of intrusiveness into male affairs; it has to do with women's self-assertion, self-direction, and will."[12] As we shall see, Porter again depicts this "flip" in "Virgin Violeta," exposing there a young girl's fear and confusion as she is named and renamed by a male artist, her symbolic status a matter of his language and desire.

"Flowering Judas" stands at the center of Porter's Mexico fiction, and at its tense erotic center is a long evening in which Braggioni watches Laura with the patience of a predator. Customarily interpreted as a story about the Mexi-can Revolution, "Flowering Judas" is also an exploration of the power relations between a male artist/spectator and a female subject. Told from the woman's point of view, the story carefully dissects her simultaneous attraction to and fear of objectification. The terrible but thrilling experience that held Alma in her seat, silent among her male admirers, here keeps Laura equally frozen and silent. Although "nobody touches" Laura, she appears surrounded by men who watch and desire her, and she defends herself against the sexual threat implicit in their gaze by erecting barriers. Like Alma, she maintains an "attitude of calm" and conceals her sexuality: her lips are "always firmly closed"; her "great round breasts" are covered "with thick dark cloth."[13] Likewise, Laura's defenses mask desire as much as resistance, for she enjoys being a spectacle (91). When a young man begins daily to follow her, "She is pleasantly disturbed by the ab-stract, unhurried watchfulness of his black eyes which will in time turn easily toward another object" (96).

Porter's depiction of Laura's self-defenses resembles her depiction of the Princess's armored body: "She has encased herself in a set of principles . . . leav-ing no detail of gesture or of personal taste untouched" (92). Laura's "notorious virginity" also sets her apart and shields her. Her ascetic denials contain her body and order her world, distancing her from emotional or physical contact. Like a saint, she "wears the uniform of an idea, and has renounced vanities" (92). Virginity is a means of self-possession in both "Flowering Judas" and "The Princess," an act of resistance to male desire to determine the status and meanings of the female body. And in both stories the woman who transforms herself into the "encased" or armored object threatens the symbolic order and thus risks being unnatural. So Laura fears, "It may be true I am as corrupt, in another way, as Braggioni . . . as callous, as incomplete" (93). Like the Princess, too, Laura is isolated and alienated from others: "She is not at home in the world" (97). Yet at the same time, her defended virginity arouses her spectators. She too is watched as she walks, and her commonest actions take on the quality of performance under the eroticizing gaze: "No dancer walks more beautifully than Laura walks, and she inspires some amusing and unexpected ardors" as she passes silently through the streets (95).

Like Alma in "The Evening," Laura's pleasure in her own objectification is combined with an "insatiable thirst" for "excitement." Her marginal participation in the revolution rises from an erotic attraction—what is dangerous is also sensual. As Jane Krause DeMouy suggests, "The revolution has the same fatal attraction for her that a flame does for a moth."[14] Laura experiences "pleasantly disturbed feelings" in "the presence of danger." Like Alma, for whom the gaze of a murderous lover provides a "fillip of pleasure," Laura too finds that "it is the remote but implied danger which gives the moment its pique." Following her desires, she lives tantalizingly close to impending violence, whether it be the revolution's chaos or Braggioni's physical assault. Hers is a "liminal state" between yielding and flight, an exciting, sustained tension. Seated across from Laura, Braggioni is the mirror in which she views what she fears and desires. His physical appearance suggests the combination of sensuality and violence that secretly attracts her. Gluttonous, oily, with yellow eyes like a cat, he exudes an erotic threat. Like Laura's masking clothing, Braggioni's costume forms a central symbol of his sexuality: "Over his lavender collar, crushed upon a purple necktie, held by a diamond hoop: over his ammunition belt of tooled leather worked in silver, buckled cruelly around his gasping middle: over the tops of his glossy yellow shoes Braggioni swells with ominous ripeness, his mauve silk hose stretched taut, his ankles bound with the stout leather thongs of his shoes" (93). Braggioni's silk and leather clothing suggests the implements of bondage in sadomasochistic sexual fantasies. His gasping body is "buckled cruelly" inside his heavy belt; his feet are bound. Braggioni represents the erotic dangers and pleasures of love for Laura, where yielding to desire requires subjection of the self.[15]

Despite the sexual bondage of his clothing, Braggioni's body expands around him. "His mouth opens round and yearns sideways"; "he stretches his eyelids"; and he "leans forward, balancing his paunch between his spread knees." In response, Laura's "knees cling together." Their two bodies, one swelling, the other shrinking, bespeak Porter's interest in the gestures that constitute gender performance. Here she accurately replicates male and female use of space: the female body confined and disciplined, the male expanding. As studies of men and women in public have demonstrated, most often "men sit with legs thrown apart, crotch visible," women "with arms close to the body, hands folded together in their laps . . . legs pressed together."[16] In every gesture, in the shapes their bodies take in space, Braggioni and Laura perform scripted gender roles about sexuality, identity, and power.

Cruel and vain, Braggioni pins Laura beneath his gaze and assaults her with his song. He plays the guitar as though it were her body, expressing through it the sexual violence implicit in his costume: "Under the rip of his thumbnail, the strings of the instrument complain like exposed nerves" (98). As a singer, Braggioni resembles the other artist figures in Porter's 1920s fiction; not only is woman his subject and inspiration, but the goal of his art is her submission to his fantasy of desire and power. Thus his song, which transforms Laura into a figure in a romantic legend, legitimizes his hunger. It represents an effort to control her by controlling the language that defines her. "'O girl with the dark eyes,' he sings and reconsiders. 'But yours are not dark. I can change all that. O girl with the green eyes, you have stolen my heart away!'" (97). Braggioni remakes the song as he would like to remake Laura; his words are a mask over his predatory gaze, the "cat's eyes" that, as he sings, mark "the opposite ends of a smoothly drawn path between the swollen curve of her breasts" (97).

Knowledge of Porter's source for Braggioni's song further reinforces the fact that she views the gluttonous revolutionary as an artist and Laura as his passive medium. Thomas Walsh has identified the song as "A la Orilla de un Palmar," a ballad in which a male speaker recalls a meeting with a beautiful woman and sings her lament: "I am a little orphan, alas. I have no father and no mother, nor even a friend who comes, alas, to console me" (Walsh's translation). As Walsh rightly points out, "The song is obvious male fantasy with the promise of sexual conquest lurking just below its sentimental surface."[17] In Braggioni's ballad, sung to the tune of his sadistic guitar, the male artist speaks the woman's desire; she is his creation, part of his fantasy of seduction and control.

Laura's silence and Braggioni's volubility further confirm her status as object and his as the controlling creator. Their verbal roles also enhance the sadomasochism implicit in their encounter: he is master, dominating language, working to control her meaning; she is silent, passive medium. As Roland Barthes once described an appropriate companion to Braggioni, the Marquis de Sade, "The master is he who speaks, who disposes of the entirety of language; the object is he who is silent, who remains separate . . . from any access to discourse."[18] Like the poet at the close of "The Princess," Braggioni uses language to shape Laura into the patterns of his own desire; in his ballad she obediently speaks of her longing for the comfort of his presence.

Laura attempts to defend herself from "the sight and sound of Braggioni's singing" by keeping "an open book on her knees, [and] resting her eyes on the consoling rigidity of the printed page" (91), as if the written word will defend her against the spoken. Her protection is ironic, of course, for there is no surety that one text will necessarily defend her against another. Yet the fixity of print seems to attract and console her, for rigidity characterizes Laura's aspirations, as it did the Princess's. Both women seek to escape inscription by the patriarchal culture that surrounds them, and Porter employs similar imagery to depict the consequences of their choice. For each woman, resistance takes the form of bodily control and rejection of sexual contact. The Princess's armored body defined her as an artist and a visionary, but it also made her unnatural, more artifact than flesh-and-blood woman. Laura too wants to be textual rather than sexual. Staring at the book, she seeks escape from Braggioni in another kind of art. But, as with the Princess, the price is alienation, the repression or denial of sexual desire. It is troubling to see Porter representing women who work to counter their objectification by choosing, essentially, to turn themselves into objects, freezing into silence and immobility, denying human connection.

Laura differs from the Princess, however, in her yearning to be a sexual object. Her immobility is a tense resistance against her own desire to yield to Braggioni's oily allure. Masochism, a thrilling attraction to violence, counters Laura's fear. As the long, slow evening progresses, her excitement grows and she moves away from self-imposed rigidity and toward her dangerous but desirable spectator. "The presence of death in the room makes [Laura] bold," and finally her desires move her to replace the book in her lap with Braggioni's pistol and gun belt. Her half-willing attraction to the combination of sensuality and danger in Braggioni becomes most apparent as she oils and loads his pistols. At his request, she takes his ammunition belt and "spreads it laden across her knees" and "sits with the shells slipping through the cleaning cloth dipped in oil" (99–100). The guns and the oil, the two elements of Braggioni's erotic appeal—violence and sensuality—completely occupy her. And when he then asks her why she has no lover, "a long, slow faintness rises and subsides in her," suggesting that her conscious defenses briefly yield to unconscious desire. The wave passes, but in that moment Braggioni's sensual but dangerous hold has tightened. Again the guitar represents Laura's passive body: "Braggioni curves his swollen fingers around the throat of the guitar and softly smothers the music out of it" (100). The moment is both climax and murder, a soft smothering. As the vehicle of his inspiration, she is killed into his art.

"Flowering Judas" has biographical ties to Porter's other fiction from the 1920s that continues her gender-thinking on the relations between women, art, and objectification. All of these stories characterize men's desire to dominate women through image and text as sadistic, and all complexly and ambivalently suggest women can find masochistic pleasure in their objectification. Braggioni's blond curls, youth, and impassioned song indicate that his character is partially based on one of Porter's admirers, the Nicaraguan poet Salomón de la Selva, with whom she was involved in 1922. Publicly, Porter claimed that she combined "four or five objectionable characters into one" when she created Braggioni,[19] and privately she was even more explicit about Carlos, the poet with predatory eyes in "Virgin Violeta." In unpublished notes on her *Collected Stories*, Porter wrote that Carlos was "based on looks, character, and malicious ways of Salomón de la Selva."[20] De la Selva's poetry shares in and likely influenced the atmosphere of her 1920s fiction. His collection *Tropical Town and Other Poems*, published in 1918, explores themes of religious and sexual devotion, often mingling the Christian and the erotic with intimations of violence. In these poems, sacred ecstasy, a dying to oneself in passionate communion with God, is connected with sexual ecstasy, losing oneself in another. Some of his poems recall the experiences of mystics like St. Theresa, others use language suggesting the rituals and implements of sacrifice, and still others are explicitly sexual, the sexuality emphatically stained with sadomasochism. Lovers' caresses are burning flames in the night; the lover is "afevered for the torture" of the beloved's touch; dawn brings death to passion; in several poems, the beloved herself is dead.[21]

Porter's papers also link de la Selva with two other acquaintances in 1920s Mexico: Diego Rivera and his model and wife Lupe Marín. According to her notes, the 1924 story "The Martyr" was directed at "Diego Rivera and his wild-woman Lupe Marín." Among her papers is a description of an evening with Rivera, Marín, and de la Selva from which she drew material for "Virgin Violeta":

> The night at Los Monotes . . . Lupe the Savage. Diego. Salomón de la Selva. our pilgrimage to the Nino Perdido. . . . The old convent in the old street, the cobblestones and broken glass, the rattle of the tinny orchestra from the pulquerria around the corner. A danzon. We dance, and afterward he makes a poem . . . something about the nuns in that convent who looked out on dancers in other days . . . and tonight their ghosts with ghostly partners, come and dance again—the nuns are dancing with small bare feet, over broken glass in a cobbled street . . . for me, he said.[22]

De la Selva's nuns dancing barefoot on broken glass—a startling image of erotic sacrifice—appears twice in these 1920s stories, in both "Virgin Violeta" and an unpublished artist narrative, "The Lovely Legend." In the latter, Amado, de la Selva's fictional counterpart, weeps briefly over a woman's masochistic devotion. "'She did, she did,' he sobbed. 'She danced for me on broken glass with her white feet bleeding. I knelt and kissed the wounds through the cold iron grill of the gate.'"[23]

The image of a dancing woman with bloody feet deserves attention, for it clearly fascinated Porter. Like Laura, the dancing nuns wear clothing that both covers their sexuality and ostensibly announces its repression or denial. External identity is erased, and one can either argue that they have found a way to control their own bodies, armoring them in an ideology, or one can read in their simple garb another form of self-erasure; they await the inscription of male desire, either the fantasy accompanying the erotic gaze or, in the case of the nuns, the patriarchal Word. The nuns' bare feet express their "freedom, sexuality and abandon"; they are in a state of nature.[24] Dancing on glass, they reveal their sexuality—the blood suggesting defloration or menstruation—and receive punishment for it. Their expression of desire is at the same time an expression of self-sacrifice. Dancing with their bloody feet, the nuns recall the little girl in Hans Christian Andersen's tale "The Red Shoes" who, entranced by her beautiful red shoes in church, forgets God; the punishment for her vanity is endless dancing, until finally she has her bloody feet amputated and embraces a self-sacrificing faith. Like Laura, the nuns are silent. They enact this erotic ritual for the male observer—"for me," the poet says. The poet both interprets their actions and claims them for his own pleasure, as did the acolyte at the close of "The Princess." The dancing nuns are de la Selva's supreme romantic fantasy, a spectacle of adoration, submission, and sexual sacrifice.

Even more than "Flowering Judas," "Virgin Violeta" reveals Porter's concern with the power of the male artist's text to contain, define, and seduce women. Violeta's awakening sexuality leads her from romantic fantasies of masochistic devotion fed by Carlos's poems, to a terrifying experience of her actual entrapment and victimization within these fantasies. Like "Flowering Judas," in "Virgin Violeta" the point of view belongs to the silent woman; controlling speech belongs to the man. Thus the story shares the same erotic tension of withholding and desire and has the same slow movement, a sense of unendurable time spent in a liminal state between boredom and arousal. From the beginning romantic love is entwined with religious ecstasy, violence, and abasement in the text. Carlos's poetry speaks of the "torment of love," and the picture above Violeta's head shows St. Ignatius before an aloof Virgin Mary, "grovel[ing] in a wooden posture of ecstasy."[25]

Violeta, passionate and imaginative, is set against her sister Blanca, whose name suggests both her purity and her docile nullity. Speaking only in whispers and dressed demurely in white, Blanca is one more blank page awaiting the inscription of her male artist/spectator.[26] Jane Krause DeMouy argues that the appearance and actions of the two sisters represent two possibilities for young women. "On a deeper plane . . . theirs is a struggle between chastity and passion and, ultimately, between woman as sacred object and woman as person."[27] However, the opposition of the two may be even more absolute. Blanca, quiet and obedient, represents passive female identity. She follows the rules of her patriarchal culture. Violeta, by contrast, is unruly, a violator, passionate as purple, speaking out of turn. Although she has spent the past year studying "modesty, chastity, silence, and obedience," her body remains restless; she fidgets, longs to "stretch her arms up and yawn," to take up the space of a Braggioni (26). On the brink of adolescence, full of ambition and desire, she must be forcibly taught her lack of power and her place.

Violeta has of course already been acculturated to receive this lesson through both the church—she attends a convent school—and literature. She loves poetry, and as a poet Carlos especially fascinates her; she longs for his approving looks and studies his poetry, seeking the images of his desire. The power of Carlos's text contends with that of the church for Violeta, giving her another version of what it means to be good. The two cultural texts come together in church, when she conceals his poems in her missal, memorizing them during religious service. The lessons about chastity and denial she receives from her education alchemize sexual desire into masochistic pleasure and guilt. Reading Carlos's words, Violeta fills with painful pleasure and her "swimming eyes" rise in adoration to "the delicate spears of candlelight on the altar." Notes De-Mouy, "her tears are an emotional release from repression of sexual desire that surfaces as she reads about chaste nuns who should not but nevertheless have loved. The titillation inherent in that image of forbidden pleasure for Violeta is only enhanced by her masochistic pleasure in the nuns' punishment."[28]

Through the long, slow evening, while she watches Carlos court her sister Blanca, Violeta dreams of a masochistic sacrifice, combining ecstasy with self-abasement. "She was certain she would be like those nuns someday. She would dance for joy over shards of broken glass. But where begin?" (24). Placing herself within Carlos's text, Violeta imagines herself to be "even one of the nuns, the youngest and best-loved one, ghostly silent" (25). Like Laura, she finds looking and being looked at absorbing and stimulating. She feels intensely exposed to Carlos's critical gaze as she sits at her mother's knee. And watching the poet watch her sister Blanca, she becomes increasingly aroused. As spectator, Violeta identifies herself with Blanca, the focus and actual passive recipient of Carlos's desire. This excited identification again resembles the potential pleasure that E. Ann Kaplan assigns to the female spectator of an erotic film: "Locating herself in fantasy as in the erotic, the woman places herself as either passive recipient of male desire or at one remove, as *watching* a woman who is passive recipient of male desire and sexual actions."[29] In Porter's text, Violeta's identification with her sister is so complete that she participates in her physical experiences. When Blanca's shawl slips from her shoulder, "A tight shudder of drawn threads played along Violeta's skin, and grew quite intolerable when Carlos reached out to take the fringe in his long fingers" (27).

Violeta alternates watching with fantasy. She imagines herself "miraculously transformed," beautiful and desirable. Like Alma in "The Evening," she longs to be a performer in a clichéd romantic scene, with an audience of excited, admiring men. Thus she imagines that "she would dance with fascinating young men . . . would appear on the balcony above, wearing a blue dress, and everyone would ask who that enchanting girl could be" (24–25). The center of Violeta's fantasy is of course Carlos; he is the most important of the admiring observers. In Violeta's mind, the poet's sexual desire would rise with his awareness that she has devoted herself to his poetry. Looking at her displayed on the balcony, "Carlos . . . would understand at last that she had read and loved his poems always" (25). For Violeta, memorizing the poet's text is one with becoming the text. Transformed into the perfect object, she becomes a poem. Just as Braggioni's guitar stood in for Laura's body in "Flowering Judas," so Violeta becomes Carlos's poem in her imagination, the perfect image of his desire.

Finally unable to restrain herself, Violeta intimates to Carlos her knowledge of his poems. The confession immediately brings both what she desires and fears: her transformation into an erotic object. When she rises to retrieve his book, the poet follows her down the dark hall, the predatory "*pad-pad* of his rubber heels close behind her" (28). Finally he traps her in the moonlight and kisses her. Although Violeta receives only a kiss, the impact of Carlos's act is equal to a rape; she is, as her name suggests, a virgin violated.

Carlos's unexpected kiss constitutes a terrifying violation for several reasons. Violeta has romantic notions of love; she turns to Carlos expecting "to sink into a look warm and gentle." What she confronts instead is the blank gaze of the predator: "His eyes were bright and shallow, almost like the eyes of Pepe the macaw." Rather than offering a communion between equals, Carlos seeks to possess and devour. Like Braggioni's predatory gaze, which belies the superficially compassionate content of his song, Carlos's eyes expose the sadistic desire that underlies his poetry. "Staring at her, fearfully close," their blank rapacity terrifies Violeta and she struggles to escape, feeling as if she's "about to smother" (29). No matter which way she turns, however, the young girl confronts another image of herself as she is perceived by the poet. She cannot escape his text: it surrounds her like a mirror, and she possesses no other language except that which defines and thus controls her. Her rapid transformations in the subsequent passages reveal the limitation of her imagination by the texts that have shaped it, as well as Carlos's overt use of those texts to control and punish her for her unruliness, her bold speaking, her apparent desire.

In the next moments Violeta's sense of her self is repeatedly transformed as she struggles to accept the changing images Carlos provides. The poet first calls her an innocent child, chiding her for overreacting to "a little brotherly kiss." His voice reveals that thinking about her innocence excites him. When he tells her that she "smell[s] like a nice baby, freshly washed with white soap," his "voice tremble[s] in a strange way." Longing for adulthood, Violeta cannot fully understand Carlos's fantasy, the pleasure he takes in imagining her innocence as a blankness, white-washed and eager for inscription. Yet she continues to watch herself as if through his gaze, assuming her cultural position as the one who is looked at and so defined and judged. She accepts the poet's image of her with shame and horror. "She saw herself before him, almost as if his face were a mirror. Her mouth was too large; her face was simply a moon; her hair was ugly. . . . Oh I'm so sorry! she whispered" (29). In her own mind, Violeta feels transformed into a round-faced infant by the poet's controlling language and look. To be undesirable, she feels, is to be without value, to not exist, and she suddenly longs "to run away," to kill herself.

Like Gordito, for whom Alma is alternately "little whore" and "adorable angel," Carlos enacts a "misogynist flip" and again transforms Violeta: "What did you expect when you came out here alone with me?" he asks, suggesting that she invited the kiss. Suddenly now she sees herself as seductress rather than innocent child—she provoked her own violation. "He turned and started away. She was shamefully, incredibly in the wrong. She had behaved like an immodest girl." Buffeted between the twin poles of male fantasy, Violeta is at one moment a sexual innocent and at the next a guilty whore. Her names replicate this polarity, for she is both Virgin and Violated. There is no escape from the constructs that surround and define her. "It was all bitterly real and unbelievable," she thinks, "like a nightmare that went on and on and no one heard you calling to be waked up" (30).

Laura and Violeta form a still center in their stories, surrounded by men who perform the actions and do most of the speaking. The willing objects of male fantasy up to a point, they alternately yield to and struggle against the defining language and erotic gaze of the more powerful male characters. In their identification with vehicles of the imagination—musical instruments, poetry—Laura and Violeta resemble artist's models, whose silent, posed bodies provide image and inspiration. In this context in two other stories dating from the 1920s, "The Martyr" and "The Lovely Legend," Porter's gender-thinking attends even more to the violence potential in male-female relations, explicitly exploring the idea that women's cultural status as symbols within male texts of desire and power deeply threatens women. She continues to suggest that sadistic and masochistic desires fuel this relation and lead women to find pleasure in compliance. Of these two stories, Porter published only "The Martyr." Unlike "Flowering Judas" or "Virgin Violeta," however, both "The Martyr" and "The Lovely Legend" are told from the point of view of the male artist. In these two works, Porter's attention turns more fully to the male artist's power. Both stories expose, with underlying irony and anger, his exploitation and objectification of women in the making of his art.

Creating Rubén, the artist in "The Martyr," Porter drew on her acquaintance with Diego Rivera. Isabel, Rubén's model, resembles Lupe, Rivera's wife and model, known for her violent temper, and the painting in the story corresponds to Rivera's mural *Creation*, which he painted in 1922 at the Preparatoria School.[30]

However, Porter draws Rubén with the exaggerated strokes of a cartoon. The "martyr" of the story, he can only speak of his passionate adoration of Isabel. When she leaves him for another artist, he essentially gorges himself to death, between bites mourning the moments when "she used to kick my shins black and blue."[31] Rubén's steady feeding not only reveals his self-destructive tendencies but also suggests his powerful desire to repossess Isabel. Thus Porter repeatedly links his eating to his loss: while he laments Isabel's absence he fills himself with substitutes: "crisp sweet cakes," "sweet wine," and "soft Toluca cheese, with spiced mangos" (36). "Eating cheese and gazing with wet eyes at the nineteenth figure of Isabel" on his easel, Rubén longs again to devour his model with his eyes but must now satisfy his hunger for her in other ways.

In his obsession with her as his model, Rubén's "consuming" desire for Isabel was apparent before she ran away. She would often "stand all day. . . . While Rubén made sketches of her" (33). His mural was to contain twenty figures of Isabel, twenty reinterpretations of her significance. In the flesh the single focus of the artist's gaze, Isabel becomes the sole subject of his language after her departure. Here she appears in the same dualistic terms—innocent child and evil temptress—that flipped Violeta across the spectrum of male fantasy. "My poor little angel Isabel is a murderess," Rubén mourns (35). She is a killer in the diminutive, "Ah Isabelita, my executioner!" (36). Ironic and exaggerated, "The Martyr" parodies the male artist's obsession with the meaning of woman. Yet even as parody, it suggests through Rubén's gluttony the artist's desire to control and consume his model through language and image. (At the same time the story alludes to Rivera's own voracious appetite for both food and sex. His frequent relations with his models—perhaps including Porter—are public knowledge.[32]) Isabel's response can be inferred from her flight, as well as from the boredom and sense of entrapment we glimpse before she escapes with her lover. Yet describing Isabel's new relationship, Porter reveals that this woman is as addicted to her objectification as is Laura in "Flowering Judas": Isabel has left Rubén for a man who will create a "mural with fifty figures" of her "instead of only twenty" (34).

The mocking tone of "The Martyr" disappears in "The Lovely Legend," replaced by anger and disgust. Here Porter portrays two male artists, friends, both using the same woman as image and inspiration in their art. The painter Rafael's relationship to this model is both overtly exploitative and sadistic; in contrast, the poet Amado is foolishly infatuated with his own fantasies of the woman. Rafael, occasionally referred to as Rubén, is clearly based on Diego Rivera; Amado, a poet and lover, takes his character from Salomón de la Selva.

The story opens with the two men discussing women as erotic objects. Amado is describing at length the color and odor of women he has desired or made love to. Rafael seems bored, mentioning finally his need for a particular type of woman to serve as a model: "I need a model for the Maya fresco. A lean tall woman who does not simper or paint her finger nails; who has long hard hands and feet, and a nose with a hooked bridge, that is the one kind of beauty I can endure in a woman: and her hair must be black."[33] According to Amado, Rosita, a dying tubercular prostitute living at Calle de la Palma, exactly meets Rafael's need. Like Isabel in "The Martyr," or like Lupe herself, according to Porter's notes, Rosita is aloof and bold, gaunt but physically powerful and often violent. Rafael takes her home as his model and paints her during the increasingly infrequent lulls between her violent rages and physical attacks.

Both Rosita's original profession and her increasing violence disrupt the reader's ability to share the complacency with which the male characters view her objectification. In fact, her first role as prostitute suggests the truth about her second as model. In both she is essentially powerless, an object that is exchanged between men and discarded when it is no longer of service. Whether standing before the two men in the artist's studio or at Calle de la Palma, she has value in her spectators' minds only insofar as she stimulates both their erotic fantasies and their art: the two are inextricably linked. Her violent attacks on Rafael suggest that Isabel resists her completely passive status. Although she does not speak, by throwing pots at the painter's head she clearly upsets the terms of their relation and attempts, unsuccessfully, to assert her presence as more than passive medium.

Rafael, however, remains entirely indifferent toward his model, unlike Rubén in "The Martyr." He does not recognize her violence or rage in any way. It is merely an annoyance, and he makes no effort either to understand or resolve it. For him, Rosita is an object, not a person, a more or less useful means for expressing his creative powers. As he tells Amado, this "empty creature, useless as a human being, has for me the value of a work of art." Amado the poet, by contrast, is deeply affected by Rafael's images of Rosita, "recreated in splendor, her likeness raised to the stature of a goddess" (213). Stimulated by his fellow artist's work, he begins to construct increasingly obsessive romantic fantasies about the model until, unable to overcome his infatuation, he flees to Nicaragua, rewrites all of his poetry, and dreams of Rosita's "magnified portraits."

Amado's obsession with Rafael's artistic visions of Rosita, rather than with the woman herself, underscores Porter's point that art serves as a dialogue between men about the purpose and place of women. During Amado's absence, Rafael tires of the model's violence because, Porter suggests, he fleetingly recognizes it as an effort at self-expression. As he tells Amado, Rosita acquired an increasing, irritating tendency to regard "those gorgeous bones as her own property" (214). He returns her to the brothel at Calle de la Palma; having taken what he needed from her, he finds her usefulness over. When an unsubdued Amado returns, Rafael tells him that Rosita is dead. The poet mourns the dead woman passionately and composes a lengthy ballad of her life, transforming her into "The Lovely Legend." But then, learning that she has been returned to her former profession, he visits Calle de la Palma only to experience an inexplicable yet complete collapse in his fantasy. She ceases to be a significant object for him, and he feels, suddenly, "as if she were really dead" (217).

In Rafael's last speech to Amado, Rosita's status as object to be appropriated and discarded becomes entirely evident. According to Rafael, Rosita herself had no identity; she existed and had value only through the forms given her by the artist's desire. When that desire disappeared, she became a thing of no value. Why mourn, Rafael asks his friend:

> You have your poem, I have my fresco: they are the ends, what else is in the least important? Rosita? pah, dead or alive, how does she figure in this now? . . . I tell you, you loved some fancy you had of her, nothing more. She is not a woman to love, she is a bitch and ugly to her core; any beauty she possesses you added to her yourself. I clothed my idea with her outlines, and I love that: but I never confused the two things. (216)

As prostitute, bitch, and ugly woman, Rosita is nothing—she has no significance except as a passive physical vehicle for the artist's vision. In Rafael's speech, Porter exposes the sadistic appropriation of Rosita by poet and painter. Rosita herself has no voice in the story—the men speak her significance and insignificance. Her only recourse is inarticulate rage. Ironically, through or by means of this silent woman, texts are produced: a poem, a fresco, a "Lovely Legend." These transform a dying prostitute, like an orphan wandering on a shore, or a nun dancing on glass, into an image that serves the male artist, expressing his desire and power.

When "The Lovely Legend" is grouped with Porter's other published and unpublished stories from 1920s Mexico, it becomes apparent that in her early fiction, her gender-thinking repeatedly returned to an exploration of the sadomasochism she saw underlying relationships in which women are transformed into symbolic and erotic objects. All of her male characters are artists: poets, painters, singers. Their poems, paintings, and songs originate in a relationship to a woman that is both violent and sensual. And their art is implicated in that violence. Although alternately seductive poetry and obsessive fantasy, it is always somehow predatory, seeking to define, objectify, and ultimately control its female subject. On the one hand, in those narratives written from the woman's point of view, the combination of attraction and danger surrounding the male artist creates such ambivalence that the female character is frozen between desire and terror, yielding and flight. On the other hand, narratives written from the man's point of view expose an attitude toward the woman that is either so fatuous or so coldly exploitative that the female characters respond with violence.

If we turn back to the question Porter asked in 1925 in her review of "Sex and Civilization," we can find a partial answer in these Mexico narratives written between 1923 and 1930. "Why did woman allow herself to be used as a symbol by man?" Porter asked. "If this difference is biological, then it may be said that nature is the implacable enemy of women and it is the duty of intelligence to combat this destructive law." Her narratives of male artists and female subjects suggest that the difference is not "biological," but it is sexual. Men find pleasure in their domination, and women—although frightened, frozen, or enraged—are deeply attracted to being dominated, to the threat of violence, to performing roles provided by men. The poems, paintings, and songs created in her stories of male artists and female models/muses either originate in the exploitation of a woman or express a man's desire to possess his beloved object—a desire that finds correspondence in her unacknowledged wish to be possessed. "Possessing," as Porter points out in a much later essay, "Marriage Is Belonging," is too often "the basis of many contracts" between men and women.[34] In short, the varying postures of seduction, infatuation, and sacrifice represented in the interactions of admiring men and admired women rise out of oppressive, violent relationships and are in actuality postures of domination and submission. Women are seduced by the allure of participating in the male-dominated art world, where they are taught repeatedly that objectification is exciting.

Caught up in the Mexican art community, Porter must have felt great contradictions between her attraction to and emotional involvement with the men she knew and her simultaneous recognition that both their art and culture sexually exploited women. She records with pleasure "Salomón repeating his poems, lightly melancholy, full of a false nostalgia, oddly enchanting."[35] Yet elsewhere her notes explicitly condemn the male poet: "I detested his attitude toward love and women." She comments wryly, "If Salomón met the Virgin Mary, he would introduce himself as the Holy Ghost."[36] "Symbols,"—"little whore, adorable angel"—or models and muses—"plastic medium[s] for the expression of some one else's ideas"—the women in Porter's Mexico fiction are objectified and exploited. Yet to grind paints and perhaps model for Diego Rivera and to dance with Salomón de la Selva and have that dance transformed into a poem were undoubtedly experiences Porter was unwilling to relinquish.

The stories Porter based on her experiences in 1920s Mexico reflect her intense gender-thinking about questions of art and sexuality. As a woman artist, she was acutely aware of the ways in which male-dominated traditions in literature and painting represented women as passive, often victimized, sexual objects, not as active creators. In these stories the male artist is dangerous, controlling, gluttonous. Yet he is also fearfully seductive. Both fantasies of power, playing a part in the long and thrilling history of a male-dominated art world, and suppressed sexual desire attract the women to these predatory men and, simultaneously, to their own objectification. These mute women from Porter's 1920s Mexico fiction provide an interesting counterpart to the Princess. Unlike them, the Princess rejected all sexual and emotional intimacy and used art to defend herself against men's desire. The implications that emerge are troubling, for the texts together seem to suggest that women can either be artists, at the expense of their sexuality, or sexual beings at the expense of everything—body and mind. The power of patriarchal narrative is everywhere evident in these texts, from the judge's sentence that sends the Princess to the tower, to the Poet's final words on her inspirational beauty; from Braggioni's smothering song, to Carlos's sacrificial nuns dancing barefoot on glass. To be the beautiful, best-loved object may be a woman's fulfillment, according to Porter's gender-thinking in the 1920s; as muse and mistress she can participate in men's creative achievement. However, it is at the price of her own independence and creativity that she receives the rewards of sexual love and social acceptance.

Katherine Anne Porter's stories of male artists do not tell how a woman can become a subject, can transform herself from passive medium to active self-creator, from model/muse to artist. Alma, Laura, Violeta, Isabel, and Rosita all feel the net of male desire that encloses them in language, image, and gaze, yet all lack the power or will to escape. Their stories tell with terrible candor what it means to be a woman who inspires the male imagination, awakening fantasy and desire. But none of these stories offers an image of an inspired woman. Porter's own words again come to mind: "The body of woman is the repository of life, and when she destroys herself it is important. It is important because it is not natural, and woman is natural or she is a failure. . . . Therefore women saints, like women artists are monstrosities. . . . You might say that if they are saints or artists they are not women."[37] Although Porter's analysis of women's symbolic role in male cultural production is brilliant and unflinching, she has not yet created a successful, undamaged woman artist. Nor has she yet found a response to Alexander Goldenweiser's argument in "Men and Women as Creators," an essay she assigned "some truth" to in her review of "Sex and Civilization." "Firmly he points out," she writes in that review, "that woman's greatest work of art is the child and that her creativeness expresses itself best in domestic craftsmanship" (23). Porter idealized motherhood, and in letters and journal entries throughout her life she repeatedly expressed a yearning for children of her own. Yet her fiction provides a more disturbing and ambivalent view of motherhood. There too she saw enormous risks for a woman artist. How can she give birth to her art and to a child? Can the two creative acts coexist? Or does one come at the expense of the other? Seeking answers, she turned the complex lens of her gender-thinking toward the subject of motherhood, in particular her own maternal legacy. What gifts do mothers give daughters? Can a childless daughter speak with a mother's tongue?

SEEKING THE MOTHER TONGUE

In one fragment of "The Princess," Katherine Anne Porter's artist heroine describes the beauty she creates as both bodily and transcendent, both in her flesh and existing independently of it. "This is the beauty I have dreamed and made," she proclaims. "If you should strip me, you will find nothing but that beauty I have made . . . and if you kill me, you cannot destroy my dream." Generative, weighted with her art, the Princess is mortal and yet the creator of something that will endure beyond her. Her language evokes both suffering and maternity: "If I am heavy with it, it is because the love of beauty is a heavy sorrow, and the making of beauty a task too great for the soul to endure for long." For the people of her father's kingdom, such misdirected female creativity bespeaks madness and heresy. As one "old lawgiver" sourly complains, "Since when has she become a god, to create with her hands?"[1] The links loosely drawn here between female artistic labor and the labor of childbirth form part of an enduring metaphorical chain in Western culture, one that represents creativity through the imagery of maternity. For women artists, these images are both attractive and disturbing, on the one hand suggesting that women are naturally creative, that in fact women artists are akin to their mothers, rather than unnaturally different. On the other hand, maternity's associations with pain and sacrifice, as well as the mere fact that motherhood has been so insistently women's rightful role, makes such imagery less compelling.

Porter looked long and hard at the relations of mothers and daughters, motherhood and vocation. Born in 1890 to a Texas family rooted in nineteenth-century social and aesthetic values, but living in the midst of the modernist world, Porter experienced fully the divide between her nineteenth-century predecessors and her twentieth-century peers. As she once observed, "I was bred to mid nineteenth century standards by a grandmother of unusual strength of character."[2] Like her foremothers, she often viewed motherhood in opposition to writing, yet like her contemporaries, she sought revisionary metaphors that would heal the gap between her present achievements and her maternal legacy. In this creative quest, Porter followed the path illuminated by other modernist women writers who turned to that maternal legacy as they sought to chart a new aesthetic of female creative power. As Heather Ingman writes of modernist women in her study *Women's Fiction between the Wars: Mothers, Daughters, and Writing*, "Their attempt to recover the maternal inheritance . . . is a quest to find a female identity which will empower them as writers."[3]

In the rich and relatively unexplored landscape of motherhood, modernist women found many possibilities for their own art. Some sought a mother tongue, a feminine language, preverbal, embodied, speaking of presence, one that could replace a masculine language of symbol and absence. Others turned to childbirth imagery, seeking affirming metaphors for women's creative labor. Perhaps writing, thought some, brings women into closer relation with their mothers: rather than becoming unnatural or unsexed by their vocation, women who write are fruitful bearers of the word.[4] "Far from being a regressive influence which has to be left behind in order for the daughter to enter the symbolic order of language and culture," suggests Ingman, "the mother and the recovery of the mother's voice in many cases frees the daughter's writing."[5] Like many of her peers exploring the question of their maternal legacy, Porter found a rich resource in Virginia Woolf.

Few writers received Porter's unqualified praise. However, her admiration for Virginia Woolf never wavered. In a 1954 letter to her nephew Paul, Porter lamented Woolf's death, naming her "one of the wonderful beings of our time." As she confessed to Paul, "I am haunted by a vision of her figure, tall and gaunt as a tower, leaving her stick and her cloak on the bank, and walking into the water on that cold March day. . . . Think of any one being so lonely as that! I still shed tears about her, for some reason her death hurt me more than any I have known in my time."[6] Of all of Woolf's writings, Porter spoke most often of *To the Lighthouse*, including this great novel of motherhood in her list of literary works she "believed in in my time." Her concluding words in the eulogistic essay she published on Virginia Woolf point to one source of her love for this literary foremother. Porter wrote, "She lived in the naturalness of her vocation. The world of the arts was her native territory; she ranged freely under her own sky, speaking her mother tongue fearlessly. She was at home in that place as much as anyone ever was."[7] Natural, at home in her art, "speaking her mother tongue," Woolf embodied much that Porter sought in her own work as a woman artist. The language Porter chose for her praise suggests she saw Woolf as successfully uniting her life as a woman and her art. Although Porter herself wrote "the body of woman is the repository of life . . . . and woman is natural or she is a failure," she can say of Virginia Woolf, "She lived in the naturalness of her vocation." In fact, Porter's praise for Woolf incorporates in the phrases "mother tongue," "naturalness," and "at home," one positive formulation of her career-long gender-thinking.

There is no need here to rehearse the many compelling discussions of Woolf's concern with the woman writer and her maternal legacy. Both *To the Lighthouse*, published in 1927, and *The Waves*, in 1931, take maternal presence and absence as their subject and find in memory a means to generate language or art. There is no writing without loss, Woolf tells us in these novels full of longing and memory. Ingman identifies Woolf as a central forger of a maternal aesthetic, writing of her "yearning after the lost mother," her efforts "to recreate the mother's presence," her awareness "of the buried mother's world pressing against the father's." Margaret Homans perceives Woolf's identity as a writer depending "not on cutting [herself] off from [her] mother's world, but on trying to retrieve it."[8] Especially in the 1930s as she passed the midpoint of her life, Porter resembled Woolf and other modernist women writers in her efforts to understand her own maternal legacy and to probe, through memory and metaphor, the connections between a daughter's language and her mother's death.

Porter's interest in the potential relations between artistic creation and maternal legacy appears as early as January 1920 in "The Shattered Star." In this embryonic tale of female creativity and alienation, the infant Nayagta reveals from birth a natural attraction to beauty. She loves to watch "the light from the oil bowl rippling in shadows on the walls of the ice hut until they shone with blue and green and silver light like stars shining in the sea. . . . Nayagta loved this almost as much as she did the warmth of her mother's neck and shoulders as she lay cuddled in the furry parka (hood) that covered her mother's head. And she loved to hear her mother sing in a low voice, the same song always, that had only three notes in it."[9] Torn from this comfortable mother-daughter world by the "will of the Moon-man," Nayagta learns powerful magic but is unable then to rejoin her people. The result, as discussed in chapter 2, is the Northern Lights, Nayagta's art. The story makes evident that Nayagta's brilliant creation may employ the magic learned from the patriarchal Moon-man, but it is compelled by and seeks to express her yearning for reunion with her mother's body. She is alienated forever, eternally homesick for this lost connection. The art she creates rises out of memory and is her attempt to replicate the lost world of the mother. Here is Porter's account of Nayagta's creative labor:

> Nayagta, wrapped in a great whirling cloud of black and gray, comes up scream-ing her homesickness in the storm rack; or lies at peace on the edge of the sea watching her shattered star as it is mirrored deeply in the snow and frozen seas. It ripples like the light of the whale oil lamp on the walls of the igloo where Nayagta's mother used to sing three little notes as she swayed with Nayagta in her hood. And Nayagta remembers forever.[10]

The mother's monotonous song, just three notes repeated over and over as she rocks the child against her body, suggests a kind of mother tongue, a commu-nication that allows no gap between speaker and listener, one that speaks of fullness and connection rather than symbolizing what is lost. In her influential study of women's gendered relation to language, *Bearing the Word*, Margaret Homans defines such communication as "literal language," language replete with the mother's presence rather than emerging from her absence. "The words matter as sounds, monotonous and rhythmic, issuing from and returning to the body. This is what I mean by literal language shared between mother and daughter: a language of presence, in which the presence or absence of referents in the ordinary sense is quite unimportant."[11] Memories of this mother tongue and the comforting security it expresses are central to Nayagta's homesick longing for the lost world of childhood. In fact, it is her desire for the lost lan-guage and absent body of her mother that induces her creative labor. Homans identifies this as a fundamental relationship: "We could locate in virtually all of the founding texts of our culture," she argues, "a version of the myth . . . that the death or absence of the mother sorrowfully but fortunately makes possible the construction of language and of culture."[12]

In Homans's work, as well as that of other scholars who have explored the connections between women writers, language, and the maternal legacy, the ideas of the French psychoanalyst Jacques Lacan provide a theoretical corner-stone. Lacan argues that infants move from a pre-Oedipal, undifferentiated, and nonverbal union with the mother into separation and speech. Male children, denied the mother's body, receive as a substitute all of language and culture, receive in Homans's summation, "what Lacan calls 'the law of the father,' or the symbolic order . . . the sign system that depends on difference and on the absence of a referent." Under Lacanian theory, the daughter does not travel the same road. Rather than joining the male child as maker of symbolic substitutes for the mother, she becomes herself a signifying object. As Homans argues,

"Women must remain the literal in order to ground the figurative substitutions sons generate and privilege."[13] Here it is not amiss to recall Porter's own description of a woman as an actress: "a plastic medium for the expression of someone else's idea."[14] In her stories of male artists and female models, we have seen how she sought to answer a key gender question: "Why did woman allow herself to be used as a symbol by man?" In her writing on mothers, daughters, language, and memory, Porter continued her gender-thinking on related questions. What is the source of language for women? Is it, too, connected to the mother's absence? Can a woman "go home" (i.e., reconnect with her lost mother), and if so, is this reconnection positive and productive or silencing, even self-annihilating?

At times it seemed to Porter that Western culture denied women any metaphors for imagining a reconnection with their place of deepest origin. Among her unpublished papers are some intriguing notes on Genesis, inspired by her reading of Simone de Beauvoir's influential arguments in *The Second Sex* (1949). Here Porter muses about what she terms "the rib myth, perhaps the most sinister, unaesthetic and evil of all myths, but endowed with a dreadful meaning." Porter reads Genesis as a story of women's homelessness and exile. Initially she feels a deep sympathy for Eve, and for all women, who, in her thoughts, are unlike men because they cannot return to the place of their birth, cannot, she feels, return to the nurturing love of a woman as a substitute for the mother. "The loneliness of women is greater than of men," she writes, "because man literally can return to the womb, and woman cannot. She is cast out once and for all, for Adam's side is closed and she cannot go back to her old home." As is characteristic of her gender-thinking, however, a second later Porter shifts her tone and perspective. Although she sympathizes with women as exiles, she despises what she sees as the solution many have chosen—identity through a man. It seems men may find rebirth and renewal through a symbolic return to the womb, but women, attempting to return to Adam's hard side, find lifelessness instead. "The woman trying to find her life and the meaning of her life in a man" gains nothing, Porter writes contemptuously. "Poor lost shivering Eve, trying to creep back inside her man and be a rib again." In the story of Genesis, which Porter calls a "strange and ominous myth, created out of the enormous male vanity," men have it all. Not only do they give birth to women, but they can return to the womb, to home, and find their "life and the meaning of . . . life."[15] Women, by contrast, can only facilitate men's regenerative return. Although they may long for a journey home, they face eternal exile, homelessness.

Homelessness, homesickness, and exile are all words that appear again and again in Porter's writing, published and private. Journeys away from or toward a variety of home places recur throughout her fiction, from "The Shattered Star" to *Ship of Fools*. And her letters are filled with descriptions of houses. Porter's peripatetic life can be viewed as an unending search for the perfect home. Each time she settled and gathered her papers and furniture about her, she wrote lyric letters to friends and family, letters filled with images of flowers, fruits, warmth, and light—the good place at last. But each time she became dissatisfied and moved on. In 1954, at the age of sixty-four, she wrote an essay titled "Here Is My Home" for the aptly named magazine *Perfect Home*. It begins with the confession, "I am still searching, really for 'home' in the accepted sense. My mother died when I was 18 months old, and my grandmother, who cared for me as a child, died when I was only 10 years old."[16] Here, as elsewhere in her work, home is closely identified with her mother and her mother's primary substitute, her grandmother. Approximately ten years earlier, Porter responded with powerful emotion to Malcolm Cowley's *Exile's Return*. Her answer to Cowley, titled "The Land That Is Nowhere," survives as almost one hundred pages of repetitive autobiographical fragments, recording her struggle with the word "exile" and providing some of her most compelling descriptions of her sense of homelessness. Here she describes herself as "the one who had lost something. . . . I was looking for the country where I should be reborn." And again, "Being a pilgrim and a stranger by birth and by experience and by the force of the times in which I lived. There is no foot of ground on this earth which I can set my foot and say, 'this belongs to me, and I belong to it.'"[17] However, "The Land That Is Nowhere" also contains Porter's crucial recognition of the permanent home she carried within herself wherever she traveled. For in these unpublished writings, "The Land That Is Nowhere" is not only a home lost but also a home gained—the home of art.

In her insightful essay on the "Origins of Power in the Fiction of Katherine Anne Porter," Shirley Scott connects Porter's writing to her earliest experiences of loss and absence, suggesting "that even as a child Porter associated the written artifact with a dialectic of the presence and absence of the self." Letters, journals, a work of fiction—all represent language signifying absence, while simultaneously embodying a new, ordering presence. Scott extends her argument from language to embrace all artifacts, finding in *Old Mortality*'s material objects that replace the dead and evoke their memory testimony of an absence and an effort "to imply and constitute a presence."[18] When Porter felt fully at home in her art, she could say of herself, "I was never, for one moment, no, not even in the place I was born, an Exile. The Land that is Nowhere, that is the true home." Or, as she writes, more explicitly, in her praise of Virginia Woolf, "She lived in the naturalness of her vocation." In the "world of the arts . . . she ranged freely under her own sky, speaking her mother tongue fearlessly. She was at home."[19]

Porter's finest work records her efforts to draw on her maternal legacy to create meaning and order, a secure home in a world characterized by disorder and absence. Memory, making the lost past present, and homesickness, a longing for a people, a place, and a childhood peace that precedes loss, proved to be her richest resources. In all of her writing, memory, home, and—at a deepest level—the lost mother are interchangeable, for memory takes her back to home, to a place that can be either terrifying and empty—the grave—or full of comforting presence. Between 1930 and 1940, at the midpoint of her life and in her most productive decade, Porter forged the creative concept of "legend and memory." These twinned terms came to describe for her the process from which her finest writing emerged. Her formulation of "legend and memory"—and the stories that arose from it—all began in her work on a projected novel tentatively titled *Many Redeemers*.

Never completed, *Many Redeemers* represented an extraordinarily ambitious plan to retell the Porter family history in fictional form. It would cover "from about 1700 to 1918," moving from European roots to the present. The work was intended to mingle historical record and family narratives with Porter's own deepest recollections, to unite, that is, "legend and memory."[20] For Porter, only the past constitutes true presence, is real, solid, reliable. As she proposes in some "Notes on Writing" dated "Paris, Fall 1936," "Of the three dimensions of time, only the past is 'real' in the absolute sense that it has occurred, the future is only a concept, and the present is that fateful split second in which all action takes place." Writing out of memory, Porter sought to enter into the "real" to connect with the concrete, determining experience of the past. For her, the 1930s became a decade of memory, in which she constantly traveled back into her past. From memory came the material for her fiction. "This constant exercise of memory seems to be the chief occupation of my mind," she wrote, "and all my experience seems to be simply memory, with continuity, marginal notes, constant revision. . . . Now and again thousands of memories converge, harmonize, arrange themselves around a central idea in a coherent form, and I write a story."[21]

Piecing together fragments of memory and legend, creating a new coherence or presence out of absence, Porter is "remembering" in the word's most essential meaning, as a "re-membering," a putting together of a lost or scattered body. So too Nayagta embodies her lost mother in the Northern Lights. So too, as Margaret Homans argues, language rises from the absence of the mother. Porter repeatedly spoke of her work with "legend and memory" as bodily, even preverbal. For example, describing her composition method for *Many Redeemers* to her friend Caroline Gordon, she wrote, "I depend precisely on what I know in my blood, and in my memory, and on something that is *deeper than knowledge*."[22] Drawing on this buried knowledge was painful. Porter powerfully depicted the process in a letter to Eudora Welty, another female friend, trying to communicate how she drew the text from the vitality of her own bodily memory: "My God, I can compare the process only to tapping my own spinal fluid, so nearly does it come to the quick of memory, that is, numberless memories all fused together . . . the real difficulty is explaining how, by the organic process of creation, the scattered and seemingly random events remembered through many years become fiction."[23]

Throughout the early 1930s, Porter referred to the various sketches and short stories that she later collected under the title *The Old Order* as portions of a projected novel. For example, she wrote her friend Robert Penn Warren, then editor of *The Southern Review* in 1935, "I could have sent you the section from my novel, *Midway in this Mortal Life*, called 'Legend and Memory.' But the *Virginia Quarterly* published two portraits from it and have accepted for April a fragment called "The Grave."[24] It was not until 1965 that "The Fig Tree," in Porter's words, took "its right place in the sequence," immediately before "The Grave."[25] With this placement Porter confirmed the importance of maternal death and memory to the sequence as a whole. However, *The Old Order* also opens with a version of Porter's creative process, the making of a work of art out of fragments of legend and memory. Grandmother and Nannie, both storytellers, spend hours with needles, old family finery, and "clear lemon floss," sewing family quilts. As the two women sew, they talk, remembering the past and analyzing the present in the light of all that preceded it. Again and again their conversation alters and organizes each new day into a version of the past, incorporating it into their old, orderly story. "Even the future seemed like something gone and done with when they spoke of it."[26]

Porter's representation of the interaction of "legend and memory" through the image of piecing a quilt connects her own creative process to women's culture by employing a traditional emblem of women's writing.[27] In their collaborative work, the two elderly women employ the material of women's lives, recounting marriages, births, and deaths and stitching together fabric worn by the family women at these central events. Their "clear lemon floss" creates a beautiful and useful object from fragments of the past: the quilt suggests how the past, when reembodied through art, becomes a comfort to the present, an enclosing warmth, and something to be passed on in a family as a thing of good use. The image, standing as Porter's sign of her creative process at the start of *The Old Order*, suggests that the compounding of "legend and memory" was, in her gender-thinking, a particularly feminine creative process.

Yet for Porter, other aspects of her maternal legacy were less positive. As is characteristic of her gender-thinking, she refused to rest in one place, here in the celebratory metaphor of female domestic labor as a sign of her creative method. Other portions of her inheritance from her mother and foremothers deeply complicated any simple effort to embrace her legacy. For Porter, in particular, traumatic exposure to the connections between childbirth and death complicate maternity as a potential metaphor for creation. Overall, memory is always double-edged in Porter's writing. At times the journey back brings loss of voice, not freedom, brings her to a preverbal state where the self risks being erased, devoured by the mother's enclosing presence. At other times the journey brings her to a fertile, comforting, and joyous place where the self feels whole and endlessly renewed. In her papers she carefully saved a few phrases that summarized this double face of the mother, linking her—as so often Western culture does—with that greater mother, Nature, Mother Earth. "Earth, my tender, soberly smiling mother, oh fruitful nourisher, oh demonic fury, oh drinker of blood, insatiable devourer of rotting flesh!" Porter dated these words "Mexico 1921, copied Basel 1932." Porter's words rather strikingly resemble those of the French psychoanalytic writer Julia Kristeva, who writes of "the desirable and terrifying, nourishing and murderous, fascinating and abject inside of the maternal body" in *Powers of Horror: An Essay on Abjection*.[28] Kristeva's description of the French author Celine's struggles with the "mother-tongue" highlight Porter's creative labors. In her evocative prose Kristeva describes how he probes within for a "buried authenticity," attempting to find language for "an unnamable truth of emotion," to "bring the depths to the surface, carry emotional identity as far as signifying appearances, raise neural and biological experience up to social contract and communication."[29] To quote again from Porter's description for Eudora Welty of her own creative work: "My God, I can compare the process only to tapping my own spinal fluid."

Often Porter depicts the journey into memory, toward the lost mother, through landscape. In her imagery the journey back may bring her to a place of death, an empty grave, or to a rich, life-giving resource, a fertile orchard.

Notes among her papers describe the two sides of memory, the tomb and the womb: "The past can be a viper concealed in the dear hoarded heap of rubbish where you thrust your unguarded hand; or the opening of a grave where you breathe in again the old sickness of which you have already once died, and now must die again; or a curtain drawn idly without thought to find a green spring landscape there, just where you left it, buttercups, the sound of running water, morning light, new-born calves, and all."[30] Porter's imagery suggests her awareness of both the delights and the dangers of journeying into the buried past. More than once she employed the double imagery of pastoral landscape and grave in her fiction, notably in two stories from *The Old Order*: "The Fig Tree" and "The Grave." Linked to these are the unpublished story "A Vision of Heaven" and a much-revised elegy she wrote for her mother and titled "Anniversary in a Country Cemetery." Along with unpublished fragments of autobiography and other notes or drafts connected to her work on *Many Redeemers*, these texts address the relations between the mother's legacy and the daughter's creative self. In all of them we find Porter's complex and brilliant gender-thinking about a maternal aesthetic. Inscribed in them as well are her anxiety about being a woman and an artist, the fear that inevitably followed her mother's death just two months after childbirth, and the painful lesions left from her own experience: an abortion and a stillbirth. For Porter the maternal as creative metaphor was dangerously close to her own fears and grief.

Porter wrote most directly about her childhood in "Pull Dick—Pull Devil," an unpublished, incomplete autobiographical essay. It begins with the central fact of her mother's death: "My mother died of her fifth child, when I was a year and a half old." The loss was kept very present throughout her childhood she records, for her father never remarried and perpetually mourned his wife, making "a cult of her memory," which he shared with his children. He brought out pictures of their mother and told them romantic stories about her: "We saw and touched her gloves, her curls of hair, her strange and charming dresses: he showed us bits of jewelry we should have when we grew up." In *Old Mortality* Porter recalls these rites: the story flows back and forth from fiction to actual memory. There it is the grandmother who "twice a year compelled in her blood" brings out the "locks of hair . . . yellowed long gloves and misshapen satin slippers"; however, the father also participates, reading young Miranda and Maria romantic poetry: "'Her tantalized spirit now blandly reposes, Forgetting or never regretting its roses. . . .' Their father read that to them."[31] Porter echoed these lines in the close of her own poem, "Anniversary in a Country Cemetery," which she buried in her mother's grave in 1936: "This shape of her love / Whose living dust reposes / Beside her dust / Sweet as the dust of roses."[32]

Repeatedly expressing to his children a wish that they had never been born, Harrison Boone Porter seems to have consistently shared with them his guilt over their mother's death, which followed a debilitating pregnancy, the fifth in seven years. According to Porter, her father frequently expressed the feeling that he had been "betrayed" by his marriage, for he was "wifeless when he had wanted a wife, and a father when he did not want children."[33] His children, replacing the lost and perpetually mourned wife, were simply a burden. Among Porter's notes is a brief entry on her mother's death, mentioning the guilt transferred from father to children: "She was very young," Porter writes, looking at a photograph, "and she died of exhaustion at the birth of her fifth child, her fifth in the space of less than seven years. Quite literally she died under torture, and the guilt of this death was never lifted from any of us, husband and father, and the children through him."[34]

Blaming his wife's death on his children, Porter's father repeatedly linked childbirth and death, a link that profoundly influenced Porter's thinking. According to her notes, his first words to his daughters when they married were, "Don't have children." Her mother "died too young and too hard a death," she wrote in "Pull Dick—Pull Devil," "and somehow this was told to me in a way that makes a sore spot in me to this day."[35] When her older sister Gay had her first child, the first birth of their generation, Porter feared that Gay would soon die. Seeing her sister quietly resting after labor, she imagined her "wounded and remote with the kind of far awayness of people who know they must die and so have nothing to say to life."[36] But Porter may have also possessed concrete early memories that connected childbirth with suffering and death. Joan Givner, who visited the family home where the mother died, describes it as "a simple two-room L-shaped log structure."[37] The children might well have overheard or even witnessed their mother's labor. Although Mary Alice Porter died two months after giving birth, Porter's words—"she died . . . at the birth of her fifth child"—indicate that the powerful impression of childbirth overshadowed everything.

Pursuing the depths of memory, linked to mother and landscape, Porter often spoke of feeling homesick, of yearning for something lost—a place, a people, security. In the early 1930s she frequently expressed to her friends a longing to revisit places from her childhood in west Texas. "I'm getting simply and childishly homesick," she wrote Janice Biala on May 16, 1935. "I want to see my family and that country once more."[38] In 1936 she made the trip, which included a special excursion to visit both the old family home in Indian Creek, abandoned after her mother's death, and the nearby graveyard where her mother was buried. The two locations—the small farm and the grave—a home lost with the loss of the mother, a landscape full of both her presence and her absence, became rich sources for imagery Porter wove through much of her fiction, letters, and journals, appearing, for example, in her depiction of memory as the open grave and "green spring landscape . . . [with] new-born calves."

In the fifteen years since Porter had last visited Texas, her memory had perfected the world of her childhood. The Indian Creek farm, with its roses and pecan and fig groves, had become an Eden and a source of perpetual longing. No other dream recurs with such frequency in Porter's private papers as does the dream of reproducing this first perfect place, secure and bountiful: she wished for an "acre where I could grow apricots and almonds and figs."[39] Her frequent descriptions of houses remembered or imagined speak of a similar Edenic landscape. "Home . . . is a continuous, deep, sunny revery," she wrote in "Here Is My Home." It is a world of absolute peace and contentment, filled with food and fragrance: "This house is in the country; and in a climate that grows figs and peaches, camellias and gardenias." It is timeless and completely fulfilling: "Everything I ever loved is there, and all my friends come and go at ease. . . . All the books and the music and the flowers and good food have gone there; and there it is, astonishingly perfected and radiant."[40] This perfect home is recalled in the grandmother's fruitful plantation in *The Old Order*, as well as in Porter's public, half-fictionalized memories of childhood in "Notes on Noon Wine" and several interviews, particularly one with the *Paris Review* in 1963. In all of her descriptions, home is characterized by its fertility; the landscape is full of fruit-laden trees, flowers, and newborn animals. Its warmth and fecundity, and the pleasure she experienced recalling it, connect it with her earliest nurturing relation. In this completely gratifying, secure place, she could live "a continuous, deep, sunny revery; a long day dream of perfect beauty."[41]

The lost childhood home replicates the lost mother, for the family moved shortly afterward and entered the unhappy years that followed Porter's mother's death. Since then, nothing could be as fulfilling and complete as the landscape of memory, no home as complete as the child's with the mother. Thus as frequently as she writes of her longing for a home buried in the past or reproduced in the present, Porter records her feelings of alienation and homesickness. As she acknowledged to a friend in 1941, "My life has been a long history of my attempts to take root in a place, to have a place to go back to, at least. . . . This has been so often thwarted and disappointed, it has become almost like a fantasy, a mere day dream, and I have resolved quite often to put it away, and think of it no more, and I have tried to persuade myself that such an apparently simple, natural, human situation was not for me."[42]

The actual Indian Creek house, which, responding to her yearnings, Porter revisited in 1936, felt shabby and rather forlorn; the orchard had been cut down, and everything seemed diminished. In her drafts for "Here Is My Home" (originally titled simply "Home"), she recalls her grief and alienation: "Old friends of the family showed me bits of furniture, but they might as well have been talking to a stranger. I went back to my grandmother's house, and home was not there, either; it was an empty forsaken house with not even a ghost in it. I have not found it anywhere since, though I have looked for it everywhere."[43] However, her visit to her mother's grave in the family cemetery felt, at least momentarily, like a homecoming. At first Porter was terrified to approach the gravesite—"shaking with fear of my own feelings"—yet the "quiet dark blue marble stone and the old calm weathered earth of her grave" soothed her. Her notes on this journey describe a sudden sense of peace: "I sat down beside her and began instantly to dig a place to plant the rosebush I had brought. I felt strangely at home, rested, eased, full of the most profound almost painful joy."[44] In her recollections of this experience, Porter claims that she wrote a poem at her mother's gravesite, which she then "tucked . . . into the earth."[45] She revised this poem repeatedly before finally publishing it under the title "Anniversary in a Country Cemetery":[46]

This time of year, this year of all years, brought
The homeless one home again;
To the fallen house and the drowsing dust
There to sit at the door,
Welcomed, homeless no more.
Her dust remembers its dust
And calls again
Back to the fallen house this restless dust
This shape of her pain.
This shape of her love
Whose living dust reposes
Beside her dust,
Sweet as the dust of roses.[47]

In the poem, a return to home clearly represents a return to the dead mother. In "repose" by this "fallen house," Porter feels eased, "welcomed," no longer alone.

Porter's claim that she wrote "Anniversary in a Country Cemetery" while at her mother's grave is fascinating and not completely true. Perhaps she composed a new version of the poem there or simply wrote down what she already held in memory. Well before the trip to Texas, however, in Paris in 1932, she had been working on the poem at the same time that she was writing portions of *The Old Order*. Yet the peace and welcome she felt, and the image of effortless, spontaneous literary composition, tell a deeper story. Here, rejoining the mother, the daughter's voice comes free.

Porter's terror approaching the grave suggests that her expectations of the visit were initially double-edged. As she had succinctly expressed in 1921, the mother is both a nourishing home and a devouring grave. In fact, the last four lines of the published version of the poem were not added until twenty years after this memorial visit. All earlier versions express the dangers and pain of reunion as much as they speak of a healing bliss. An early version of the poem, dated "Paris, 1932," provides a more disturbing image of the mother's power. It opens, "But this time of year brings me back, / As though she cried / From her deep grave upon me."[48] Here the mother's cry oppresses; her grave is "upon" her daughter, like a burden to be endlessly carried. The mother's voice from the past continually pulls the daughter back into the anguish of memory. This earlier version of the poem and all subsequent versions until the poem's 1956 publication in *Harper's* lack the last four lines, which greatly soften what was initially a more bitter, painful statement. The additional lines especially soften the phrase "the shape of her pain" by restating it in the next line as "the shape of her love." The original closing phrase, with its implications of guilt, is central.

One other significantly different, undated version of the poem sheds even more light on the phrase that here, too, appears at the poem's close:[49]

Time has heaped a bitter dust
Over her name:
Ashes are sagging on the hearth
She breathed to flame.

Her path from fire to cradle
Measured the earth:
She served the stern necessities
Of death and birth.

I take all roads and each road
Is strange to me:
I claim no kin with any wave
On any sea.

Nowhere do I stop and say
"This much is done:"
Still I fly before the winds
And the staring sun:

But this time of year her voice
On the wind's track
Follows me from her deep grave
And hails me back.

Her dust remembers its dust and calls again
back to her side this prodigal shape of her pain.

This earlier poem makes more clear that the mother died after childbirth, died serving the "stern necessities / Of death and birth." Even clearer, too, is that the speaker, or wanderer, believes herself to be the cause of the mother's death. Although her mother died when Porter was almost two, shortly after giving birth to Porter's younger sister, Porter could never free herself from the belief that she, and not her sister, was the "shape of her [mother's] pain." Thus rather than associating her mother or her mother's grave with home and house, this poem associates her mother's death with Porter's own feelings of exile and alienation, which seem to have been fed by a profound sense of guilt. Cast out and kinless, she flies from her original home, trying to escape the place of destruction, the place that she destroyed. In her solitary flight, alienated from sea, sun, and sky, this speaker resembles Nayagta of "The Shattered Star," who also hears her mother's voice as she paints her anguish across the northern sky. Like Nayagta, this speaker cannot free herself from memory, the mother's voice; it returns with the seasons, calling her back again each year to the place of death.

It is striking that Porter's poem evokes two very different stories of familial return, one masculine, the story of the returning prodigal son, the other feminine, the cyclical story of mother and daughter, Demeter and Persephone. Just as, in her gender-thinking, she saw reunion with the mother complexly, as a dangerous fall into silence and a loss of self, or as a nourishing reconnection with a maternal legacy, so she saw opposing meanings in her break from her maternal home. The prodigal son is traditionally a story for young men. As Nancy Corson Carter suggests in her meditative essay "The Prodigal Daughter: A Parable Re-Visioned," "the prodigal role is accepted for males in our culture. Under the rubric of 'sowing wild oats,' we allow our young men to be prodigal for awhile. . . . and then we welcome them back home with that 'phase' behind them. . . . In contrast, the prodigal daughter is still an anomaly in our so-called liberated culture."[50] Affiliating herself with the prodigal son, Porter presents her journey away from home as part of a male narrative. For her, there was no available narrative of the daughter leaving home to discover herself, to become an artist. In fact, such an extravagant, wasteful act required forgiveness akin to that given the son of the biblical parable, for to leave home to be a writer was to leave behind the mother's example. Carter writes of her own journey, "It was probably the artist self that 'drove me forth' from the socially acceptable women's masks I had been hiding behind."[51] Returning home, this prodigal daughter may experience the peace of her mother's forgiveness, and may even give to her mother a gift from her journey—the poem a sign of her artistic achievements—but she cannot remain. "To re-gain home in a patriarchy as a daughter was quite a different matter from returning as a son," Carter notes.[52] So too for Porter, who describes herself as "restless dust," unable to stay at home, in the mother's world, without losing the freedom and selfhood she associates with the prodigal son.

More haunting in Porter's poem is her evocation of another story of family separation and reconnection, that of Demeter and her daughter Persephone. This myth proved especially rich for modernist women writers and deserves special attention, for it underpins some of the fiction that emerged from Porter's gender-thinking about memory and maternal connection. Marianne Hirsch describes the tale of Demeter and Persephone as a "mother-daughter narrative" and extensively annotates its appeal to women writers of Porter's generation: "Its motifs—the preexistence of timeless bliss vaguely identified with a matriarchal past, the descent to the underworld and the conflation of marriage and death, the connection of femininity with fertility and procreativity, the idealization of maternal power, the resolution of plot in cyclicity—carry a particular resonance for modernist writers. They connect to the images of Freudian psychoanalysis, such as the pre-oedipal, and to the anthropological and archaeological research of matriarchy theorists of the 1920s."[53] It is remarkable how many of the motifs Hirsch identifies appear in Porter's complex and personal exploration of her maternal legacy. The Edenic landscape she finds in memory, expressive of the rich and blissful bonds of maternal love, appears with the imagery of springtime renewal, the mythic sign of Demeter's reunion with her lost Persephone. Yet for Porter, procreation could signal death as well as life—both for her are the mother's legacy. In "Anniversary in a Country Cemetery," the mother's grave is a "fallen house" and she sits at its door, comforted on the threshold of an entrance to the world of the dead. To return to the maternal was as much a journey to the tomb as to the womb.

In her poetic revisioning of her visit to her mother's grave, Porter expressed much of her ambivalence about her maternal legacy. Her mother retains immense power in these poems; her voice calls from the grave, and each year her daughter follows a cyclic pattern of returning to her mother, sometimes for healing, sometimes in pain, only to return to her endless flight. Mother love embraces and suffocates. Nancy Corson Carter describes the father's forgiveness of the prodigal son as a form of *agape*, a love that erases all boundaries, "making no distinction between I-you-s/he-thou. . . . The return of the prodigal, of any one lost, then, is the restoration of oneness."[54] Is such a reunion with the mother equally desirable? Or does it carry "with it the danger of non-meaning, a sinking back into a night of non-differentiation," the threat Hirsch identifies in her work on modernist women, mothers, and daughters. Does the maternal legacy give the daughter a voice, or do "death and non-meaning, and *not* a different narrative model, emerge from the perpetuation of infantile plenitude"?[55] Porter's allusions to the prodigal son as well as the myth of Demeter and Persephone suggest her double-minded viewpoint. Like other female modernists, she struggled with her identifications, whether she should attempt to replicate male narratives of independence and creative power or find new narratives for her life as a woman artist. As Hirsch reminds us in her discussion of modernist women's use of the cyclical Eleusinian tale, "The story of Demeter and Persephone does not simply reverse heterosexual plots of disconnection in favor of a model of female connection. More complicated affiliative patterns are revealed here, patterns which describe the affiliative intricacies of female modernism."[56]

When Porter's gender-thinking focused most fully on her maternal legacy in the 1930s, she found a knot of associations woven about her mother, childbirth, creativity, and death. The words she found emerging from herself at her mother's grave expose this knot in all its intricate and contradictory connections of birth and death, home and the grave, fulfillment and absence, nurturing and emptiness. All are bound together in this much-revised poem as they were bound in Porter's own memories. Portions of her story sequence *The Old Order*, in particular "The Grave" and "The Fig Tree," represent explorations of this same knot, providing visions and revisions of the connections between a dead mother and her artist daughter. In another unfinished story, "A Vision of Heaven," Porter wrote about a related loss, the death of her niece Mary Alice, a child she had adopted in her heart as her own.

The world of *The Old Order* is governed by the grandmother, a Demeter or great mother figure who performs, yearly, a seasonal, cyclic journey of homecoming and renewal. The opening sketch of the sequence, titled "The Source," identifies the grandmother as the wellspring of order and love in her extended family. For her grandchildren "she was the only reality to them in a world that seemed otherwise without fixed authority or refuge, since their mother died so early."[57] The grandmother's seasonal journeys evoke the seasonal cycles of Demeter and her daughter, moving between a fertile springtime world and Hades, the world of the dead. At the start of "The Source," Grandmother readies herself for her annual spring journey to the farm. The same leave-taking reoccurs at the opening of "The Fig Tree," where Persephone's descent to Hades is explicitly invoked; the family refers to the farm as Halifax, and their seasonal journey begins with Old Uncle Jimbilly "yelling like a foghorn," turning the "steeds" around "so they would be pointing towards Halifax" (355).

For the grandmother, the source, each journey is a journey toward home, for she instills order, security, and fruitfulness wherever she travels. Creating home everywhere, she is always coming home: she arrives at the farm in summer "with an indefinable sense of homecoming" (322); yet after setting the place to rights, she heads back to town, arriving there "with the same air of homecoming she had worn on her arrival in the country." Here, too, she immediately "set[s] to work restoring . . . order" (325). Central to the grandmother's identity as a great mother, a fertile life source, is her ability to "bring forth fruit": to bear and feed children. The birth mother of eleven children and caregiver of many more, she continues to find fulfillment in old age watching the seeds she has planted reproduce as well. In "The Source," "when the Indian cling peach-tree against the wall of the town house begins to bloom," the grandmother thinks of the five orchards she has planted, and stands "quite still for a moment looking at the single tree representing all her beloved trees still blooming, flourishing, and preparing to bring forth fruit in their separate places" (322).

The grandmother's fertility, her cyclical patterns of renewal, make her a symbol of maternal power. Her procreativity sustains the family, bringing it successfully from the past to the present. In notes on her family's story, made for *Many Redeemers*, Porter mentions several times the failure of the women in the generation after the grandmother either to bear children or to survive childbirth. Evidently Porter feared that her family faced complete extinction with her generation and at times saw herself as at least partially responsible. The fruit tree, especially the fig, becomes a symbol for her of familial fertility, that of both the women and the land, reproducing and nourishing the same blood through generations. She responded powerfully to a passage from the King James Bible, "when the fig tree does not bear it must be cut down and cast into the fire": "I was thinking of my own family, and at the words a deep shudder went all through me, as if all the dust of the dead quivered and communicated with my flesh . . . terror, too. I do not want us to die and be altogether dust . . . the roots mustn't be destroyed, there must be a replanting."[58] But how replant when the source is gone, the fertile Great Mother has died, the mother has passed on a legacy linking childbirth with death, and the daughter, childless, has only words for her creation? Such questions lie behind "The Fig Tree" and "The Grave," two stories in which Porter's gender-thinking focuses on the interrelations of the maternal legacy, knowledge, and art.

In "The Fig Tree," a young Miranda ritualistically buries baby animals in flower-draped graves. Having just lost her mother, Miranda is preoccupied with both nurturing and death. Shortly after the story opens, she runs off alone, musing on her recent loss:

> Sometimes [her father] called Grandmother "Mamma," but she wasn't Mama either, she was really Grandmother. Mama was dead. Dead meant gone away forever. Dying was something that happened all the time, to people and everything else. Somebody died and there was a long string of carriages going at a slow walk over the rocky ridge of the hill towards the river while the bell tolled and tolled, and that person was never seen again by anybody. Kittens and chickens and specially little turkeys died much oftener, and sometimes calves, but hardly ever cows or horses. (354)

Miranda's thoughts move from her grandmother, who has replaced her mother yet is not "Mama," to burial rites, and from these to the baby animals she frequently finds dead at the summer house and on her grandmother's farm. To the child, death seems everywhere, "something that happened all the time to people and everything else." The carriages and tolling bells fascinate her, and in an effort to gain some control over her insecure, death-filled world, she has developed a ritual of burial corresponding to those she has seen adults employ.[59] She must rigidly repeat her ritual each time a small animal dies: "she always buried it in a little grave with flowers on top and a smooth stone at the head. Even grasshoppers. Everything dead had to be treated this way. This way and no other!'" (354). Through her rule-bound burial rites, Miranda repeats her mother's burial, and as the story progresses we see that the correct performance of the rites has become her way of coping with the terror and loss connected with her mother's death.[60]

Because she is thinking about death and burial, Miranda's steps lead naturally to the fig grove of the town house, a symbolic landscape in the story, representing the nurturing mother's body. It is dark and comforting in the grove, and Miranda's favorite tree reaches down to her height, feeding her without effort on her part: "the deep branches bowed down level with her chin, and she could gather figs without having to climb" (354–55). A later description of the fig grove at the farm makes the connection even clearer; the trees, with their soft round fruit, smell milky, like a mother's breast: "They took the dewy path through the fig grove, much like the one in town, with the early dew bringing out the sweet smell of the milky leaves. They passed a fig tree with low hanging branches, and Miranda reached up by habit and touched it with her fingers for luck" (361).

However, the fig grove, like the mother, now dead, no longer nourishes; it is now also a grave as well as a fertile garden, and all of Miranda's efforts are directed toward preventing the "fruitful nourisher" from becoming the "insatiable devourer." When, under the shelter of her favorite tree, Miranda finds "one little chicken [that] did not move," she fears that death threatens to transform the nurturing grove into a place of terror. Miranda urgently begins an especially elaborate burial, but pressed for time because of the family's imminent departure to the farm, she cannot complete it. The hasty ritual proves inadequate, and just as Miranda is called to the carriage, she hears "a very sad little crying sound. It said Weep, weep, weep, three times like that slowly, and it seemed to come from the mound of dirt" (356). As the family leaves for the farm, Miranda, distraught, imagines the trapped chick crying in the grave: "She had to go back and let him out. He'd never get out by himself, all tangled up in tissue paper and that shoebox. He'd never get out without her" (357).

Implicit in Miranda's distress for the chick is the fear that the nourishing world of the grove is also the grave; the lost maternal care for which the fig trees provide a milky substitute is also incurably the world of death. If Miranda cannot perform her burial ritual adequately, she cannot comfort and silence the voice calling from the grave. Her failure seems inescapable, for the cry is even clearer in the milk-scented fig grove at the farm. Just as Miranda touches a low-hanging tree for luck, "From the earth beneath her feet came a terrible, faint troubled sound. "'Weep weep, weep weep . . .' murmured a little crying voice from the smothering earth, the grave" (361). Nurturing has again been transformed to death; the once comforting trees are full of a voice calling from the improperly made, suffocating grave.

"The Fig Tree" offers one resolution to the problem of the mother's legacy being both the springtime renewal that greeted Persephone and the return to Hades. Porter creates a new kind of woman in her story, intellectual, modern in her interests, fulfilled without childbirth. Great-Aunt Eliza, unmarried, and somewhat masculinized, with a large frame, "grizzled iron-colored hair," and a "growly voice," is the grandmother's sister, and her clear counterpart. "Grand-mother turned pink as the inside of a seashell . . . she had always been the pretty one and was pretty still," Miranda realizes at one point, "but Great-Aunt Eliza was not pretty now and never had been" (359). Eliza defies convention; she dips snuff and pursues scientific interests. Whether she is scrutinizing bits of her dinner under a microscope or watching the stars through the telescope she mounts on the chicken house, Eliza is associated with vision, seeing the world in new ways.

Great-Aunt Eliza fascinates young Miranda and provides her with a model for another way of being a woman besides motherhood: "Miranda almost for-got her usual interests, such as kittens and other animals on the place, pigs, chickens, rabbits, anything at all so it was a baby . . . for Great-Aunt Eliza's ways and habits kept Miranda following her about, gazing, or sitting across the dining-table, gazing" (360). The clear vision of Eliza's rational, scientific mind, represented by her microscopes and telescopes, releases the child from her maternal legacy, pushing the buried world of the mother back with the language of reason and the application of science. When again, walking with her aunt "through the fig grove," Miranda hears "'weep, weep, weep' . . . a little crying voice from the smothering earth, the grave," Great-Aunt Eliza offers a new explanation "in her most scientific voice":

> "They're not in the ground at all. They are the first tree frogs, means it's going to rain."
>
> Miranda took a deep trembling breath and heard them. They were in the trees. They walked on again, Miranda holding Great-Aunt Eliza's hand.
>
> "I'll show you one some time under the microscope" Eliza promises the com-forted child, forging a new alliance on which Miranda can now depend (361–62).

In the figure of Great-Aunt Eliza, Porter offered an alternative to the mother's legacy that momentarily can comfort young Miranda. But for a modern woman, the alternative Aunt Eliza represents fails to resolve essential conflicts. Eliza is clearly masculinized, and she is associated with the traditionally masculine world of scientific rationality, dissection, and observation. Although she is free of the twinned ties of childbirth and death, she is also unsexed, grizzled, "growly," and odd. Aunt Eliza releases the child from her maternal legacy of death, but she also breaks her away from the legacy of nurturing. In Porter's gender-thinking, motherhood and such intellectual independence as is signified by Great-Aunt Eliza seems still to be completely incompatible.

"The Grave," the story that Porter placed at the close of *The Old Order*, contains the same struggle to resolve the double edge of maternal legacy but offers a far more ambitious resolution. Like "The Fig Tree," "The Grave" re-enacts the seemingly inevitable movement from nurturing and fulfillment to violence and loss. The "time" of the story provides an example. Miranda and her brother have recently lost their grandmother; "the motherless family" is now doubly abandoned, "with the Grandmother no longer there to hold it together" (365). The grandmother's death, though, means more than the loss of a second mother; it means also the loss of land and a house. The published version of "The Grave" records only the loss of the land: "After the grandmother's death, part of her land was to be sold for the benefit of certain of her children, and the cemetery happened to lie in the part set aside for sale." Little more is told about this loss except that, significantly, the cemetery was also a garden: "a pleasant small neglected garden of tangled rose bushes and ragged cedar trees and cypress, the simple flat stones rising out of uncropped sweet-smelling wild grass" (362). Yet even these small clues reveal the cemetery as a place containing the two sides of memory, the nurturing and destruction that together constitute a woman's maternal legacy. In a page Porter once intended for inclusion in the final story, it becomes increasingly clear that the lost land contained not only the cemetery but also the fruitful garden and the family home. The page, among Porter's papers and headed "to be added to 'The Grave,'" describes the children responding to the loss of the land after their grandmother's death. Here it is clear that with the land, a peach orchard and the grandmother's first house were also lost. After the grandmother's death, the children are humiliated trespassers when they return to their former garden to gather fruit:

> Something more than her physical presence had disappeared from the children's lives with the death of their grandmother. They puzzled over the loss of land, over the sale of the finest orchard where grandmother had planted her finest peaches. Even the empty cemetery was no longer theirs. They felt like trespassers. . . . The summer after the grandmother's death, they remembered her Indian cling peach

trees in the orchard that was now sold. The three of them went boldly, walked into the orchard and filled their baskets with the fruit as they had done the summer before. The woman who owned the orchard saw them from her vegetable garden nearby. She and her husband had been renters, sharecroppers but in twenty years' time they had saved enough money to buy the first old house the grandmother had built, and her first beautiful orchard.[61]

Each image of loss corresponds to another: the nourishing fruit, the family home, and the fertile land are all lost with the grandmother's "physical presence," and that loss recalls the original loss of the mother's nurturing body.

In its use of memory, "The Grave" itself illustrates Porter's own creative process, seeking in memory and legend rich resources for her art. Here, however, the double nature of that legacy is explicitly drawn. At the story's close, Porter assigns to Miranda the sudden experience from which a memory/text originates. Like the mother's voice calling from the dead, this is a moment of rebirth or resurrection, as memory—sudden, vivid, and painful—springs from the dead past into the living present. The moment recalls the "spinal tap" of creative production Porter described to Eudora Welty. Miranda stands in a busy marketplace when suddenly, "without warning, plain and clear in its true colors as if she looked through a frame upon a scene that had not stirred nor changed since the moment it happened, the episode of that far-off day leaped from its burial place before her mind's eye. She was so reasonlessly horrified she halted suddenly staring, the scene before her eyes dimmed by the vision back of them" (367). Miranda's involuntary memory, evoked by the "smell in the market, with its piles of raw flesh and wilting flowers," brings back a day in early adolescence when she and her brother went hunting together and found the emptied graves on their family's former land. Like the marketplace, full of flowers and spoiling meat, the graves also smelled of life and death, "mingled sweetness and corruption."

The losses, first of their mother and then their grandmother and then the land on which the graves lie, form the context for other moments in "The Grave" when fertility yields to death rather than fulfillment. The two children playing in the empty graves find treasures: Miranda a silver dove, Paul a ring. They promptly swap. The ring Miranda covets and then gains carries all of the complex interweaving of sexuality and death that runs throughout Porter's fiction. "Carved with intricate flowers and leaves" (363), the gold band links the fruitful garden with marriage. Yet the children find the ring in a grave. Marriage and adult sexuality may be the source of life, but they are also closely bound with death, as childbearing brings both life and death to a woman. The story records Miranda's first move into puberty, recognition of her own connection to female sexuality and womanhood. Admiring the gold band on her grubby thumb, she longs to shed her rough clothing, to dress and act like a "proper" young lady. Immediately she wants "to go back to the farmhouse, take a good cold bath, dust herself with plenty of Maria's violet talcum powder . . . put on the thinnest, most becoming dress she owned, with a big sash, and sit in a wicker chair under the trees" (365).

However, Miranda's fantasy is abruptly interrupted when her brother shoots and then eviscerates a pregnant rabbit. Here is the counterpart to a wedding ring in a grave, a mother's body as the place of death. Looking down at the tiny rabbits, lying beautiful and blood-covered in the open womb, Miranda gains sudden, clearer understanding "of the secret, formless intuitions in her own mind and body, which had been clearing up, taking form so gradually and so steadily she had not realized that she was learning what she had to know" (366–67). Hers is not a simple lesson in the facts of human sexuality; it is a symbolic realization of her bondage to childbearing and death. Split open, the body of the rabbit corresponds to Miranda's own new split, severing her from her former childhood innocence. Moving toward adult sexuality, she moves inexorably toward death. "Quietly and terribly agitated . . . looking down at the bloody heap," Porter's character rejects the vision. Her brother "buried the young rabbits again in their mother's body," and Miranda buries the vision deep in her memory "for nearly twenty years" (367).

Many readers have explored the content of Miranda's memory in "The Grave," seeking an answer to the puzzling images of the story's close in the recollected events that precede it. Although the interpretations vary in emphasis, many express similar insights. Both Jane Krause DeMouy and Darlene Unrue emphasize the gendered meanings of Miranda's lessons in "The Grave." "She has discovered her own mortality and her own femaleness, with its frightening, awesome burden of procreation," Unrue concludes.[62] DeMouy extends the point to include the daughter's assumption of her foremother's legacy: "Giving life means risking death. This is her true legacy from her grandmother and her society. . . . The story does not state that Miranda remembers the death of her own mother in childbirth, but certainly she recognizes for the first time the blood rites of womanhood."[63]

In "The Grave," Miranda's anguished response to her vivid memory finds comfort in another recollected image that brings the story to a close: "the dreadful vision faded, and she saw clearly her brother . . . again twelve years old . . . turning the silver dove over and over in his hands" (368). Like young Paul, Porter's readers have meditated over this concluding symbol, carefully turning it over in their readings of "The Grave." At least twice, Porter herself acknowledged the richness of the dove as a literary symbol. During a 1960 panel discussion, she uses the dove as an example of a symbol's potential multiplicity: "The dove begins by being a symbol of sensuality, it is the bird of Venus . . . and then it goes through the whole range of every kind of thing until it becomes the Holy Ghost."[64] Again in 1961, during a classroom conversation at the University of Wichita, she commented on the dove's richness as a symbol, this time explicitly addressing its role in "The Grave." As she told a curious student, "Of course the dove is a symbol. It's symbolic of peace, security, love, and lechery. But it's also the Holy Ghost and the innocent love of children."[65]

Intriguing in Porter's comments on the dove is the range of meanings, from sexual love—even "lechery"—to innocence and spiritual love. Most readers of "The Grave" have emphasized the spiritual aspects of the symbol. For example, in one of the finest readings of the story, "Myth and Epiphany in Porter's 'The Grave,'" Constance Rooke and Bruce Wallis see the story as a "miniature myth of the Fall" and find in the dove the promise of "redemption and resurrection" brought by the Holy Spirit.[66] Yet studies of symbols, both encyclopedic and theoretical, point attention, as Porter does, to the dove's rich connections to sexuality as well as Christian doctrine. Summarizes one, the dove can represent the "Cosmic All Mother: The Great Goddess of Fertility," or "the spermatic Word or Spirit" impregnating the Virgin Mary or any Christian soul.[67]

If we turn back to "The Grave" as a text in which Porter's gender-thinking explores questions of her maternal legacy, we can find in the dove a new solution to the problem of childbirth's connection to death, a solution akin to but far more affirming than Aunt Eliza's scientific vision. In this reading, it is important to recall that Miranda first drew the dove from the family graves, but encouraged by her gendered upbringing, she traded this treasure for the ring and the visions of traditional, passive womanhood it evoked. Only after the harsh lessons of the eviscerated rabbit, and the subsequent recognition of her own ties to birth and death evident in the images and smells of the marketplace, does she recognize the dove as a better choice, one that can provide, on a symbolic level, a resolution to her conflicts. In her introduction to *Gender and Religion: In the Complexity of Symbols*, the noted religion scholar Caroline Walker Bynum suggests that symbols can perform several tasks "in the context of gendered experience . . . not merely reflecting and shaping, but also inverting, questioning, rejecting and transcending gender as it is constructed in the individual's psychological development and sociological setting."[68] For Miranda, and for Porter herself, who pointed out to her students the symbol's great range of meaning, the dove unites the physical and the spiritual, or, to quote again from the meanings listed above, the "Cosmic All Mother: The Great Goddess of Fertility," and "the spermatic Word or Spirit." Through the dove, Porter can wed the oppositions she found so troubling. For unlike the ring, which leads its wearer directly to traditional womanhood, the dove unites the female and the male, the fertile mother and the powerful word.

Both Darlene Unrue's and Jane Krause DeMouy's readings bear on and enrich a view of the dove as a symbol that can represent both the mother's body and the father's word. In *Truth and Vision in Katherine Anne Porter's Fiction*, Unrue notes that the ring has "evocations of superficial womanliness," while the dove "remains the primary representation of art in the story." The closing vision of Paul, "'turning the silver dove over and over in his hands' . . . confirms both the dynamic process of knowing and also the perpetual yielding of new meanings by the work of art."[69] DeMouy sees an active reclamation occurring in the final image of the boy holding the dove. For her the dove represents freedom, a gendered freedom traditionally belonging to men. Thus in the final scene, when Miranda finds peace recalling the dove, she is claiming her own right to fly free rather than follow the paths walked by the women in her family before her. Concludes DeMouy, "It is not the gold ring which hangs in her mind's eye nearly twenty years later. It is the image of Paul . . . full of potency and possibility, handling the silver dove which was hers first, before she ignorantly traded it away. This time she trades her ignorance, reclaiming the dove in its positive image: the spirit's ability to fly free."[70]

Without question, the dove offers a resolution for Miranda and, perhaps for a time, Porter as well. Offering a cluster of meanings, the symbol frees Miranda from the "mingled sweetness and corruption" that is her maternal legacy. In the dove's range of meanings she can find freedom, traditionally belonging to young men, and claim it for herself, an ambitious young woman. Through the dove she can also unite fertility and the word, her body and her art, into a new whole. She need not follow the path of Great-Aunt Eliza, choosing abstraction and rationality at the expense of her womanhood, nor need she choose womanhood at the expense of all else she desires. Momentarily at the close of "The Grave," the story Porter chose to conclude the portion she published from *Many Redeemers*, her gender-thinking provides a vision of a new possibility for a woman artist, one that revises but does not reject the mother's legacy. In Christian iconography the dove is indeed the "bearer of the word," symbol of the Holy Spirit impregnating a Virgin Mary so that she may birth that Word as flesh. Just as the dove makes carnate the father's word, so too a woman artist might replicate the mother's fertile labor, creating through words a new order out of the dismembered fragments of legend and memory.

Like much of the other material Porter grouped together to form *The Old Order*, "The Grave" is in part an elegy, a recollection and celebration of a lost world, full of memories and the graves of the dead. Those graves yield treasures, the golden rings and silver doves that the woman artist transmutes into language, like the poem she tucks into the earth of her mother's grave, returning the gift. The epiphanic moments of reunion, when memories coalesce and become text, poetry, fiction—concrete and orderly expression—are marvelous, but fleeting. What is constant, however, is the homesickness, the yearning for connection that drives memory into language. There is no way to return fully home for a woman artist, no way to replace the lost mother's body. Likewise, there is no way to return to the blissful, Edenic childhood home, that perfect embracing landscape. For Porter, the closest she can come to a "true home" is in her art, a land that is truly nowhere, yet everywhere. The recognition is not resolution, but as with the dove in "The Grave" it is a momentary comfort. As she wrote in her drafts of "The Land That Is Nowhere," "being a writer by vocation and by fate, a fate I had no chance of escaping by any sort of strategy—I carried my breathing life with me wherever I went, and that is an indestructible 'hearthstone.'"[71]

It is tempting to rest here in the assurance and solidity of Porter's phrase "indestructible hearthstone," but as always she complicates any such surety. Being a writer may be her "hearthstone," but note, too, it is as "inescapable fate," and as ephemeral is "breathing life." Likewise the dove and the knowledge it imparts are both fleeting and liminal. Examined closely, the experience at the close of "The Grave" is extraordinarily complex, a mingling of visual and olfactory memories, the present and the past, before her eyes and behind them, neither here nor there. Miranda's brother is just twelve, on the brink of adolescence, and she is on the brink of her own self-knowledge. He holds the answer; she made another choice; and the key symbol she recalls in his hands is in constant motion. Memory shows the dove turning, "over and over." This impermanence characterizes all the moments of peace and homecoming in Porter's writing, all the moments of union with her maternal legacy. To quote just one more passage from her essay "Here Is My Home," "I have had what I think may be the feeling of being at home. . . . just for a moment of delight that illusion that here was the center, the beginning and the end, the visible shape of the inner reality." "A moment of delight," and an "illusion"—"the way the light fell in a room at certain hours" (3)—home, that "indestructible hearthstone," is as illusory and weightless as a vision.

Katherine Anne Porter found much that was fruitful in her maternal legacy. She found the rich resources of memory, the language that rises from yearning and homesickness. But she recognized as well the insubstantiality of this resource and its roots in loss. Both the ring and the dove of her finest story of memory's rewards come from a grave. In her mind, birth seems too closely knotted to death to embrace as the metaphor for her creativity. Yet she continues to consider the meanings of motherhood in her gender-thinking. As we shall see in the next chapter, her remarkable story "Holiday" continues her exploration of the union of woman and artist.

CHAPTER FIVE

A LITTLE STOLEN HOLIDAY

When the High Priestess and the gathered powers of her kingdom finally bring the Princess to trial for her unnatural crimes, the masked and bejeweled female artist responds with laughter. Proclaim the judges, "We accuse Her Royal Highness with the following offenses against the dignity of the throne, the peace and welfare of the sovereign realm, and the Temples of the most High Zerdah and of the Woman God." As the judges list the Princess's offenses—"unholy practices," "corrupting the youths and maidens of her court," and more—she answers each accusation with a loud "Ha, ha, ha." The audience is shocked that "the enchantress, the stone image, the heretic, was laughing at her sacred tribunal." But as the offenses mount in number and the verdict is proclaimed, the Princess's laughter becomes infectious. When the judges "pronounce sentence of death," the spectators momentarily lose their solemnity: "'Ha, ha, ha, ha, ha,' laughed the Princess, so gayly and lightly that some of the people forgot themselves and [laughed] with her [then] suddenly [they] remembered things that hurt, and wept."[1]

The Princess's laughter disrupts the solemn tribunal. Shocking and infectious, it answers the law with lawlessness, countering the judge's order with the Princess's disorder. Masked and mysterious—"enchantress," "stone image," "heretic"—the Princess suggests both fixity and change; she is plural in identity, full of possibility, wonderful and terrifying. Set against the established order of her kingdom, this laughing Princess can be fruitfully linked to Bakhtinian concepts of carnival. In his influential book *Rabelais and His World*, Bakhtin argues that carnival, with its manifestations in laughter and the grotesque, is decidedly antiestablishment: "Carnival celebrated temporary liberation from the prevailing truth and from the established order; it marked the suspension of all hierarchical rank, privileges, norms, and prohibitions."[2] Although they may differ in form and content, literary works employing the tropes of carnival share certain fundamental goals: "In all these writings," Bakhtin argues, "in spite of their differences in character and tendency,

> the carnival-grotesque form exercises the same function: to consecrate inventive freedom, to permit the combination of a variety of elements and their rapprochement, to liberate from the prevailing point of view of the world, from conventions and established truths, from clichés, from all that is humdrum and universally accepted. This carnival spirit offers the chance to have a new outlook on the world, to realize the relative nature of all that exists, and to enter a completely new order of things.[3]

Feminist theorists have employed Bakhtin's concepts of carnival to illuminate the often powerful and ambivalent depictions of female laughter and unruliness in women's writing. A woman out of bounds may be admonitory and her fate a warning to the restless, yet at the same time she may herself represent momentary liberation, her existence destabilizing and calling into question assumed orders. A woman laughing, a woman making a spectacle of herself is disturbing and provocative. As Mary Russo argues in "Female Grotesques: Carnival and Theory," "The masks and voices of carnival resist, exaggerate, and destabilize the distinctions and boundaries that mark and maintain high culture and organized society."[4]

Katherine Anne Porter's Princess deliberately makes herself into a spectacle, her ornamental, armored presence a visible protest against cultural norms of what constitutes a natural and obedient woman. Her laughter before the massed judges and citizens of her kingdom carries all the tonal complexity "of carnival laughter." As Bakhtin describes it, "This laughter is ambivalent: it is gay, triumphant, and at the same time mocking, deriding. It asserts and denies, it buries and revives."[5] Such laughter includes the laugher and the listener in its mockery; both the Princess and her gathered people alternately laugh and weep.[6] It is important to note, however, that the match between Porter's laughing Princess and a figure of Bakhtinian carnival is not at all exact. In her mocking gaiety, spectacular presence, and subversive intents, the Princess affiliates with the social disruptions and liberations of the festive, yet her rigid, intensely crafted, and sterile art opposes the carnival-grotesque body. As Mary Russo describes that body, "the grotesque body is the open, protruding, extended, secreting body, the body of becoming, process, and change."[7] In Porter's gender-thinking, hegemonic concepts of woman's natural place and function can constitute a confining order, as manifested in the rituals of her Princess's imaginary kingdom that mark and define the female body in its changes and becoming. Against such social definition and control of the natural she sets a higher form of control—rather than a Rabelaisian disorder. Through her Princess, Porter creates a closed form of the grotesque rather than an open one. Her disorderly woman artist is an artifact, her mocking and disobedient fixity simultaneously subversive and tragic, a liberation and a prison. The laughing Princess's rejection of the patriarchal forces of legality and order is neither simple nor painless. To be forever an outsider is both liberating and lonely, this story tells us, and there is pain in the pleasures of rebellion. When the judges "pronounce [their] sentence of death," "those who stood near the Princess saw with amazement how tears suddenly streamed from the emerald eyes of the mask, as if it wept for the Princess while she laughed." And those who listen to the Princess are infected by her laughter, but they also are overcome with memories of "things that hurt" and they weep as well.[8]

In her gender-thinking about women, art, and the woman artist, Porter returned several times to carnival tropes, depicting the female artist as a kind of grotesque figure, deploying the subversive powers of female laughter, exploring the dangers and attractions of the carnivalesque. However, she never embraces what might be termed a fully Rabelaisian carnival spirit. She imagines momentary or limited disruptions, clarified alternatives, and is drawn to mockery as a form of protest, yet at the same time she fears sustained disorder and misrule. Ambivalence is everywhere apparent in "The Princess" and reappears in a later text that draws on carnival in its gender-thinking, the long, aptly named "Holiday."

One of Porter's most successful works of fiction, "Holiday" presents a wonderfully rich coming together of many strands of Porter's ongoing exploration of gender, culture, and female creativity. Written in 1923 and 1924, the story sets an anonymous narrator down on a black-land Texas farm in early spring. Like "The Princess," "Holiday" probes the relations of a woman artist and a patriarchal order. The story traces its artist-heroine's quest for healing knowledge in the face of her belief that marriage and parturition bind women to the natural order, and that she, choosing another path, is grotesque, "mutilated," or unsexed. While the natural world unfolds into spring in "Holiday," Porter's narrator must come to terms with her own feelings of alienation and sterility. Through the narrator's relationship with nature, and with her double, Ottilie, the handicapped Müller daughter, "Holiday" explores what it means to be natural and unnatural. The moments when the story expresses joyous acceptance of the maimed, alienated self are remarkable. In a sequence of epiphanic moments, the narrator realizes that although her life choice may separate her from traditional womanhood, it does not separate her from nature, and thus, the story suggests, her difference does not make her unnatural. In fact, "Holiday" momentarily celebrates her liberation from the demands of motherhood, opening up an alternate path in which she can experience an equally rewarding, free, and festive relation to the natural world.

"Holiday" has been discussed in detail by several scholars. In its first full-length critical reading by George Core in a 1969 essay titled "'Holiday': A Version of the Pastoral," the story emerges as a text about "universals": life and death, order and disorder. Core's Empsonian reading finds irony, ambiguity, and paradox within the perfect "wrought thing," which is "Holiday." The story is "about suffering and labor, about the labor of the farm, the labor of childbirth, the labor of life, and the labor of death."[9] The final realization of both narrator and narrative, Core concludes, is that you cannot escape life, for "in both its manifest forms and unpredictable nature [it] continues any and everywhere, despite man's best efforts to avoid it."[10] This eminently New Critical reading traces some of the story's larger outlines and marks a path for subsequent readers to chart in more detail. Another reader to give the story lengthy attention, Darlene Unrue, follows in Core's footsteps: her fine formalist reading specifies some of the elements that make up "life" as "Holiday" describes it. According to Unrue, "Holiday" is built around the oppositions of order—the Müllers—and disorder—Ottilie. The schism marking this fundamental opposition reflects a larger rupture of communication and meaning: "At the same time that the story illustrates the insufficiency of patterns and systems to lead to truth and life's meaning, it also shows the separateness of humans and the inability of one person to completely understand another."[11] Both Unrue and Core find "Holiday" a dark story, about mutability, alienation, and disorder.

Interesting in these readings is the tendency to condemn the Müllers while focusing on the larger structures of their world. Core argues that "at the heart of the story" is the paradox that "Ottilie is the most human and sympathetic character in the story . . . she ironically achieves humanity in inhumanity whereas the rest of her family does not."[12] Likewise, Unrue's reading treats the Müllers harshly. The family's dedication to external order subverts "human love" and denies "the dark, unfathomable side of life" symbolized by Ottilie. The Müllers are unable "to give sufficient love," Unrue argues. "They never acknowledge that Ottilie is their own."[13] Yet both internal and external evidence suggests another view, raising the possibility that in the Müller family's "use" of Ottilie, Porter saw healing and even joy, not a failure of love. "Holiday" explores not just the alienation that comes with difference but also the absurd joy that can accompany that difference, no matter how terrible and disabling it may be. Throughout the narrative lies evidence that Porter viewed the Müllers' treatment of Ottilie in a positive light, seeing it as a way of providing this different daughter with an important, meaningful place through service to the family. As the narrator tells us, the Müllers show a "deep right instinct" in "their acceptance of Ottilie. . . . I found great virtue and courage in their steadiness and refusal to feel sorry for anybody, least of all for themselves."[14] Porter herself was even more explicit about her admiration for the family. In unpublished notes, part of drafts for her introduction to her 1979 Collected Stories, she wrote that the "question of morality and humanity" surrounding Ottilie was resolved in her own mind: "Her family's treatment of Ottilie, their use of her life for the family purposes had shocked me deeply, running violently against the grain of my traditions, religious teachings, my own natural feelings—everything. In my society invalids were coddled, kept in bed or wheel chairs, waited on perpetually, and I am afraid, were not allowed to forget for a minute that they were—invalids, that is, useless even though loved." She identifies the Müllers' "use" of Ottilie as far better, manifesting a positive human instinct to "save somehow for the uses of human love and daily living even the most fragmentary of the maimed, the deformed, the Ottilies of this world," to make "valid" a life her culture invalidated.[15]

Through the relationship of the narrator to Ottilie, "Holiday" extends beyond the familial concerns of the Müllers to explore another equally positive potentiality: the acceptance and good use of the fragmentary, maimed, and deformed portions of the self. From this perspective, the story is about a handicapped woman in a patriarchal family and a narrator who has chosen to disable herself from traditional roles. Like Ottilie, the narrator is a woman alienated from her past and her culture, who also lives on the margins, or in the attics of the patriarchal household, and who also cannot speak the patriarchal language. Joan Givner's appraisal of Ottilie's fate suits the narrator as well: "There is no room in the patriarchy for a woman who cannot fulfill the roles of wife, mother, and bearer of children." The narrator is, in Givner's term, Ottilie's "alter-ego"; however—and crucially—unlike Ottilie, she can and has made choices. The narrator is a woman who has chosen not to participate in the cycles of marriage and parturition that characterize women's lives under patriarchy.[16]

Because the manuscript evidence of "Holiday" not only contributes to a reading of the story but also has been somewhat misrepresented in critical accounts, it is important to briefly survey what records we do have of Porter's composition before turning to the specifics of the text. According to Porter herself in her 1965 introduction to her *Collected Stories*, "The story haunted me for years and I made three separate versions, with a certain spot in all three where the thing went off track. So I put it away and it disappeared also, and I forgot it. It rose from one of my boxes of papers, after a quarter of a century, and I sat down in great excitement to read all three versions. I saw at once that the first one was the right one" (v). Porter uncovered the manuscript in 1960, while digging through boxes in her Georgetown home in the company of a neighbor, Rhea Johnson. Drawing on an interview with Johnson, Joan Givner gives an account of the published story's origins that confirms Porter's 1965 comments. Furthermore, according to Givner, the "certain spot" that always stymied Porter was the conclusion; she "wrote three versions of the ending and set it aside indefinitely." Then in 1960 she reread her typescripts, "saw how the story should go, [and] triumphantly finished it."[17]

Although the archival evidence confirms the rediscovery of the text, marginal dating in Porter's hand suggests a different sequence of composition than Givner provides. Of the drafts of the story housed at the Harry Ransom Center, University of Texas at Austin, one typescript carries Porter's marginal comment: "Written 1923. Rhea, this is my *first* draft. The *others* are attempts to rewrite it. I have returned very much to this version in my final copy. I destroyed the first five pages, alas!"[18] This typescript, missing the opening pages, begins with the first dinner table scene and continues unbroken all the way to the story's conclusion. Except for the addition of a few words, that conclusion is identical to the one in the final copy. Clearly the "certain spot" that troubled Porter was not the ending. Another far less complete typescript, labeled by Porter "paper scraps of second draft," begins with the narrator's entrance into her attic room and continues for a page beyond the dinner scene. It is interesting that the first page of this typescript is numbered "2," as though the story began only shortly before the entrance into the attic. Finally, a third typescript, labeled "Part of 3rd draft begun in Georgetown, July 1960," begins at the train station: "For half an hour I waited on the station platform, seated on my small trunk." This draft then moves back to the conversation with Louise (that conversation precedes the station scene in the final version). This four-page typescript continues to resemble the opening of Porter's final version fairly closely; it describes her journey to the farm and ends with her entrance into the attic room. What the typescript evidence suggests overall is that the "certain point" that stumped Porter was the beginning of "Holiday," not the conclusion. Her first draft lacks the opening pages, as does her second, which builds the description of the attic bedroom.

Only in 1960 could Porter resolve her story's opening and decide what to do with that "certain spot . . . where the thing went off track." Both the manuscript evidence and the opening of the published story suggest that she struggled with setting up a context for the narrative, in particular describing the "troubles" that brought her narrator to the Müller farm. Her decision in 1960 was to sidestep the entire problem, and she does this by choosing silence. The published story begins with a cryptic allusion to "troubles" and then a refusal to tell: "It no longer can matter what kind of troubles they were, or what finally became of them" (407). The voice here originates in Porter herself in 1960, at least thirty-seven years after she first started "Holiday." At the age of seventy she could truthfully say of her troubles when she was twenty-three and twenty-four (her age when the story's source events occurred) or thirty-three and thirty-four (her age when she wrote the story), "It can no longer matter what kind of troubles they were, or what finally became of them." That Porter did have troubles at both times in her life, and that both times have bearing on "Holiday," is very clear from biographical evidence. Both moments, a decade apart, probably underlie the narrative's opening silence. Of the two, the earlier biographical background to "Holiday" is most important to the issues to be explored in this chapter. The events occurring at the time of the actual composition of "Holiday" will be discussed in chapter 6.

Both the setting and concerns of "Holiday" reflect the time when Porter first labored to fulfill and then broke away from the traditional gender roles of her conservative west Texas upbringing. The story is rooted in an event Porter rarely mentioned and seems to have hoped would disappear from her biographical record: her nine-year-long early marriage, begun at age sixteen, to John Koontz, a young Texan from a wealthy Swiss family.[19] John Koontz proved an unhappy choice for Porter, and the marriage was full of disagreements, likely some violent. Looking at photographs from these nine years and reading the biographical record of 1906 to 1915, one discovers a young woman full of romantic notions, engaging, flirtatious, eager to dress well. She also longed to begin a family and romanticized her relationship to her sister Gay's first child, Mary Alice, dreaming that she would become the child's "Tante" and pretending "to herself that she and not Gay was the child's mother."[20] Unhappily, the marriage met few of her expectations. John Koontz seems to have been a steady but conservative husband, and his family on the whole disapproved of Porter's flirtatious personality and spendthrift pleasures. Furthermore, there were no children. The marriage to Koontz likely provided some of the setting and family characterization of "Holiday," from the Koontz ranch, which Porter enjoyed visiting, to the death of the family patriarch, Henry Koontz, after exposure in a winter storm while tending his cattle.[21]

According to Joan Givner, the opening of "Holiday" reflects Porter's final response to her marriage—flight. Givner draws language from that opening to describe Porter's personal decision: "Once she faced the fact that her marriage was 'trouble that did not belong to her' she hardened her resolve to run from it 'like a deer.'"[22] All of Porter's "tradition, background, and training"—to continue quoting from "Holiday"—had certainly taught her otherwise: that a wife stays loyally by her husband's side no matter what troubles occur. Such is the practice of the heroic women in her fiction, like Grandmother Sophia Jane, the matriarch of Miranda Gay's family and the fictional counterpart to Porter's grandmother who raised the Porter children after their mother's death. In *The Old Order*, Porter wrote of the grandmother Sophia Jane that although she "despised men," she followed her husband without question, loyal to him alive and cherishing his memory after death, despite the fact that she "watched him play away her substance like a gambler." According to this grandmother, spokeswoman of family values in *The Old Order*, "It was the business of a man to make all decisions and dispose of all financial matters"; as a woman, her "natural activities lay elsewhere."[23] As the grandmother's eleven children confirm, women's "natural activities" were the creation and nurturing of children. Set against a background constructed on such values, Porter's flight from John Koontz when she was in her early twenties was a dramatic and devastating flight away from the expectations surrounding the life of a young woman of her time and place. This flight from her first marriage was a crucial step for Porter: her first step onto the different road of the independent woman artist.

In "Holiday," the narrator's friend Louise identifies the Müllers' as "a household in real patriarchal style—the kind of thing you'd hate to live with" (408). Old Testament figures, the Müllers seem larger than life, solid, physical, bound to the natural cycles of the earth and the body. Obedient to these cycles, the family women follow lives devoted to marriage, childbirth, and the care of men and children. Porter is unabashed about her heroine's entrance into an ultimate patriarchal order; she has Louise, a friend, describe the Müller farm as ruled by "old father, God almighty himself, with whiskers and all" (408). By placing her female artist within such a context, Porter highlights her alienation in a culture where gender relations are traditional in structure and unquestioned.

In such an environment, the woman artist's choices and struggles stand out clearly for examination, and in the course of "Holiday," Porter considers questions of women's roles under patriarchy, at times seriously opening up these roles to question, at other times describing them with longing or reverence. On the surface, the fecundity of the farm world suggests that the family's patriarchal order is not just natural but even blessed. Yet throughout "Holiday," Porter's gender-thinking troubles this smooth surface, providing glimpses of the limitations for women under patriarchal rule.

Like "The Princess," "Holiday" expresses resistance to patriarchy. Its ruling patriarch, Father Müller, is the ultimate authority in his family. His economic and legal power, both in his family and his community, continually expands, built on shrewd dealings and careful control of his children's marriages. The labor of his offspring, their spouses, and their children contributes to his profits. Seated at dinner, the "patriarch . . . at the head of the table," Father Müller heads up a hierarchical organization in which all other men and women are ranged, each in their place, beneath him, obedient to his word. In his book-length study of Porter's intellectual growth, *Katherine Anne Porter's Artistic Development: Primitivism, Traditionalism, and Totalitarianism*, Robert Brinkmeyer suggestively describes "Holiday" as "a parable of the totalitarian state, with the Müller family representing the emerging power of Germany under Fascist ideology." He continues, "There is little room for individual identity within the tight-knit and systematically organized family. All work as one, and the corporate identity supersedes the individual's. The narrator observes that the entire family, even the men who married into the family, give the impression of being 'one human being divided into several separate appearances.'"[24] Such unified ideological control, enforcing obedience to a single order while denying and even erasing difference, invites the disruptive laughter of Bakhtinian carnival.

Under Father Müller's patriarchal rule, women's lives are closely tied to cycles of fertility and nature. As Jane Krause DeMouy notes, all the Müller daughters are "absorbed in bearing, rearing, and nurturing life, like their mother."[25] Throughout, Porter loads her narrative with imagery of maternity: women marry, give birth, care for human and animal offspring, milk cows, and feed men in a landscape moving from winter to spring, where the fields lie "ploughed and ready for the seed" (410). As DeMouy rightly points out, "Maternity is the mark of this tale, made in so many places it astounds. Imagery, symbolism, setting, time, character, even gesture communicate maternity in 'Holiday.'"[26] Porter's artist-narrator has complex interest in the Müller women. On the one hand, they represent women's lives within patriarchal tradition, devoted to the domestic and nurturing labors. They represent a possible life choice she could make. On the other hand, as simple figures of endurance and renewal, they suggest ways for her to live and find her own labors. She also finds "the almost mystical inertia" of the Müllers' minds relaxing—it releases her from her own intense mental activity. Their "muscular life" provides "repose" for her intellectual one. Yet it is not a life she would choose. In the course of the narrative, she notes how repetitive and unreflecting this family's day may be and recognizes that they lack the intellectual and aesthetic awareness that is so central to her own consciousness. Even the play of the Müller children repeats the laborious demands of constant nurturing. In silence they move their toys through a day's tasks: "They fed them, put them to bed; they got them up and fed them again." For variation, the children "would harness themselves to their carts," an image that confirms what the text everywhere else suggests, that the Müllers' life is little different from animal life. It is physical, instinctive. The women in particular exist in a state of mental sleep, or half-waking. For example, Gretchen, the family's favorite daughter, "wore the contented air of a lazy, healthy young animal, seeming always about to yawn" (416). Raising their children, the women "were as devoted and care taking as a cat with her kittens" (419).

In her portrayal of Mother Müller, the matriarch, Porter suggests the negative side of traditional womanhood. While Father Müller possesses legal and economic power over his family, Mother Müller works to sustain the gender roles, which order and perpetuate that power. Called "the old mother" by the narrator, she emerges from the descriptive language surrounding her as a powerful, fearsome woman, looming behind her husband "like a dark boulder" (412, 415). Her control and power are most evident in the milking scenes that dominate her characterization. That she is fully bound to this labor is suggested by the description of her daily passage to the barn wearing a "wooden yoke, with the milking pails covered and closed with iron hasps." Her unmarried daughter Hatsy does not yet carry the full maternal burden; thus she is described as running beside her mother, light-footed, swinging two tin pails. When later Hatsy's new husband tries to carry the full pails of milk, relieving his wife of this labor for a moment, the mother loudly stops him, shouting, "No! . . . not you. The milk is not business for a man" (430). Milk is women's business; money is men's in this story. Both Father and Mother Müller work to maintain these distinctions around which gender has historically been structured. When she dies, the family is thrown into disorder and the children break into a "tumult utterly beyond control" (431). However, the mother's death represents a disruption, not a collapse. As in "The Princess," women's lives must follow natural cycles, and thus grief must yield to necessity: "they would hurry back from the burial to milk the cows" (433).

In his 1979 introduction to *Katherine Anne Porter: A Collection of Critical Essays*, Robert Penn Warren stated that concern for the "alienation of the artist" is "implicit over and over" in Porter's fiction, "and in 'Holiday' it finds something close to an explicit statement." Warren describes one passage in "Holiday" as a "little poem celebrating the artist's doom."[27] In that passage, the narrator reflects on her inability to understand German. Her meditations form part of Porter's continual examination of language, identity, and the woman artist. In "Holiday," the language of Father Müller, and thus the patriarchal tongue, is German. The narrator's knowledge of this tongue is small but significant. All the German she knows is "five small deadly sentimental songs of Heine's learned by heart" (413).[28] The language of sentiment, of romance with its emphasis on traditional gender roles, is both deadly for women, Porter suggests, and deeply indoctrinated, something "learned by heart."

Porter's artist heroine seeks another tongue. She longs to escape the words she has "learned by heart" and, returning to the preverbal, emerge with a truer tongue, one that can name her own choice and experience. As she sits in her attic room and hears the murmur of German beneath her, she finds pleasure listening to the "muted unknown language which was silence with music in it." "It was good not to have to understand what they were saying," Porter's narrator realizes, for relieved of the possibility of communication, she imagines she can travel toward a more essential self: "I loved that silence which means freedom from the constant pressure of other minds and other opinions and other feelings, that freedom to fold up in quiet and go back to my own center, to find out again, for it is always a rediscovery, what kind of creature it is that rules me finally" (413).

The narrator's journey from her troubles is also a journey toward freedom, and that freedom entails not only discovering her own authority, what "rules [her] finally," but also her own "opinions" and "feelings." As Anne Goodwyn Jones brilliantly observes of the movement away from language in "Holiday," in her break from the ruling tongue, the narrator breaks "from the stable and coercive representational structures, relational possibilities, and dichotomous subject constructions of the patriarchal . . . household." It is precisely such a break that the narrator desires: she is looking for a new way to define herself as a woman, outside of those constructions. She seeks her authentic tongue:

"From her descent into a state free of language's structures and ingrained, controlling meanings, the narrator can emerge essentially linguistically newborn." She can "re-enter the symbolic so that eventually she can tell us this story."[29] However, never one to endorse a single answer in her gender-thinking, Porter refuses to embrace fully the concept of an authentic mother-tongue emerging from a return to a preverbal silence. Outside of language, a woman artist may find freedom from its constructed verities, but she may also find herself outside of all meaning, mute and chaotic. Such a condition characterizes Ottilie, the narrator's handicapped double, with her uncontrollable body, "formless mouth," and eyes "strained with anxiety" (420). Ottilie is unintelligible, and for the narrator she seems outside of meaning, incomprehensible. Ottilie's alienation is at first too great for Porter's narrator; the girl seems to her to exist without any reference to reality: "Her muteness seemed nearly absolute; she had no coherent language of signs"; "nothing could make her seem real, or in any way connected with the life around her" (421, 425). Outside of coherence, unconnected to the dominant culture—its signs and meanings—what is there? A new order? Or incoherence and chaos?

When the narrator of "Holiday" arrives at the Müller farm, she feels she has no part in the natural cycles that structure this traditional agrarian household. She is a winter figure who comes to this fecund place seeking healing and renewal. She rides to the farm on the felicitously named spring wagon, whose mysterious harnesses suggest her own interest in finding a way to attach herself to the positive, forward movement of the season. It is no accident that later, in her triumphant and comic exit from the narrative, she manages not only to harness but also to drive the spring wagon off toward new beginnings. At the start of her story, however, this narrator is presented as in every way separate from the Müller family, isolated, unhappy, outside of their language, an oddity of sex and vocation. The double nature of silence, as disconnection or reconnection, finds parallels in the narrator's haven at the German farm. Assigned a small room with a single window, high up under the eaves, she inhabits a space rich in symbolic potential for reading a woman writer's text—the attic of the patriarchal household. Although the narrator could sleep downstairs with the family, in what Hatsy clearly thinks is a "better place," she loves the attic. Besides her storytelling friend Louise, who has guided her to the Müllers', at least one other literary woman previously found shelter in the small sloped-ceiling bedroom. Piled in a corner are the writings of nineteenth-century women: "*The Duchess*, Ouida, Mrs. E.D.E.N. Southworth, Ella Wheeler Wilcox's poems." The inhabitant before Louise was "a great reader," who passed on these women's texts to her successors.

The description of the attic room in Porter's "Holiday," with its shingled ceiling, "stained in beautiful streaks, all black and gray and mossy green," recalls the inscribed walls of Gilman's "The Yellow Wallpaper." In fact, the room as a whole, tucked up at the top of the patriarchal household, is a familiar location in women's writing: the place of retreat and creativity. For many women writers, an attic room, or small private chamber, provided an escape from household demands. One thinks of Emily Dickinson's small bedroom, or Willa Cather's rose-papered nook, where she—and later her fictional counterpart Thea in *Song of the Lark*—read and escaped her family. From the attic in *Jane Eyre* to the nursery in "The Yellow Wallpaper," such a room in women's fiction has represented the condition of women under patriarchy. At times it is a prison, suggesting the isolation and oppression of creative women in the patriarchal household. At times it is a symbolic location, suggesting the suppressed, enraged, and even insane creative impulse within the silenced woman artist. Sandra Gilbert and Susan Gubar's *The Madwoman in the Attic* explored the attic and related images extensively in women's texts, concluding that the room signifies women's entrapment "in the architecture—both the houses and the institutions—of patriarchy."[30]

Porter's manuscripts indicate that she worked at length on her description of the attic: it was in fact the location of most of her revisionary labor. Not only does she place it atop an especially patriarchal household, but she also describes the house itself in a way that recalls the Gothic manor houses in which fictional women guilty of too much imagination so often have languished. In the final version of "Holiday," the house is "staring and naked, an intruding stranger" in the landscape. "The narrow windows and steeply sloping room oppressed me," the narrator confesses; "I wished to turn away and go back" (411). In contrast to the house, the attic room is far from alien. In her drafts, Porter took pains to exactly describe the room's welcome: "It was as homely and familiar as a place revisited, long remembered" (third draft); "it was not even a strange room, but a homely place revisited, though I had never set foot in it until now" (second draft). The attic comforts the narrator. Although it is a place the narrator has never physically been, she knows well the place of creative women within the patriarchal household. Joan Givner likewise suggests such a reading, describing the narrator's relation to the house and its inhabitants as "that of the woman writer in the larger world. She occupies the attic of a household where her own language is not used; she plans to write letters to which she expects no answer; she finds reading material that she expects will connect her with a series of foremothers."[31] It is interesting that in her drafts of "Holiday," Porter's description of the attic contained images of the sexual renunciation and deathliness she associated with her vocation. In both the second and third draft, she elaborates on the room's bed. To draw from the third draft, "The puffy big bed suggested goose feather under the white knitted counterpane, the flat white pillows stood up like small marble tombstones."

In "Holiday," Porter's exploration of a woman writer's anxiety about vocation and patriarchal expectations coalesces in the narrator's relationship with Ottilie, the Müllers' handicapped daughter. The narrator powerfully identifies with Ottilie, feeling that she and this mute woman are "even a part of each other" (426). The text invites a reading of Ottilie as the narrator's double, a doubling that DeMouy extends further when she reads the unnamed narrator as Miranda, Porter's fictional counterpart.[32] In a reading of "Holiday" as a narrative about a woman writer's search for identity within the confines of patriarchal culture, Ottilie emerges as a figure of the oppressed creative woman inhabiting the margins of women's texts. She is, in a phrase coined by Sandra Gilbert and Susan Gubar, a "dark double." As they explain, "In projecting their anger and dis-ease into dreadful figures, creating dark doubles for themselves and their heroines, women writers are both identifying with and revising the self-definitions patriarchal culture has imposed on them."[33] Both Porter's narrator and Ottilie are alienated from the patriarchal household, from its language and strict gender roles, especially the generational cycles of marriage and parturition. Like Ottilie, this self-conscious, literary narrator is "a stranger and hopeless outsider" (421).

The divisions within Porter's gender-thinking underpin her narrator's feelings about Ottilie. Just as freedom from patriarchal speech is viewed with ambivalence, and the madwoman/artist's attic is both free space and potential tomb, so Ottilie is both compelling and terrible. In the mute, physically handicapped girl, the narrator sees a woman free from sexual and emotional attachments, silent and unknowable, and she sees a woman who is unsexed and disfigured, barred from participating in the traditional life patterns of the other Müller women. According to the narrator's divided mind, Ottilie could be either the most complete or the most damaged human being in the patriarchal household. In short, her feelings toward "the servant" are deeply ambivalent. In an extended passage, she meditates on the consequences of Ottilie's isolation: "I got a powerful impression that [the Müllers] were all, even the sons-in-law, one human being divided into several separate appearances. The crippled servant girl . . . seemed to me the only individual in the house. Even I felt divided into many fragments. . . . But the servant girl, she was whole, and belonged nowhere" (417). To be bound or to have been bound to others is to lose one's wholeness and individuality. Yet in the common mass there is comfort, familiar ritual, shared love. Ottilie represents a location outside patriarchy; she "belonged nowhere." Like the intellectual or rebellious woman in the nineteenth-century attic, this mute, painfully crippled girl in the Müller kitchen and her counterpart, the solitary, observant narrator with her secret wound, inhabit "the marginal life of the household" (417). It is appropriate that Porter kept the original name of the young woman on whom she based her character, for Ottilie, correctly pronounced O-teel-ya, sounds much like the more familiar Ophelia, a name associated with a woman driven mad within the patriarchal household. She was a common figure in nineteenth-century painting's obsession with beautiful, insane women, sisters of the literary madwomen spinning words in their attics.

Porter establishes the narrator and Ottilie's distinct difference from the patriarchal Müller household with a single, sweeping visual image. The two women literally stand out from the mass life of the family and the animals. Out for her morning walk, the narrator looks back toward the farm and sees that "the women were deep in the house, the men were away to the fields, the animals were turned down into the pastures, and only Ottilie was visible" (424). This moment of recognition leads to her deeper recognition of her bonds with Ottilie. In response to Ottilie's gestures, the narrator follows her into a cloistered room, a dark double to the attic. In contrast to the attic, which suggested the intellectual inheritance of literary sisterhood, Ottilie's room suggests the prison of silent, unwanted women's lives. It is "bitter-smelling and windowless," with a "blistered looking-glass"—an image suggesting Ottilie's distorted reflection of the narrator. Here the narrator learns that Ottilie is the eldest of the Müller sisters and simultaneously recognizes her own kinship with the servant. Looking at the photograph of Ottilie as a sturdy child, the narrator feels for "an instant [how] some filament lighter than cobweb spun itself out between that living center in her and in me . . . so that her life and mine were kin, even a part of each other" (426). Ottilie flees such intimacy, and the narrator is left with her knowledge of their deep, human connection; she is indeed bound to this woman who is as much Other to patriarchy as she is herself.

Throughout "Holiday," Porter's narrator displays painful, contradictory emotional responses to Ottilie. At times it seems to her that Ottilie is whole and unplaced, "neither young nor old, living her own secret existence." At other times she sees the girl as a victim, "mutilated," her face broken in "blackened seams as if the perishable flesh had been wrung in a hard cruel fist" (420). In her identification with Ottilie, the narrator draws up waters from her own well of unhappiness. For she and Ottilie are the women in the Müller house who do not marry and bear children. Artist and "crippled servant girl," both are outsiders, "mutilated" by the hard fist of a tight patriarchal order, unsexed. This view of the solitary woman artist as unnatural, even monstrous, recurs as we have seen in Porter's gender-thinking. In her discussion of "Holiday," DeMouy makes this connection well, noting that the story's narrator—like Porter—"cannot change her ingrained view of femininity and its fulfillment; neither can she live that way. Thus in her mind she is like Ottilie, an arrested and crippled figure of a woman who will never bear life."[34]

Yet "Holiday"—an aptly named narrative—manages first to work through this terrible confrontation with the mutilated female self to some reconciliation and then, rather wonderfully, to set aside the whole problem. Ottilie may indeed be the narrator's double—in whom she recognizes that internalized cultural view of her self as the alienated, unnatural woman. But Ottilie also helps the narrator come to the joyous realization that her life choice brings not only losses but also rewards. "Holiday" presents one of Porter's most affirming visions of the woman artist on her different path. To counter the term "unnatural," she turns to the actual natural world and allows her narrator to be blessed by its beauty. Furthermore, in "Holiday" Porter joins other women writers in depicting the marginal location of creative women as not entirely negative. Isolated from patriarchal culture, they are often more free to pursue their own visions, to take, quietly, another road than their sisters.

Porter shows us a woman free from domestic labor. Her narrator neither cooks, nor scrubs, nor cares for children. Unburdened by a woman's traditional labor, she looks around with fresh eyes and has time to contemplate, to dream. This woman artist often spends her days following a narrow lane down to the river, "passionately occupied with looking for signs of spring." She seeks both renewal in herself and in the corresponding natural world, and she receives both in one, glorious gust of beauty. Returning late to the house, she finds the orchard "abloom with fireflies"; she had never seen "anything that was more beautiful": "the flower clusters shivered in a soundless dance of delicately woven light, whirling as airily as leaves in a breeze, as rhythmically as water in a fountain. Every tree was budded out with this living, pulsing fire as fragile and cool as bubbles" (419–20). The soundless, intricate movement of the fireflies evokes thoughts of art as much as nature in the narrator. She is touched both literally and figuratively in their transforming light: "When I opened the gate, their light shone on my hands like fox fire. When I looked back, the shimmer of golden light was there, it was no dream." Entering the house, she immediately meets Hatsy "on her knees in the dining room, washing the floor with heavy dark rags," doing her labor at night so that "the men with their heavy boots would not be tracking it up again" (420). The juxtaposition is vivid and intentional. Bound to her domestic labors, particularly her service to men in the household, Hatsy may be part of the cycles of parturition, but she is also alienated from nature as a source of aesthetic beauty and from the blessing it can lay on the hands of the woman artist. Her hands are full of "heavy dark rags," not visionary light that is yet "no dream."

In "Holiday" Porter presents the woman artist, a woman free from domestic duty, as an outsider and a visionary, a woman free to watch the "soundless dance of delicately woven light" that nature creates; her hands are touched with the same creative power. But as in Porter's other gender-thinking texts, libratory visions are countered by physical facts. Artist, saint, or princess, visionary women are unnatural, sterile, and grotesque. In "Holiday" darkness swiftly follows light: as spring brings new life to the story's artist-narrator, death comes for the great Mother Müller. It is the death of Mother Müller that brings the narrator to a final sequence of confrontations with her fears of alienation and sterility, her own life choices. While the funeral procession gathers outside the Müller home, Porter's narrator, alone in her attic nook, undergoes a vicarious experience of dying. Porter rewrote this moment several times in her drafts; it is a crucial, cryptic passage. The published narrative tells us that the narrator realized, on the funeral day, "for the first time, not death, but the terror of dying." And overcome by that terror, she lay in her room and felt that she too was passing away—"it was as if my blood fainted and receded with fright, while my mind stayed wide awake to receive the awful impress" (433). In her first draft Porter was even more explicit about the death experience: "I went to my room and lay down, an awful foreboding certainty closed over me like a vast impersonal hand. Life was squeezed away drop by drop, a cell at a time I was dying as I lay there." In both versions, when the funeral procession moves off, she is relieved: "As they receded, the noises grew dimmer, I lay there not thinking, not feeling, in a drowse of relief and weariness." As we have witnessed repeatedly, Porter associated both her own silence and death and her creative voice with motherhood and the mother's death. In "Holiday" the female narrator's vicarious experience of the mother's passing encapsulates the passing away of all the mother stood for in the story. Lying on her white bed, with its pillows like "small marble tombstones," the narrator lets go of her own motherhood. With the passing of the matriarch's body, she too is set free from the rigidity of Mother Müller's view—that milk is the business for a woman.

Relinquishing once essential, self-defining beliefs about womanhood, Porter's narrator experiences a personal death and release. Falling asleep, finally relaxed and at ease, she is wakened by a terrifying howl; it is Ottilie crying out in the kitchen below. Ottilie's grief is a mirror image of the narrator's. Both women are experiencing—as internal and external fact—the loss of the mother.[35] In the passages that follow, Porter suggests that Ottilie is her narrator's child, the grieving, crippled self she has given birth to with her aspirations. When the narrator enters the kitchen, Ottilie comes to her and lays her "head on [her] breast," babbling and howling with grief. Gathering the helpless woman together, the narrator loads them both into the spring wagon. At first they head for the mother's hearse; the narrator imagines that Ottilie wishes to be a part of the funeral procession, to belong to and be governed by the family rituals. Rather than finding her own self through difference, she will attempt to bring that crippled and anomalous self back into the old order.

But as the narrator guides her wild, swaggering spring wagon toward the dark procession, she touches Ottilie and confronts fully and irrevocably this other woman's difference from traditional womanhood and similarity to her alien-ated artist self: "My fingers slipped between her clothes and bare flesh, ribbed and gaunt and dry against my knuckles. My sense of her realness, her human-ity, this shattered being that was a woman, was so shocking to me that a howl as doglike and despairing as her own rose in me unuttered and died again, to be a perpetual ghost" (434). In an intriguing discussion of "Holiday," Givner reads this moment in a biographical light. Touching Ottilie's bare flesh, she argues, the narrator touches the possibility of love between women, particularly women artists, a love that frees them to take paths other than those laid out for traditional womanhood. And after this touch, this figurative recognition of a potential different life path, the narrator turns the spring wagon off the main traveled road. Says Givner, "For Porter, the road less traveled was the world of women without men." Considering the power of Porter's homophobia and the power of her association of natural womanhood with childbearing, it seems almost astounding that she would consider a lesbian relationship as a personal possibility. Givner is quick to qualify her reading: "It was one [possibility] that she did not consider for very long. However much she felt alienated from the mainstream world, the idea of all-female associations and the idea of physical contact between women was distasteful to her."[36] For this reader, it is more likely that touching Ottilie, the narrator experiences not potential physical relations but rather pure anguish, touching once again what she viewed as her own crippled womanhood. The howl that rises in her is again grief at the loss of the mother within herself, echoing Ottilie's earlier howl at the mother's death without. The narrator's "unuttered" yet "despairing" howl expresses a never completely comforted grief that repeatedly articulated in her creator's own gender-thinking.

What is marvelous in "Holiday"—and lacking in much of Porter's other gender-thinking as it appears in both her published and unpublished writings—is a sudden hilarious celebration of the grotesque, unnatural self. While the narrator yet reverberates with the shock and despair of intimacy and recognition, Ottilie, her counterpart and companion, breaks into laughter and "clap[s] her hands for joy. . . . The feel of the hot sun on her back, the bright air, the jolly senseless staggering of the wheels, the peacock green of the heavens: something of these had reached her" (434). "Jolly senseless staggering"—the two women roll down the roadway in their spring wagon. Like a baby, Ottilie "gurgled and rocked in her seat"; she leans on the narrator and marvels Miranda-like, waving "loosely around her as if to show me what wonders she saw." Soon the narrator joins in the celebration, recognizing that both she and Ottilie are "equally the fools of life." A small parade, just two fools laughing in a wagon, Ottilie and the narrator join in a moment of Bakhtinian carnival, their grotesque, celebratory procession aptly described by the phrases that define such carnival at the start of this chapter: "temporary liberation from the prevailing truth and from the established order"; "suspension of all hierarchical rank, privileges, norms and prohibitions."[37] While the traditional funeral procession of the patriarchal family inches away like a "train of black beetles," Ottilie and the narrator have their own parade, full of the laughter that accompanies the rollicking wagon and Ottilie's wagging head. One answer to life's punishing limitations is just such laughter, "Holiday," tells us. Laughter deflates power and points up absurdity. In Bakhtin's words, the carnival-grotesque "consecrate[s] inventive freedom" and "liberate[s] from the prevailing point of view of the world, from conventions and established truths."[38] "We had escaped one more day at least," Porter's narrator exults. "We would have a little stolen holiday." With these words, the narrative repeats itself, but with a difference. Whereas the narrator's first holiday from her troubles took her only to the margins and attics of the patriarchal household, this second springtime holiday takes her completely away from that household toward new, less charted possibilities.

"Carnival spirit offers the chance to have a new outlook on the world," Bakhtin writes, ". . . to enter a completely new order of things."[39] And in its final paragraph, "Holiday" turns toward that "new outlook" with an echo of Robert Frost's poem "The Road Not Taken." Porter's narrator turns the spring wagon away from the "main traveled" road where the funeral procession still marches in the distance. She and Ottilie turn to a road less traveled, a narrow lane that heads toward the river. It is a joyous escape, a holiday from oppressive gender roles. Rollicking down to the river through the blooming meadows, the narrator need not scrub on her knees with dark rags, nor yoke herself with iron-hasped pails of milk. Instead, she can marvel with Ottilie at the unfolding natural world, and perhaps share with others the "wonders she saw."

"Holiday" represents Porter's most positive fictional resolution of the conflicts between being a woman and being an artist. The story does show the alienated narrator inhabiting the symbolic space of her nineteenth-century predecessors; like them she risks social condemnation—"madness"—by her choices, risks always being a "hopeless outsider" to traditional women's lives. Yet for this narrator, brought into existence in 1924, the attic of her literary foremothers is a "homely and familiar place." In the same way, she can come to terms with her dark double, the expression of her fears of alienation and unwomanliness—her monstrous, unsexing vocational choice. The road less traveled takes these two women, shoulder to shoulder, wagging and clapping in joyous irreverence, away from the rituals of motherhood, the demands of patriarchy. They are an absurd, grotesque couple, off on their own little carnival parade, a "stolen holiday . . . on this lovely, festive afternoon" (435).

So often in her gender-thinking, Porter embraced traditional ideology and felt her vocation and creative power simply condemned her as a woman, yet the carnivalesque offered a more complex response to narrow convention. Through it, she found a way to respond to tradition—the patriarchal family or the Princess's massed judges—not with despair or anger or even negation. Like Porter's other fiction from the earlier part of the 1920s, "Holiday" explores questions of female identity and vocational choice. Unlike the other works from this period, however, "Holiday" takes a different path, momentarily raising the possibility of simply rejecting the whole patriarchal narrative that has historically governed women's lives. Unlike the frozen women of Porter's Mexico fiction, both the narrator and Ottilie seem free from the destructive compulsions of sexual desire. Unlike the Princess, they need no glittering armor to protect them from sexual experience. Outside of language and thus free from its constraining definitions, inhabiting the very margins of the father's household, their lives are not inscribed in the narrative of patriarchy. There is power in their mocking laughter that, like the Princess's, can momentarily turn over the old order and shake it into something new. Wagging, rollicking, grotesque but free, Ottilie and the narrator of "Holiday" simply ride, laughing together, out of the whole story.

"Holiday" comes as a happy surprise in the midst of Katherine Anne Porter's fiction from the earlier 1920s. Perhaps because the story suggested such a radical departure from traditional values, its completion eluded Porter for decades. At the age of seventy, when she returned to and completed "Holiday," she was almost as free as Ottilie from cultural definitions of womanhood. The story stands in Porter's work as an anomalous narrative—for in it she joins parties with the unfixity and difference represented by Ottilie. In the majority of her other fiction, the horror Ottilie also represents dominates her mind. In fact, "Holiday" forms part of a group of stories connected to painful personal events in Porter's own life. And the resolution she eventually gained when she completed "Holiday" in 1960 eluded her when she first worked on the narrative. It is to the deepest biographical roots of "Holiday" that we now turn, tracing in rumor and speculation the underlying origins and aspirations of an interconnected group of texts. We find here, in the events of Porter's most private life, some of the tensions and tragedies that shaped her gender-thinking and gave birth to crucial personal metaphors for female creativity.

CHAPTER SIX
RUMORS AND REPRESENTATIONS

Made hopeful by the Princess's sudden willingness to marry the young acolyte, the Queen expresses her heartfelt wish, "May I live to dandle my grandchildren upon my knee." But the Chief of the Royal Council remains baffled by the Princess's strange vocation; he cannot understand why she would reject motherhood for her glittering and painful art. "Why" he asks, as have so many others in this strange story, "Why do you suffer the torments of these robes and the dark mask and the sharpened jewels of your gloves?" The Princess responds in her familiar cryptic fashion: "I will make beauty after my own secret thought . . . and I will also devise my own cruelties, rejecting utterly the banal sufferings imposed by nature."[1] Her art, it seems, is simultaneously personal creation and punishment; it replaces the bodily pain of physical relations and maternity. What can be made of the Princess's beautiful yet masochistic dream? Creation and defense, prison and self-punishment, her art is a lover, an enemy, and—most significantly for the rumors and speculations that make up this chapter—her alternative to a child. As Jane Marcus once rather bluntly summed up such a concept, "The virginal vagina was the place and the space for the production of female culture. Women could not be the producers of culture while reproducing humankind."[2]

At the end of chapter 4 we saw how the silver dove, embodying both the father's word and the mother's fertile potential, could become an icon for a woman artist. Her art becomes her creative labor, the child of word and body fused into one. "The Grave" ends in comfort; the sun shines on the young boy whose hands slowly turn the shining dove. Yet preceding this peaceful resolution is the marketplace with its evoked terrors, and these lead not only back to the story's epiphanic evisceration but also outward from the text to Katherine Anne Porter's own life. In their work on "The Grave," both Darlene Unrue and Jane Krause DeMouy speculate on the connections between the content of Miranda's memory and the Mexican marketplace in which it suddenly springs, painfully, back into her mind. On the surface, Porter provides clues in the linked smells of the market and the graveyard. Visually, too, the dyed sugar sweets shaped like baby rabbits connect the past event with Miranda's present. However, a biographical connection, unacknowledged in the text, provides another level of relatedness. Submerged beneath the Mexico scene, binding the hot marketplace to the eviscerated rabbit, is an event that explains the anguish associated with Miranda's memory: an abortion Porter had in Mexico sometime in the early twenties. Mentioned in an autobiographical fragment and confirmed by Mary Doherty, one of her closest companions in the 1920s, the abortion repeats the pattern of fertility transformed to death that informs "The Grave."[3]

The connections of Porter's own personal struggles and her story do not transform "The Grave," but they do deepen the significance of the resolution found in the symbolic dove. From the empty womb, the grave, comes the fertile word, a source of comfort, a means of closure, and a treasure that outlasts mortality. To draw such connections between an author's life and her writing is compelling, often illuminating and almost as often suspect, for the connections often rely on felt associations; speculations; private, cryptic records; and rumor. Yet, this said, it is intriguing to probe two other places where Porter's fiction is interwoven with her own personal, painful relations to maternity, children hoped for, loved, and lost. In each, art provides a potential alternative creation or healing resource. The first of these is again "Holiday." Like "The Grave," this story emerges from the loss of a child and is, in a fascinating, wonderfully indirect way, connected to Porter's greatest work of art, her heroine Miranda. The second is an interconnected pair of unfinished stories, "A Vision of Heaven" and "Season of Fear," both faintly yet clearly tied to the originating events and emotional resonance of "Pale Horse, Pale Rider." In the places where life and art intersect, it is possible to trace with a light hand the threads that bind experiences to their textual representations, and from such connections to enrich our understanding of Porter's gender-thinking at a deeply personal level.[4]

The heroine of "Holiday" so much resembles the Miranda of stories like "Old Mortality" and "Pale Horse, Pale Rider" that readers consistently link her with this central Porter character. Like Miranda, the heroine of "Holiday" is alienated from her surroundings and acutely observant of them; she suffers because of her isolation, yet simultaneously she cherishes her sense of difference. Porter wrote "Holiday" between 1923 and 1924.[5] While she was working on the story in 1924, she was involved with Francisco Aguilera, a romantic Chilean studying for a PhD at Yale University. Her relationship with Aguilera, and the events that surround it, has important ties to "Holiday." According to Porter many years later, Aguilera was the source for naming her fictional alter ego Miranda. As she told the scholar Edward Schwartz in 1958, "Once a long time ago I had a very romantic (though fickle) Spanish beau. I received a letter from him beginning: 'Ariel to Miranda: Take this slave of music for the sake of him who is a slave to thee!'" This address, she informed Schwartz, led to Miranda's name: "Well it was all foxfire and soon over, but just the same, that is why the young woman (and the child) named Miranda represented me, or rather the observer, in those stories you know. All this happened several years before I published a book . . . yet from that far-off episode I took my alter-ego name, which now I can never abandon."[6] Looking at the evidence remaining from 1924, it is clear that the experience of creating Miranda, her "alter-ego," was far less lighthearted. By the end of the summer that year, Porter and Aguilera were no longer involved; however, according to her letters to Genevieve Taggard from that fall, Porter was pregnant.

Joan Givner thinks that this pregnancy never actually occurred; in fact, Givner speculates that Porter could not bear children.[7] None of Porter's friends from the time ever noticed any physical changes, and none of Porter's letters—except those to Taggard—mention the pregnancy. What is intriguing is the convergence of three incidents in the letters to Taggard: the pregnancy, the appearance of Miranda, and the creation of "Holiday." Crucial passages are excerpted below:

October 31, 1924: I am completing two stories, both far too long in germinating.

November 14, 1924: I have finished my story "Holiday" in a bath of bloody sweat, and am resting. . . . dear darlin', had you heard, out of the air, maybe, that I am going to have a baby about the middle of January? Now I've passed the danger period of losing it I can't keep silent any longer. Write and tell me how mad I am.

November 28, 1924: Jedsie darling—you're not to trouble about me. I'm doing well enough, I have been a madwoman, and I know it, but I can't possibly come out of my trance to establish any mood of regret. So far as the child is concerned, it is all more than well—but everything else in my personal life has been a blank failure—in all, I mean, that touches my love.

But I will see you afterward. I will bring Miranda. (Her name and sex have been definitely chosen for seven months at least) and we will talk about everything for days.

Thursday, undated: On December second my child was born prematurely and dead, and though I have never been in danger, still it is better in every way to be quiet. . . . My baby was a boy. It was dead for half a day before it was born. There seems to be nothing to say about it.[8]

Certainly there is much here that we can never know; the letters are cryptic, and so far they form the only record of these events in Porter's life. Yet after acknowledging that rumor and speculation can only partially unravel this mystery, it is useful to trace the few threads that seem to form a pattern.

The letters first break silence, and then reinvoke it. There is "nothing to say"; it is "better in every way to be quiet." They twice confess madness: "tell me how mad I am"; "I have been a madwoman and I know it." They suggest that Porter was in a disturbed mental state, a "trance." She views the child who she knows will be female and named Miranda as "more than well," a mark of success in a "personal life [that] has been a blank failure." All the positive birth imagery in the letters, however, belongs to her writing, not to her pregnancy. Two stories are "germinating" and "Holiday" comes to birth, "in a bath of bloody sweat," a labor so great that after it Porter is "resting." The arrival of "Holiday" coincides with the end of the "danger period" of losing the baby; each is at least a viable rough draft.

Porter's letters to Taggard as much suggest the potential birth of the fictional character Miranda as they do an actual pregnancy. The bloody labor of creating "Holiday" and the long foreknown gestation of Miranda lead Porter to describe herself as a madwoman in a trance—a familiar figure of female inspiration. Yet on at least one level, the joyous achievement is short lived. The physical child, a boy, is stillborn; and even the work of art, "Holiday," lay unfinished for thirty-six years. Dead and male, the child is a bitter conclusion to Porter's hopes to create a child as much of her body as of her mind, one whose name evokes the "brave new world," and "many wonders" anticipated by her namesake in *The Tempest*, and thus places her creator, or Miranda-maker, shoulder to shoulder with Shakespeare the preeminent literary artist.

Was Porter ever pregnant? Any answer rests on a shaky foundation of rumor and speculation. What cannot be questioned is Porter's isolation and emotional anguish during the winter of 1924. What also cannot be questioned is her marvelous achievement, Miranda, young girl and heroine, rocking joyously out of the pages of "Holiday." In this literary work of art, Porter does fulfill her Princess's expressed hope: "I will make beauty after my own secret thought . . . and I will also devise my own cruelties, rejecting utterly the banal sufferings imposed by nature." The gender roles Porter encountered at the turn of the twentieth century presented a woman artist with versions of the High Priestess's proclamation that through childbirth alone a woman gains legitimacy: "If she scorns and rejects the natural office of motherhood it is written that she will never rule over the kingdom. For the fruitless woman may not inherit the throne, no, not even if she is the sole child of her father."[9] Yet from the child aborted or the child stillborn, from the grave of memory, or the bloody sweat of writing, Porter birthed the words, the silver dove and Miranda, child of a new world.

Lost children also lie behind a linked pair of unfinished, elegiac stories, "A Vision of Heaven" and "Season of Fear," and, less directly, behind her masterpiece "Pale Horse, Pale Rider." Here too, we can see how Porter wove a response to her identity as woman and artist out of her own painful relations to maternity. Witnessing her gender-thinking at its deepest personal level, we can understand how she imagined art providing a potential alternative creation for a woman artist and a healing resource for her seemingly unavoidable confusion and grief.

In October 1954, while living alone in Liege, Porter turned again to the unfinished typescripts of "Season of Fear" and "A Vision of Heaven" begun approximately thirty years earlier. As she sought inspiration, she probed some of the stories' deepest sources only to discover that the experiences from which the two texts sprang were, in fact, interconnected:

> Both stories are based upon, grew out of, terrible and tragic experiences of my own; almost mortal wounds. And neither would allow itself to be told. . . . I was looking over the mss. . . . I read the notes and the three beginnings, and the long passages . . . and then read again Season of Fear, in almost exactly the same state of incompleteness, and I realized that the two losses, were almost seven years apart, and that I had responded to them in almost exactly the same way, that one event was part of another, and that indeed, *they were one story!* How did I not see this before? Why has it taken me so long? Well, I am still the same stubborn soul that I was; oh how terribly [sic] it was for me to accept the truth about all that— and I must remember too that these two things followed close on to the Plague of 1918. I wrote that, in Pale Horse, Pale Rider, but there was, is, some residue of truth I could not tell—maybe now I shall be able![10]

The events Porter recalls are three: the stillborn baby in December 1924, the death of her niece Mary Alice in July 1919, and her own near-death illness in October 1918. These connections tie "Pale Horse, Pale Rider" to the unfinished stories: "Season of Fear," emerging from her winter alone on the Connecticut farm after the stillbirth, and "A Vision of Heaven," exploring her deep maternal bond to her niece Mary Alice and her prolonged mourning after the child's death. However, as her personal notes recognize, Porter was never able to "tell" the "residue of truth" that bound together "Season of Fear," "A Vision of Heaven," and "Pale Horse, Pale Rider." Her drafts of the unfinished stories are a jumble of disconnected scenes, powerful in emotional quality but never completely unified.

Of the two unfinished typescripts, "Season of Fear" is the least realized, the most fragmented. Along with "A Vision of Heaven," it contains many images that also appear in "Pale Horse, Pale Rider," in particular descriptions of death as bearing a double face, at once evil and alluring. We can gain a general sense of Porter's intentions for "Season of Fear" through a typescript titled "The Dark Forest," written in Santa Monica, California, in 1947, as perhaps plans for a screenplay. In this simplified, emotionally and visually flat version of the story, the unnamed heroine has chosen to spend a winter alone in an isolated New England farmhouse. She has just been through a failed love affair. As Porter summarizes, the woman "knows she is going to have a child, and at this point he tells her he cannot marry her because he is married already. As a result of this shock she loses her child" and runs off to the country.[11] The drafted fragments of "Season of Fear," clearly following the same narrative line, are far more richly imagined and compelling. In one, Porter describes her heroine: "The woman frozen like Satan in the dark lake of hell (evil). Begin with the eternal painful cold, her memories of warmth, spring, light, fertility (false spring, her love was false)."[12]

In the complex layering of Porter's imagery both in published texts and unpublished materials, life events repeat and fuse often through shared images. It is intriguing that in one letter to Francisco Aguilera, her lover and the supposed source for Miranda in name (if not the father of Porter's stillborn child), Porter offers Aguilera her love and alludes cryptically to her pregnancy. Using a mingling of poetry and enigmatic prose, she describes herself moving toward death with images much like those in "Pale Horse, Pale Rider." In the poetic passages, Aguilera sounds rather like the death figure at the start of "Pale Horse, Pale Rider": "Bundle of myrrh, o, my ascetic rack o' bones, my love thin and dark and tortured as an olive tree, will you not love me?" The child at first brings the promise of spring, an escape from winter: "Little child, solitary seed buried in my heart, will you not waken even for spring?" And the poem promises Aguilera immortality through offspring, if he will only pledge love: "If you love me, your very life shall be a pulse in the wrists of children to the latest times of the earth." But as the letter breaks from poetry into more disturbing prose, love becomes death, pregnancy a terrible disorder: "I die daily, and my love song is a funeral song too. Something mysterious and terrible is going on in me, deeply hidden, implacable; I wake in the night frightened as if I were dropping into an endless pit."[13]

In "Pale Horse, Pale Rider," death is a figure of horror who "rides beside Miranda in her dream" and regards her without meaning, "the blank still stare of mindless malice that makes no threats and can bide its time."[14] A similar figure appears in "A Vision of Heaven" as "the enemy who lives in eternity, whose chronology is not ours. . . . Blind and silent, insatiable and giving no reasons."[15] And the same silent menace moves through "Season of Fear," raising the hackles on the dogs and immobilizing the solitary woman. In the scenes Porter sketched for this winter tale, the unnamed heroine is infected with terrible feelings of guilt and terror. Her mental state is contagious and spreads to the animals crowded into the isolated small farm with her. All experience a growing, pervading sense of horror, of an evil presence that surrounds the house and stalks them through the winter woods. The woman struggles to rationalize her fear and understand her isolation and grief. To quote from one set of notes:

That night—this can be one of the pretexts for the dogs and cats fear: walking out, in the silence, the pure full moon, the pure bright frozen world, a gleaming pulse and movement in it, strange recurrent sound, like the blows of an axe against a frozen tree trunk . . . far and near, all around her, irregularly recurring. Her instant fright. Started to walk back slowly, the animals huddling near her, listening, seeming to watch her, dog's hackles on end. . . . Trying not to terrify them, afraid to speak for fear they would catch fear from her voice. . . . Gets them all back into the house safely, they settle down, though uneasily. She thinks it over: of course, branches crackling under the ice weight, striking the frozen surface of the snow. She listened for it. Yes.

The woman in "Season of Fear" drifts toward death in much the same way Miranda does in "Pale Horse, Pale Rider," feeling "ill all the time, without pain . . . a pervasive, relaxed drowse like slowly lapsing consciousness." She resists her condition in many ways, forcing herself to walk out at night, to explore the frozen countryside, to face her fears. During the day she writes "desperate letters" to friends, hoping to alleviate her loneliness by invoking their presence. "She struck the typewriter with a great clatter: Dear Jane—Dear Mary—Dear George—Dear Brack—Dear Judd—dear, dear to her they all suddenly became, she tried with the words to draw them near her by writing their names on paper." During the night she wakes frequently, hearing "some strange noise, unheard, actually, by her waking mind . . . coming out of sleep, unwilling, with the same monotonous shock of terror."

Ghosts in the storeroom, patterns of footsteps in the snow, a strange starving man in rags who bears away her fears, a small golden snake that dies suddenly and mysteriously—the fragmented typescripts that make up "Season of Fear" are full of mysterious images as Porter sought a way to embody in metaphor her character's losses and recognitions. She never succeeded, and the typescripts remain confused and disturbing, their fears uncontained, efforts at resolution incomplete, and their heroine caught in an endless textual winter.

Although also set at a New England farm, "A Vision of Heaven" is a story of warmth, joy, and presence—at least momentary presence—rather than of cold, terror, and isolation. The drafts name the central female figure Miranda and describe her on the anniversary of a beloved child's death, spending a peaceful, healing summer day with her housekeeper's daughter, a trusting, blonde-haired little girl who bears an uncanny resemblance to her lost Mary Alice. Through the course of this quiet day, Miranda mourns for the lost child (in most drafts her sister's but in some her own) yet at the same time finds joy and a sort of maternal relief caring for the visiting child. The biographical context for much of this story is well recorded. Mary Alice was the daughter of Porter's sister Gay Holloway and the firstborn child of the next generation of the Porter family. According to Porter's various records of events, she believed Mary Alice instrumental in saving her life. To quote one account of the relationship as drafted for "A Vision of Heaven":

The first child in that generation, much hoped for, loved and named before she was born. And the mother of this child had a sister who loved the child almost to the point of claiming it for her own, indeed, in her thoughts she did claim it, but was careful not to let the mother know. The sister, the aunt of the little girl, had been disappointed of her own child, born dead: and though she knew that such extravagant notions must be curbed, still her love for the child was perhaps the most important thing in her life. . . . When this child was five years old, the aunt was sick to death, there was no hope of her life, she was left at last to die behind the screens in her hospital room. The little girl asked her mother to have a Mass said for the recovery of her dear aunt, whom she loved. The Mass was said, with the child present in her white veil. She had gone into the Chapel whispering to her mother: "She will not die, she will not die," and she had come out again and said aloud in a gay voice, "She will live."

And the woman had got well.

Years later, as this account continues, the child had become desperately ill and had asked that her aunt likewise pray for her. The letter conveying this request was delayed and the child died. Porter's niece Mary Alice died in July 1919 at the age of six.

Porter worked on "A Vision of Heaven" over the course of many years. It was a story meant to bring about healing, and yet she never was able to complete it. Her letters and journals record again and again her grief for Mary Alice; each year she noted the child's death day and mourned again. As her biographer Joan Givner notes, she "longed to write a story that would be a lasting memorial to her niece. . . . She meant to call the story 'A Vision of Heaven by Fra Angelico' and to use as the central image a picture by Fra Angelico of a circle of angels. The epigraph to the story was to be 'I will show you sorrow and the ending of sorrow.'"[16] Among Porter's are three Fra Angelico prints. One is of the Annunciation, depicting a delicate Mary, open book on her knee, gazing at an arriving angel. Poised in the air above Mary's head is a dove, circled in light—an image of obvious significance for the close of "The Grave." Two other prints are enlarged portions of the tabernacle from the San Marco in Florence, both depicting angel musicians. Perhaps the most famous Fra Angelico at San Marco is *The Last Judgment*, a triptych with the damned on the right, the saved on the left, and Christ surrounded by angels and saints between them. The saved are welcomed into a flowery meadow. Behind the angels who encircle them is a shining gate to which each is gently led. This is the scene Porter chose for "A Vision of Heaven." The story opens with Miranda waking on a July morning, a morning that marks the "peak of her most bitter memory," for it is the anniversary of Mary Alice's death. As she rises from her bed, her eye falls on a "colored print of Fra Angelico's heavenly meadow patterned with small golden flowers and peopled with sedate crowned angels receiving the reborn happy souls into eternity." As she works in the garden, this image returns to Miranda's mind, a source of comfort amidst her painful memories.

Like "The Fig Tree," "A Vision of Heaven" records the struggle to sustain life and fertility in the face of death. The landscape is painfully fecund: "the orchard stood patiently tired under the tyranny of the sun and the burden of fruits, waiting for relief." Miranda resolves to spend her day gardening, creating order amidst the "warm tumbled rank grass," vowing to "tie up every vine of the tomatoes." But beneath this fertility, at all times threatening the labor to grow fruit and create order, is death. After she greets her housekeeper and meets the housekeeper's child, whose uncanny resemblance pains her with the thought, "It could have been, oh, so easily, her own daughter Alice," Miranda walks with the older woman through the rich, burdened landscape "under a sky that might fold upon them at any moment upon the treacherous earth that might open suddenly without warning and swallow them." A Demeter figure, Miranda knows that at any moment fruitfulness may turn to death, the rich garden into a frozen winter. Just as Fra Angelico's triptych balances the flowery meadow with the dark struggles of the damned, so her "Vision of Heaven" can change at any moment into "Season of Fear." As she spends her day, Miranda ponders her own failed maternity. She buttons the small girl's clothing, "proud of her learned maternal hands that carried store in them, though unused," and mourns her childlessness, "the sense of loss, of famine, of parched desolation that dried her own throat and no water could quench."

Porter never finished "A Vision of Heaven," although she returned to the typescript many times, just as she returned each year to the anniversary of her niece's death and her grief. Among the typescripts are a series of commands to herself for structuring the tale. They begin, "Tell this extraordinarily complicated story like looking into a succession of mirrors. No, no images. Have her looking through old papers, folder of drawings, looking for letters requested by a friend. Comes upon a colored print of Fra Angelico's Heaven . . . begins to remember the child." As with the dove at the close of "The Grave," the work of art is a vehicle for memory and healing. It encapsulates the painful loss, transforming it into something orderly and beautiful. Porter's "learned maternal hands" never held the child she longed for. But they did create: uniting word and spirit, giving enduring life to her work of art, Miranda.

At this point we come as far as is possible in exploring the deeply personal dimension of Porter's gender-thinking. To say the lost children become the literary work is too simple a resolution, and indeed, such textual connections are tenuous and may only be delicately traced with the aid of rumor and speculation. Perhaps the steely rebellious Princess, heavy with her dream, can obdurately proclaim, "I will make beauty after my own secret thought . . . and I will also devise my own cruelties, rejecting utterly the banal sufferings imposed by nature," but her jewels emerge from pain and cover over more than they heal. Thus at her death sentence, when she laughs, "tears suddenly streamed from the emerald eyes of the mask." For brief, luminous moments the work of art seems more than enough, a shining dove incarnate, containing word and spirit, a fleshing forth of the woman artist's dream. Yet Porter never finished either "A Vision of Heaven" or "Season of Fear." The two other stories that share ties to her life events of maternal hope and loss, "Holiday" and "Pale Horse, Pale Rider," provide only oblique resolutions. In the former a laughing Miranda rides off with her crippled companion, heading in the opposite direction of the mother's death. But this ending found its form only thirty years after the story's original birth "in a bath of bloody sweat." Neither this Miranda, nor her counterpart in "Pale Horse, Pale Rider," chooses the maternal dream that suffuses "A Vision of Heaven."

Leaving behind the rumors and speculations that connect Katherine Anne Porter's creative work on "The Grave," "Holiday," "Season of Fear," and "A Vision of Heaven," we turn now to her far more clearly inscribed analysis of another culturally endorsed desire that draws and disappoints women—romantic love. At the close of "Pale Horse, Pale Rider," a deeply alienated Miranda rises from her deathbed, dons the trappings of womanhood, and heads into the 1920s, her first dream of romantic love dead behind her. Like the heroine of "Holiday," she binds up her wounds and carries on, modern and independent. This Miranda joins the other women in stories Porter wrote in the late 1920s or early 1930s who inhabit a wasteland world, where all around them they see tradition broken and corrupted. Dedicated and solitary, yet hoping still for love, they are alternately vulnerable and defensive women struggling to build lives in the postwar modern world. In much of her fiction from the late 1920s and the 1930s, Porter turned her attention to the compromises and self-deceptions love seems to ask of women, particularly women artists torn between modern independence and traditional female roles. It is in her analysis of romantic love—and its consequences for women—that Porter achieved some of her most acutely critical and insightful gender-thinking.

CHAPTER SEVEN

ROMANTIC LOVE

For a time, the acolyte in Katherine Anne Porter's "The Princess" proves the perfect lover for a woman artist. Although he longs for a physical expression of their love, this young man willingly subordinates his desires to his beloved's dreams. At their marriage altar, the Princess refuses to undress, to set aside her ornate and beautiful robes, her consummate works of art. Instead she turns to the acolyte and announces, "This is the beauty I have created out of a dream and a vision, and I shall wear it until my death. But if you will, let us be betrothed, in a way I shall devise." The acolyte agrees that her artistic creation not only comes first but that he will serve it rather than any vision of his own. He unhesitatingly replies, "I accept all, for the sake of our dream."[1] Unfortunately, Porter found her male contemporaries far less willing to subordinate their desires to her art. In her personal experience of and related gender-thinking on the conflicts between her art and her desire for love, Porter joined many of her female contemporaries for whom the liberation of modern womanhood proved a mixed blessing. Her recurring struggles between emotion and aspiration are echoed by many of her peers, for example Isadora Duncan, who bitterly observed, "My life has known but two motives—Love and Art. And often Love destroyed Art, and often the imperious call of Art put a tragic end to Love. For these two have no accord, but only constant battle."[2]

From 1919 through the course of the 1920s, Porter was a frequent resident of New York's Greenwich Village, and she participated fully in the decade's labors to reform Victorian views of the relations between women and men. Like many of her contemporaries, Porter was both inspired by and unsure of the social changes she observed. As Leslie Fishbein notes of New York's early-twentieth-century bohemian community, "Prewar rebels were in a quandary regarding the political implications of personal behavior. Many of them were

Freudians uncertain of the relationship between art, normality, and rebellion."[3] For the idealistic men of Porter's generation, a central arena for enacting their generational rebellion was sexual relations; in Esther Newton's summation, "For male novelists, sexologists, and artists rebelling against Victorian values, sexual freedom became the cutting edge of modernism."[4]

Eager to be on the "cutting edge," Porter embraced the idea of sexual freedom but found the actual practice less than ideal. As Ellen Trimberger observes in her essay on "Feminism, Men and Modern Love," "Even the more independent and successful women in Greenwich Village—women like Susan Glaspell, Mary Heaton Vorse, Mary Austin, Crystal Eastman, Dorothy Day, Edna St. Vincent Millay, and Margaret Anderson—operated in a setting where men articulated cultural and ideological positions" and women found themselves still struggling for autonomy. "Women might give each other private support, but there was not at this time a women's movement that publicly discussed changes in personal life, marriage, and sex, nor one that helped women articulate what changes were in their interests."[5] Many women in this time period found the pressure to be sexually active as confining as it was liberating. Furthermore, the new liberation was itself still male-defined; it did not end the social convention of judging a woman by her sexual status, it merely changed the terms of the judgment. As Porter bitterly observed much later in unpublished comments on the twenties, "If you did not want to expose yourself to every passerby, it was because you were deformed. If you did not want to sleep with every man or woman who asked you, you were sexually a cripple in some way. The strangest blackmail went on in this line."[6] Her frustration with social pressure toward sexual experimentation also echoes that of other women from the period. Lillian Hellman, for example, once told Jay Martin, Nathanael West's biographer, "In those days, in the late 20s and 30s, we all thought we *should* be sexually liberated and acted as if we *were*, but we had a deep uneasiness about sex too."[7]

Most of Porter's friends and acquaintances were on quests similar to her own, and most viewed freedom from family and tradition as prerequisite to a career in the arts. Yet many of the women of her generation found it a wrench to reconcile the values they brought from home and those they encountered. They experienced, one historian speculates, a "continuing emotional adherence to the nineteenth century norm of female chastity and service to men, even as they rationally embraced the new belief in sexual fulfillment and companionship."[8] The results, for an ambitious woman artist, could be devastating. The traditions from home led to dreams of romantic love and feelings of confusion or shame about sexual activities. At the same time, women's traditional roles of serving and emotionally supporting men—which Porter's male contemporaries were not so adamant that their female companions relinquish—meant women often experienced conflict and compromise between their love and their art.[9] In *Women, Art, and Power*, Linda Nochlin provides insight into the situation of many women during the twenties. As Nochlin argues, women hesitated, as they do even now, to criticize male representations and practices in part because they feared negative labels. "Rejection of patriarchal authority is weakened by accusations of prudery or naiveté," she writes. In the 1920s, a time that celebrated women's newfound freedom and sexual pleasure, such accusations could condemn a modern woman to life outside the in crowd. Nochlin's words are further relevant: "Sophistication, liberation, belonging are equated with acquiescence to male demands; women's initial perceptions of oppression, of outrage, of negativity are undermined by authorized doubts, by the need to please, to be learned, sophisticated, aesthetically astute—in male defined terms of course. And the need to comply, to be inwardly at one with the patriarchal order and its discourses is compelling."[10] At its most immediate, the urge to please, sustained by physical desire, hopes of romantic love, and a wish to be liberated and modern, could lead to some terrible morning-after blues for Porter and her female contemporaries. An unpublished poem she wrote some time near the close of the 1920s provides a painful record of female vulnerability and male betrayal. Clearly the male speaker drew on the language of love to seduce his "laid lady," only to exult in his power over her. His words suggest that the dichotomous language of pure and fallen women still holds the power to shame an ostensibly modern woman:

Morning Song

He speaks:
Come, my laid lady, whom I wooed with words,
And called my Star—
Since you proved that you loved me, I
Know what you are.

For, knowing what I am, I have a rod
To measure by
If you mistake what I gave you for love, you are
More beast than I.

And having eased in you my ambiguous lusts
I now can prove
That you're a dupe who let me wallow you
And call it love.

If I have feet of clay, yet you are now
The dirt they trod—
And in that moment when I brought you down,
I was a god![11]

During the 1920s, Porter struggled to fit in, to enact the rebellions and liberations of her generation while remaining true to her art. What she experienced
was—she felt in retrospect—at best unproductive, often self-destructive. As the
decade receded into the past, she repeatedly returned to it in published and
unpublished writings, attempting to understand the complex gender issues that
shaped her own passage through the twenties and to thereby clarify her relation
to the decade's embraced ideologies. The result was an increasing tendency to
condemn its central male ideologues and practitioners while affirming her ultimate immunity to the decade's changes. Published essays, looking backward,
often express a hardening conservativism, a tendency to reject the freedoms
of that time and to dissociate herself from their history. In these essays Porter
often emerges heroically unscathed by the turmoil of the twenties. However,
her fiction and her unpublished papers—personal notes, incompletely drafted
essays—tell a more complex story. As one set of notes records, "These were the
years in which only the unexpected happened. . . . and almost always difficult
unpleasant and wasteful things."[12]

In her efforts throughout the 1920s to establish herself as a woman artist, Porter found herself divided between two profoundly different cultures: that of her
family in turn-of-the-century Texas and that of her rebellious contemporaries.
In 1940, while composing a preface for a new edition of her stories, Porter tried
to sum up her relationship to her historical moment. "I have lived all my life
in a period hostile to my nature," she decided, "[and] not until now have I felt
myself in a contemporary world." The 1920s were particularly alienating, she
wrote. It was "a decade which seemed horrible to me then, and in memory is
as horrible, for literally there was no spot where I could feel at home, and no
human association which offered any etc."[13] Disconnection and alienation
emerge here as Porter's predominant feelings. Having fled her own background,
denying the verities on which its social practices were grounded, she was buf-

feted by the shifting values of her contemporary moment, particularly by that decade's rejection of traditional structures—those truths of love and life—that had formed the foundation of her upbringing. To quote Porter's description of her "old-style" education:

> There was a moral order based on Divine Law, which was changeless, and, properly understood, respected and obeyed, could bring only the highest order of good to mankind. This law, if you directed your attention rightly, could be seen working flawlessly in everything. In mathematics as well as the eye of a fly and the habits of the ant, the sprouting of the seasons. . . . I am not being frivolous. Some very great and beautiful beings in this world have believed in this doctrine, have lived by it, acted upon it to the best of their ability, and have died in it and for it, and they helped to form social systems . . . as well as a stupendous body of art.[14]

Looking back, Porter felt the 1920s threw "moral order" into question if not out the window. With it went not just the order of "social systems"—particularly the gender system—but also, Porter's words suggest, the order on which "a stupendous body of art" had been grounded. The result, when Porter viewed the decade in retrospect, was chaos.

In a 1952 essay, "Reflections on Willa Cather," Porter indirectly presents her own wished for story of a painless passage through the twenties. The essay begins with Cather's childhood. In her Virginia farmhouse she seems to have received much the same moral grounding Porter ostensibly received in Texas. Cather was brought up to "reverence that indispensable faculty of aspiration of the human mind toward perfection called, in morals and the arts, nobility." Cather's family character overall was "shaped in an old school of good manners, good morals, and the unchallenged assumption that classical culture was their birthright." "Rock-based in character" with a "vein of iron," Cather represents the inheritor of solid traditional values—old, good, undeniable, and "unchallenged."[15] During her upbringing in Texas, Porter writes, she read Cather. Porter too lived in this solid world and shared its values. But security and solidity came to an end when she made the choice to flee north (away from her marriage to John Koontz) and pursue an independent career. According to her essay, she stopped reading Cather when she left home and did not pick up her novels again until Paris in the 1930s: "Those early readings began in Texas, just before World War I, before ever I left home; they ended in Paris, twenty years later, after the longest kind of journey," after the 1920s had well ended.[16] The return to Cather, the essay suggests, marks the end of Porter's own wandering and represents the acknowledgment of a former possession, a fundamental set of traditional values and beliefs. However, between Texas and Paris, the departure and the return, lies a descent—the 1920s described at the center of "Reflections on Willa Cather." According to this essay, Porter managed to pass unscathed through the decade, holding like a princess in a fairy tale to a slender thread that guided her steps: "You find that all along you had held and wound in your hand through the maze an unbreakable cord."[17]

Porter's essay on Cather represents one of her many efforts to simultaneously define and distance her own experience of the 1920s. Perhaps the most ambitious is an unfinished essay titled "The Twenties" that she worked on extensively after reading Malcolm Cowley's irritating and brief summation of her career in Exile's Return: "Mexico City was her Paris and Taxco was her South of France."[18] Porter's lengthy drafted essay "The Twenties," both a personal assessment of the decade and a personal response to Cowley's quip, represents an extraordinarily frank, often angry, and as often funny, woman's view of the roles her contemporaries played during that period. Porter came to see several of the key male modernist players as fundamentally spoiled and selfish. She particularly despised the young men who hurtled off to Europe to become artists, and her feelings are tinged with resentment for their gender and class privileges. These young men were not artists, to Porter's mind. They were manifesto makers who assumed the role of artist without having the vocation: "There were simply too many young men who decided to lead the literary life: and were so busy leading it they sometimes never got around to living it." Unlike Porter herself, they were secure with their "allowances from home" and able at any point to retreat back to their "respectable middle class . . . homes and families." Thus to her mind they took no real risks and merely made a "deliberate cult of chaos," indulging their emotions and their appetites. Such indulgence she viewed as mere narcissism. As she sums up in one paragraph from her unfinished essay: "They lacked richness because they had cut away from themselves all that traditionally gave meaning to human sorrow, to love, to all experience. They had no point of reference except their own unsupported emotions. . . . Swathed in all that drunkenness, clouded in all that much advertised love-making, I surmised one true emotion—self-pity." Turning to Henry Miller as an example, she concludes, "Such feeling is worth exactly a spit in the river."[19]

The views Porter expressed in her drafts for "The Twenties" correspond to the findings of Ellen Trimberger in her study of the heterosexual relationships of key players in Greenwich Village during the teens and twenties. Looking at the published autobiographies of men in these relationships, she writes, "Reading between the lines of the men's autobiographies, I sense that their women wanted not so much sexualized intimacy as fidelity, autonomy, and emotional support to develop their own intellectual and artistic talents."[20] Porter's words confirm Trimberger's suppositions. She felt particularly outraged by the sexism of some of her male contemporaries, believing these men pressured women into the role of liberated sexual companion while at the same time belittling the women's creative achievements. She was angered when, for example, John Middleton Murray praised Katherine Mansfield for her "peculiarly instinctive art," recognizing the sexist underpinnings of such praise. Malcolm Cowley's claim that the twenties were "a man's world" almost put Porter at a loss for words. It is apparent to her that men made the twenties a "man's world" by denigrating the achievements of their female contemporaries. As she wrote in response to Cowley's views: "The lack of generosity, the bias, the lack of aesthetic appreciation, the vulgar conceit (find other words) etc of this confession; which is to say, the men in that time, in that peculiar little group, saw to it that women artists, no matter how talented, should go neglected by them. Not then at all a question of art but of sexual vanity. Fie for shame on the lot of them then."[21]

At times laughter helped Porter deflate the "sexual vanity" of her male contemporaries, and her notes on them can be funny and even outrageous, particularly her assessments of writers who cultivated masculine poses. She does away with Hemingway in her published essay "A Little Incident in the Rue de l'Odéon," only adding in her personal notes that he is a "Big Bully . . . with prematurely grey hair on the chest." She describes Norman Mailer's *The Naked and the Dead* as "the most prolonged fart in publishing history one couldn't say literature," and she liked this appraisal so much that she initialed it "K.A.P."[22] However, the male contemporary who received Porter's most sustained contempt for his attitude toward women was D. H. Lawrence. In her several published comments on Lawrence, Porter exercised a great deal of restraint. Her 1937 essay "The Art of Katherine Mansfield" merely notes that Lawrence "did his part to undermine" Mansfield. However, personal comments in her drafts express real antipathy: "Lawrence, who always seemed shrill and shallow to me, now seems a (well, disgusting little nasty minded gutter snipe. But restrain yourself)." To Porter, Lawrence's particular exaltation of masculinity was reprehensible, and she described his personal philosophy as a "repellant doctrine of instinctiveness and intuitiveness, prompted by his inflated erotic imagination."[23] Throughout her career, Porter took on Lawrence, reviewing *The Plumed Serpent* in 1926 and writing a lengthy and funny critical response to *Lady Chatterly's Lover* in 1959, when she was almost seventy years old.[24]

Throughout her fiction as well as her letters, journals, and essays, Porter revealed her awareness that the gender roles requisite to traditional romantic love interfered with her aspiration to be an independent, creative woman artist. Perhaps because of a family delight in revising the past into romantic narrative, perhaps because of her father's prolonged mourning for her mother, Porter was raised with a particularly dramatic view of heterosexual love. In a brief, undated journal entry, she lamented her upbringing in this tradition and alluded to the shock she experienced when she entered "real life" in the 1920s.

> LOVE. My earliest notions of love were founded alas, for me in the world I was about to encounter, not on Freud, but on Harry King's poem to his dead wife, on Heloise's letters to Abelard on Wuthering Heights . . . and on my father's perpet- ual mourning for my mother, who died young and fair and never faded as mortal women do. This is no preparation for what we are pleased to call real life as I was to learn.[25]

The romantic ideals Porter learned first explain the Poet-acolyte's raptures over the Princess's corpse in her tale "The Princess," as well as Amado's ado- ration for the ostensibly dead Rosita in "The Lovely Legend." The ultimate idealization of nonphysical love in Western culture is often represented in the adoration of dead women, from Dante's Beatrice to Poe's pale female corpses. Such a view of romantic love is neither modern nor revolutionary, Porter came to understand. Rather, it is distinctly unliberating. It seemed impossible to be both beloved and free.

Porter's unpublished personal notes—especially those from the 1920s—force- fully record her recurring frustration with emotional relationships. Of her lov- ers, she once wrote, "Not one of them wished me to live as I must live, given my nature and my vocation. . . . They wished to put my whole life to uses for which it simply was not intended." Impelled by her own desire for love, she often complied with her companion's expectations. The results were painful. She saw herself, rather like the models or muses of her early fiction, transformed by the other's fantasy of her: "Under the strain of trying to live in the vise in which they could fit me," her notes record, "I took on, you might say, the shape of their own distorted desires."[26] Lovers consumed or destroyed her, Porter's journals from the twenties suggest, leaving her "withered" and "mangled." At times Porter felt the only alternatives were solitary dedication to a life of art or relinquish- ing her aspirations for the sake of a demanding lover. In a journal entry dated "Monday 27th of February 1928," she describes her struggle between these two unsatisfactory alternatives, and vows to end a period of self-imposed isolation and "face the world." "I found much there to frighten and discompose me," she writes, "but only because my sexual impulses led me into situations that I could not control or battle with. . . . Certainly my doubts of human beings and their motives is [sic] founded in a fear of their power over me."[27] Despite her critical understanding of the romantic love tradition, Porter never escaped its lure. It seems as if two discourses on love existed simultaneously in her mind: love is self-fulfilling, love is self-destroying. The first she learned from her upbringing, the second she evidently learned from experience.

Several stories Porter composed during the late 1920s and early 1930s are intriguing for the ways in which they at times participate in and at other times reject the language and practices of her 1920s compatriots. This fiction reflects a period of intense conflict in Porter's gender-thinking as she struggled to reconcile her traditional views on love with the challenges of Greenwich Village culture and as, equally significant, she attempted to reconcile the seeming conflicts between art and love. In these stories, her heroines are all scarred by love. They inhabit a threatening environment where—alienated, embattled, and alone—they witness love reduced to shallow performance and exploitation, both love and sexuality mere means to power, debased, even ridiculous. Much of this fiction evidences the influence of T. S. Eliot's poetry. Characters move through a wasteland infected with Eliot's modernist vision of intertwined personal and cultural malaise. "Theft" and "Flowering Judas" contain allusions to Eliot poems. "The Cracked Looking Glass" connects through its title to Joyce's *Ulysses* and ends as well with the language of Prufrock. In "Pale Horse, Pale Rider," a story begun during the twenties but published later (1938), Porter depicts an alienated Miranda, poised at the brink of the 1920s, already painfully aware of the impossibility of romantic love in the modern world. Several of these stories share a retrospective quality, what might be termed a double vision. Like Porter's many drafted essays on the twenties, they not only record the world of that decade but also comment on it from a distance, looking back at the self, returning to and reevaluating experience.

T. S. Eliot's influence on Porter's language and imagination is apparent in her writing throughout the 1920s and on into the early 1930s. Her unfinished story "The Evening," woven from events that occurred between 1921 and 1930, ends with echoes of "The Love Song of J. Alfred Prufrock." Here the spectator Gordito suffers a version of Prufrockian despair. He has resolved to go to the desert and fight for the revolution but longs, much like Prufrock, to escape to another, more innocent and renewing watery world: "He had meant to spend the summer at Lake Chapala in the village where time forgets to move, and it is always a clear summer, and the girls came down at early morning to bathe in the rosy-lighted lake, splashing and calling to each other without disturbing the white herons at the water's rim. Now, nothing." "Calling each to each," the village girls, like Prufrock's mermaids, are a vision of communion and fertile youth. But there is no escaping the deathly atmosphere of the modern world. The close of this section of the manuscript, which clearly represents a possible conclusion to Porter's story, echoes the first lines of "The Love Song of J. Alfred Prufrock" as well, underscoring through allusion the impossibility of escape from the loveless present: "The evening was dead. It had been slain at last, it sprawled there clammily on the table between them."[28]

Likewise, in "Flowering Judas," Laura longs to escape but finds herself immobilized in the threatening present. Porter describes her as "not at home in the world,"[29] a phrase that brings to mind Porter's descriptions of her own experiences in the 1920s, "a decade which seemed horrible to me then, and in memory is as horrible, for literally there was no spot where I could feel at home, and no human association which offered any etc." As has been pointed out several times in readings of this story, "Flowering Judas" also owes a debt to Eliot's poetry. As Ray B. West noted in 1947, the story takes its title from Eliot's "Gerontian" and like that poem depicts "a view of life as a wasteland, sterile and barren as old-age, because of the absence of any fructifying element."[30] Here too we find the tension between traditional and modern viewpoints. Laura's comrades tell her that she is "full of romantic error, for what she defines as cynicism in them is merely 'a developed sense of reality'" (91). However, it seems impossible for Laura to fully relinquish "a set of principles derived from early training" and replace them with modern disillusionment. On a scrap left among her papers, Porter assigned the same plight to another unknown woman, writing in the third person, "She suffered a great deal from love, or rather, the impossibility of finding an adequate substitute for illusion."[31] Caught between illusory principles and a cynical reality, Laura feels deceived. As Porter describes her, "She cannot help feeling that she has been betrayed irreparably by the disunion between her way of living and her feeling of what life should be" (91). Like the heroine of "Theft," another story from this same period, Laura lives without commitment. Immobilized, frozen, unable to bridge past ideals and present practice, she compromises both and in the process betrays herself while being exploited by those around her.

Of these stories in which Porter drew on her vision and re-vision of the 1920s, "Theft" provides the most developed record of her retrospective gender-thinking about women artists during that decade. The 1929 story appears to be connected to some painful self-analysis Porter undertook in 1928. According to a journal entry among her papers, she saw herself as constantly acquiescing in her own exploitation, masking her passivity with a stance of righteous noninvolvement: "I have allowed all sorts of people to trespass on my human rights because I was too timid to fight for them, and too lazy and indifferent to put up the battle that I knew was necessary to hold my proper ground. I always rationalized this timidity and weakness by putting a moral construction on it." At the same time that she allowed her "human rights" to be taken from her, refusing to force trespassers off her "proper ground," she also allowed her creative material to be taken, seemingly unable to use to advantage what she could gather herself: "I have suffered a good deal because, of what I have had to give, other persons have been able to make some use, more use than I have at any rate. Whereas my disorderliness and lack of self-discipline have made my material, got from others, almost useless to me."[32] In every way, Porter acknowledges, she has been defrauded, both by her own failings and by the resourcefulness of her contemporaries. To be silent, masking her losses behind a stubborn, silent stance of moral repudiation, only condones what should instead be resisted with loud protest and vigorous struggle.

"Theft" offers in somewhat cryptic form Porter's analysis of the role of detached spectator she tried to cultivate during the 1920s. Set in a hostile urban landscape, this 1929 story moves its unnamed protagonist through a sequence of encounters, each clarifying that the titular "Theft" is far more than the loss of a gold purse. After the opening, where the woman realizes the purse is lost, the story takes on the form of memory, offering a double vision, simultaneously a review of the preceding day and a self-analysis. In this way it mirrors Porter's own retrospective stance toward the 1920s, compacting into a day's losses her summation of the decade's betrayals. The story's laconic, alienated protagonist is an artist who allows both her creative material and her material possessions to be taken from her. Withholding judgment and thus tacitly condoning the loss of values she witnesses everywhere around her, she repeatedly allows herself to be shortchanged by refusing to honor her own feelings or meet her own needs. As a woman and an artist, she is exploited by others, and, the story suggests, because of her passivity, ultimately she alone deserves blame.

The recollected encounters that make up most of "Theft" touch on the same personal losses Porter identified in her 1928 journal entry. The first encounter is with Camilo, an admirer, who customarily pays the female protagonist's way on the Elevated. By such acts as dropping a dime in a turnstile, Camilo "managed to make effective a fairly complete set of smaller courtesies, ignoring the larger and more troublesome ones."[33] He has established an economy of relationship, in which small payments ensure a superficial appearance of emotional caring while allowing him not to recognize a larger debt of commitment. With his dime he buys her acquiescence. Unhappy with the superficiality of her relationship with Camilo, the woman resolves to begin paying, and thus she hopes to purchase a more honest relationship. However, despite her plan to refuse the small change of Camilo's attentions, she continues to focus almost entirely on his needs rather than her own. She justifies stifling her own desire for independence and honesty by telling herself that Camilo "would take it badly" (60). Overall, through such self-denial, she allows herself to be bought with "little ceremonies" and "smaller courtesies." The first recollected encounter in "Theft" exposes the first thief: this woman shortchanges herself.

Camilo indicates something of the superficial, inadequate emotional relationships that Porter's protagonist lets suffice. Her next companion, Roger, extends attention from her needs as a woman to her needs as an artist. Of the men she encounters in "Theft," Roger most resembles the female protagonist—both are struggling artists, and their affinity is clearly apparent in their initial companionable exchange of glances. As the two share a taxi, Roger shares his professional problems: his show is not selling. He tells her his response to such failure: avoidance and a stubborn refusal to change. "I don't go near the place," he says. "Nothing sold yet. I mean to keep right on the way I'm going and they can take or leave it" (61). Both Roger and the woman approve his negative stance, perceiving it as a purity of intention and translating his avoidance into independence. His refusal to yield to the demands of the marketplace elicits the woman's commendation; this is her refusal as well. Like him she believes "it's absolutely a matter of holding out." Their brief encounter makes clear that as artists both Roger and the woman are out of fashion and choose a stubborn loyalty to their artistic integrity over popular success. But adherence to independent ideals in this world also leaves one shortchanged; when they part, Roger needs a dime for taxi fare.

The nature of the world that these two artists "hold out" against is evident in their surroundings. As they ride through the rainy streets, they overhear the conversation of three intoxicated young men, "cheerful scarecrows" in "seedy snappy-cut suits." The incident recalls the bar scene in The Waste Land, where drunken, lower-class speakers reveal the absence of either love or commitment in their personal relations. In "Theft" one of the young men confesses to a romantic hope: "When I get married it won't be jus' for getting married, I'm gonna marry for love, see?" But his companions do not see and "hoot" and mock "that stuff" (61). Love, like other high ideals such as following one's own artistic vision, has no place in this world. His drunken response to their mocking gibes—"Aaah, shurrup yuh mush"—reduces words to gibberish. This is what love has become, "mush," foolish language and nothing more. These young men also reflect the woman's situation. Like them she lives in a world where idealism invites mockery. In her bitterness and alienation, she too destroys the language of love. Later she tears a lover's letter into fragments, actively destroying the words, which might create a meaningful connection between her and another. "Why were you so anxious to destroy?" the letter asks (63).

In the story's third encounter, we learn that the woman may approve of Roger's "holding out," but her refusal to yield to the marketplace has not been so complete. Bill, her downstairs neighbor, is a successful playwright, paid seven hundred dollars in advance because he can produce "a good show." Although the woman contributed a scene to his last play, Bill will not give her a part of the advance he received, for the play was rejected in rehearsal. Stingy and full of self-pity, Bill asks for sympathetic attention while refusing outright to offer concern for the woman's difficulties, or the money he rightly owes her. It is not just a failed play that brings Bill to cry in his cups, however. He also complains about alimony payments, claiming that his wife has "no right to alimony and she knows it," despite the fact that "she keeps on saying she's got to have it for the baby" (62). Weeping in comfort, surrounded by his expensive possessions, Bill resembles the safely affluent young men and self-proclaimed artists Porter excoriated in her drafts of "The Twenties." Like the outpoured feelings of Henry Miller, whom she described "leaning on bridges sobbing about himself," Bill's selfish emotions are also "worth exactly a spit in the river."

By offering a scene for Bill's play and then letting go of her own right to payment from the advance, the woman allows Bill to continue his exploitative ways. When he asks her to forget the money he owes her, the woman's response is bitter and self-denying. "'Let it go then' she found herself saying almost in spite of herself" (63). What she lets go are her own needs; she will injure herself rather than confront others or openly condemn a wrong. Yet by remaining passive, while accepting drinks from Bill, as earlier she would have accepted Camilo's dime, she again shortchanges herself, this time more seriously, and by her passivity she tacitly condones the abuse.

The losses in "Theft" are multiple, and by the story's conclusion the gold purse comes to suggest them all. With Camilo the purse seems to represent the woman's independence; it contains enough money for her to pay her own way if she would only allow herself to do so. With Roger the purse is something "beautiful," a "birthday present." Here it suggests her talent and artistic integrity, the gifts from birth she would like to be loyal to, holding out against the demands of the market. After her meeting with Bill, she thinks of the purse as "empty." She compromises her talent in her relations with Bill, and like Porter herself, according to the self-reflections of her 1928 journal entries, she sees another profit by her talent while she gets nothing. Bill certainly makes better use of the woman's creative material than she does, enjoying a seven-hundred-dollar advance on a script to which she contributed without recompense.

All of these losses mass before the woman's eyes as she slowly pieces together her day and decides that it is the janitress of her apartment building who has stolen the purse itself. Hoping to regain it, the woman descends to the building's basement, where she finds the janitress, a satanic figure "with hot flickering eyes," stoking the flaming furnace. Confronting her, the woman confronts her own devils; her descent to these infernal regions is a descent into her own private hell, and again she betrays herself. When the janitress at first denies the theft, the woman responds bitterly, "Oh, well then, keep it." But this last incident proves too much for her, and she suddenly recognizes that "she had been robbed of an enormous number of valuable things, whether material or intangible." Obeying principles of a "baseless and general faith which ordered the movements of her life without regard to her will in the matter," she has managed to spread a moral cover over her hollow and even cowardly passivity. Her recognition also echoes Porter's own insight, recorded in her 1928 journal entry, that she placed a "moral construction" over her "timidity and weakness," likewise allowing others to take her property from her. In "Theft" what the woman loses through her silence is what she most values—her own dreams, both dreams of love and of talent. What she receives instead are "bitter alternatives and intolerable substitutes worse than nothing" (64).

Porter turned thirty-nine years old between her painfully honest journal entry and the publication of "Theft." There seems little distance between the gender-thinking shaping this story and her own reality. It is likely the story summarizes what she felt in her darker moments about her achievements as both a woman and an artist in the 1920s. As an artist, she struggled to "hold out," attempting to preserve the integrity of her talent. Yet over the years she paid out that talent, dime by dime. In the course of the decade, she saw the Bills of the art world flourish. As a woman she has received little more: Camilo's "smaller courtesies," rather than larger commitments, and the drunken "mush" that has replaced romantic love in the modern world. Inevitably too she is aging. In "Theft" the janitress finally admits that she stole the purse for her seventeen-year-old niece but exonerates herself by stating that her niece—unlike the narrator—is "young and needs pretty things." In the words she gives her satanic spokeswoman—"You're a grown woman, you've had your chance"—Porter cuts to the bone. Last and most painful of all the losses that come flooding to mind at the close of "Theft" is "the dark inexplicable death of love" (64).

The women of Porter's 1920s fiction are "bogged in a nightmare," as Laura describes the sensation in "Flowering Judas" (99). Braced against the world that surrounds them, almost immobilized by their resistance, each "cannot help feeling"—again in Laura's words—"betrayed irreparably by the disunion between her way of living and her feeling of what life should be" (91). The gender-thinking that Porter undertook in her retrospective view of the 1920s exposed a grim truth. In their efforts to reconcile their needs, emotional, physical, and financial, women artists slowly, incrementally but inevitably, compromised their talent and shortchanged their ideals. At their best, she and her peers might have described their conflicts and losses in heroic terms—as Isadora Duncan does in her dramatic lament: "Often Love destroyed Art—and often the imperious call of Art put a tragic end to love." But the lived reality was often less dramatic, more resembling a "series of compromises," each eroding personal commitments, diminishing hope—a story of petty losses occurring on the small personal battlefields of self-esteem. Porter lays them out for the heroine of "Theft":

> She felt she had been robbed of an enormous number of valuable things, whether material or intangible: things lost or broken by her own fault, things she had forgotten and left in houses when she moved: books borrowed from her and not returned, journeys she had planned and had not made, words she had waited to hear spoken to her and had not heard, and the words she had meant to answer with; bitter alternatives and intolerable substitutes worse than nothing, and yet inescapable: the long patient suffering of dying friendships and the dark inexplicable death of love—all that she had had, and all that she had missed, were lost together, and were twice lost in this landslide of remembered losses. (64)

The gender-thinking central to Porter's retrospective analysis of the 1920s brought her to write fiction illuminating the bitter accretions of compromise that eventually deface the lives and art of ambitious women. Her retrospective vision is apparent both in the relations of her unpublished writings on the decade to her published fiction, and in the formal qualities of that fiction. "Theft," for example, is located between two time periods, a past, which contains the sequence of encounters culminating in the loss of the golden purse, and a present in which the woman realizes all the complex implications of her loss and struggles determinedly for some kind of retrieval. This double perspective, comprised of an immersion in experience and a subsequent ironic review, corresponds to Porter's struggles during the postwar years and to the acts of distancing and control she undertook in essays during the forties and fifties. These are stories that depict things "twice lost," once in actual experience, then again in the understandings that come with distance, the truths found while quarrying in that "landslide of remembered losses."

Among Porter's writings on the 1920s, "Pale Horse, Pale Rider" stands out, providing a retrospective summation of Porter's emotional progress from approximately 1914 to 1936. As she wrote Glenway Wescott on December 3, 1937, "Just now, within this quarter hour, I have finished 'Pale Horse, Pale Rider'. . . . Nearly twenty thousand words, darling, laid neatly in rows on paper at last. . . . I began this story in Mexico, went on with it in Berlin, Basel, Paris, New York, Doylestown, and now New Orleans . . . what a history."[34] Although its composition spans the postwar decades, "Pale Horse, Pale Rider" records the demise of romantic idealism on the brink of the 1920s, depicting a Miranda figure passing through the death of her dreams and emerging empty but armored on the threshold of the modern wasteland.

Like "Theft," "Pale Horse, Pale Rider" tells a story of loss. Adam, the ideal young man of this story, represents a precious possession. His "extraordinary face" is "smooth and fine and golden," and he is a "fine, healthy apple."[35] Porter's descriptions equate him with the golden apples of the sun, prizes hard-won by fairy tale heroes and heroines who thereby gain a "happily ever after." "Pure" all the way through, "flawless and complete" (295), Adam evokes an Edenic perfection. Such perfection cannot exist in the wasteland world the war brings into being. From the first Miranda sees Adam as doomed, "beyond experience already, committed without any knowledge or act of his own to death." Joan Givner has rightly argued that Adam Barclay does not correspond to any one man in Porter's life. Much like the purse in "Theft," he represents the pure gold ideal of romantic love.[36]

The same wasteland that fills "Theft" also fills "Pale Horse, Pale Rider." There is only the terrible monotony of the present; it is "no good thinking of yesterday," Miranda realizes (277). "I wish I could lose my memory and forget my own name" (289). The future cannot be thought of either, for "there was nothing at all ahead for Adam and for her. Nothing." Only the present exists, and a growing sense of doom: "the beginning of the end of something. Something terrible" (290–91). As the story progresses, Miranda travels deeper into the wasteland. Funerals pass by; Adam moves toward death. As in her other fiction expressing her vision of the 1920s, Porter borrows from T. S. Eliot to characterize her landscape. Seated in a bar, Adam and Miranda overhear a conversation that again reveals the absence or failure of love in a modern world without faith or meaning. "I don't like him because he's too fresh," a young woman complains, "he kept on asking me to take a drink and I kept telling him, I don't drink and he said . . ." (296–97). Her lament continues, monotonous and interminable. As if Eliot's poetry was not enough to characterize this world as the modern wasteland, Porter also echoes the close of Fitzgerald's *The Great Gatsby*, describing Adam and Miranda struggling to be together yet finding that "every step they took towards each other . . . [drew] them apart instead of together, as a swimmer in spite of his most determined strokes is yet drawn slowly backward by the tide" (292).

At the end of "Pale Horse, Pale Rider," Miranda awakens from her near-death illness only to enter the world of Porter's 1920s. Like Laura or the young woman of "Theft," she possesses a faint memory of life lived according to the dictates of love and idealism, for she retains her memory of Adam. But that memory of lost perfection is now only "the last intolerable cheat of her heart . . . the unpardonable lie of her bitter desire" (317). She tries, urgently, to call forth Adam's ghost, for like Laura she longs for a sign, something to which and for which she could pray. Even the shadow of what Adam represents would allow fragile belief some life in this hollow world. "She said, 'I love you,' and stood up trembling, trying by the mere act of her will to bring him to sight before her. If I could call you up from the grave I would, she said, if I could see your ghost I would say, I believe . . . 'I believe,' she said aloud. 'Oh let me see you once more'" (317). But Miranda must now endure the seemingly eternal, repetitive, and meaningless present. Like T. S. Eliot's doomed hero in "The Love Song of J. Alfred Prufrock," who knows "there will be time / To prepare a face to meet the faces that you meet," Miranda now has nothing but time; nothing will begin or end, and nothing needs to be done. She leaves the hospital for the empty street: "No more war, no more plague, only the dazed silence that follows the ceasing of the heavy guns; noiseless houses with the shades drawn, empty streets, the dead cold light of tomorrow. Now there would be time for everything" (317). Looking about "with the covertly hostile eyes of an alien who does not like the country in which he finds himself . . . and yet is helpless, unable to leave," Miranda steps into the 1920s.

For Porter, the casual bohemian lifestyle of the modern men and women of Greenwich Village and its environs proved far more painful than liberating. Hopes of love led to losses and betrayal, and the labor to form lasting relationships repeatedly sapped the energy she needed to write. In the decade following the twenties, she not only wrote retrospective fiction about the death of ideal-istic, romantic love but also directed her increasingly bleak gender-thinking toward the landscape of marriage. The long progression of a relationship is something Porter's Princess never had to endure. Her devoted acolyte may assure the Princess that he will "accept all for the sake of our dream," but these two fairy tale lovers are never put to the test. Somewhat conveniently, the Princess drowns, and her acolyte finds fame writing poetry about the perfection of an untested love. For Porter's views on the success rate of tested love, it is neces-sary to look at the stories that she wrote from the late 1920s up to 1940 that fol-low the course of love beyond the altar. One of the most interesting of these, begun in the midtwenties, is "The Cracked Looking Glass." The story depicts a passionate, expressive woman in a fading marriage and also presents some of Porter's more complex yet less hopeful gender-thinking on the relations of art—in particular the art of storytelling—and desire, whether that desire be for romance, physical satisfaction, or a child. Ultimately, "The Cracked Looking Glass" conflates all three.

According to Joan Givner, Porter found the seed for "A Cracked Looking Glass" during the summer of 1926, when she was staying in a Connecticut farmhouse with her then husband Ernest Stock. Local gossip described the house's former owner as "a rich Irish widow" with fancy furniture and a re-puted fancy for young boys. Writes Givner, "The story fascinated Porter and she thought of calling her version of it 'St. Martin's Summer'. . . . Later she preferred the title 'Dark Rosaleen in Connecticut.'"[37] The title Porter finally selected, however, alludes to far more than season or locale. When she sent the story off to *Scribner's Magazine* in 1932, she called it "The Cracked Mirror." Shortly thereafter she sent an urgent letter to the magazine's editor asking that the title be changed before publication. Her explanation:

> Yesterday I ran across a copy of *Ulysses* and saw again that phrase of Joyce's which had stuck in my mind: about the Art of Ireland being "the Cracked Looking glass of a Servant." I had remembered the word as *Mirror*, and so have called my story "The Cracked Mirror" when it should be "The Cracked Looking Glass—."
>
> If it is not too late, I beg of you to have the title changed, and anywhere in the story that the word *Mirror* occurs, please have the proofreader change it to "look-ing glass."[38]

On its surface, "The Cracked Looking Glass" appears to be a January–May tale framed in a slightly comic, ethnic context; the depiction of ethnicity, here Irish-American immigrants, is more superficial than in "María Concepción."

However, as the allusion to Joyce's text suggests, in this story Porter's interest in the mirror has as much to do with the role of art as it does with female appearance. Once again her gender-thinking addresses questions of creativity and femininity, telling the story of an aging creative woman, a storyteller, who is childless yet full of physical desire, rich in verbal skill yet trapped in disappointment and sterility. The story also contains one of Porter's strongest condemnations of romantic love. The fantasies flowing from her youthful erotic energy lead the heroine, Rosaleen, to marry Dennis, a dapper but much older man. When motherhood eludes her, she is left with little release for her fertile mind or body. Furthermore, much like Porter and her modern female contemporaries, Rosaleen must contend with the tensions between her sexual desires and a traditional upbringing that binds ideal love to strict moral codes. In the light of Porter's gender-thinking on the tensions of art and love during the 1920s, "The Cracked Looking Glass" appears a grim tale. For here too we can see her recognition that women are in a trap created by their ambitions, their newly acknowledged sexual desires, and their still entrenched, deeply internalized social mores. As in much of her earlier work, Porter allows but two central outlets for female creativity: art or childbirth. If a woman chooses the former, she not only is denied the latter but also becomes unsexed, sterile, no longer fully a woman.

The heroine of "The Cracked Looking Glass," Rosaleen, is as voluptuous in body and language as Joyce's Molly Bloom, but her husband, Dennis, is past desire, "all gone, and he had been so for many years . . . there comes a time when a man is finished and there is no more to be done that way."[39] What remains for this richly generative woman is the pleasure she finds in verbal play, sparring with Dennis until he falls asleep like a stone, flirting with visiting salesmen, telling and retelling with great feeling stories from her past. As she informs Dennis after regaling a visiting salesman with a tale, "He wanted a story so I gave him a good one. That's the Irish in me" (105). Although a gifted storyteller, Rosaleen is also a naive one, unaware of the longings inscribed in her effusive texts. Her art works to transform past disappointment and present desire into palatable romance. Like so many women, Porter tells us in this story, Rosaleen was herself seduced by the cultural myth of romantic love, and she cannot relinquish this ideal, for to do so would be to face the disappointments and failures of her own life. Significantly, when Rosaleen passes through New York on her way to Boston, she initially wishes "she had an hour to visit her old flat in 164th Street—just a turn around the block would be enough, but there wasn't time" (123). However, there is enough time to consume chocolates, "ice cream with strawberry preserves on it, and two movies, *The Prince of Love* and *The Lover King*" (124). Rosaleen has no time for the real past; she stuffs herself with sweetened romance. The plot of *The Lover King* parallels her own youthful, thrilling courtship with Dennis. In the movie, "a king in disguise, a lovely young man with black wavy hair . . . married a poor country girl who was more beautiful than all the princesses and ladies in the land" (124). Likewise, Rosaleen, herself "a country girl" from Sligo (107), was bedazzled by richer, older, urban Dennis, a Dublin man: "such a gentleman in his stiff white shirt front" (108). It is no wonder that "the love songs" of *The Lover King* went to Rosaleen's "heart like a dagger" (124).

In Rosaleen's oft-told tales, two topics frequently recur: the death of her cat, Billy-cat, and memories of "a lad named Kevin," a housepainter who stayed one summer with Rosaleen and Dennis. The cat's death and the young man's departure mingle in her mind; grieving for the cat, she expresses her yearning for the young man, a potential lover and son. In her excellent detailed reading of this story, Jane Krause DeMouy argues that Rosaleen is a "thwarted mother": "Her life seems in the twenty-fifth year of her marriage unfulfilled and attended by losses, most unfortunately the loss of the child that could have transformed her from maiden to mother."[40] In Rosaleen's mind, her baby son "that died in two days" also mingles with Kevin, for "now [the child] would be a fine grown man and the dear love of her heart. The image of him floated before her eyes plain as day, and became Kevin" (114). Unfulfilled sexual desire and unfulfilled motherhood live confused in Rosaleen's mind, as Unrue suggests. Lost sons are lost lovers, and lost lovers are lost sons. When she travels alone to Boston, ostensibly seeking her sister but in fact yielding to undefined desires for freedom and a return to her lost youth, Rosaleen is vulnerable to the attentions of a young Irish man, misreading his seductions in maternal terms. She cries out, "You might be Kevin, or my own brother, or my own little lad alone in the world." However, this green-eyed "hostler"/hustler penetrates her effusive maternity and responds to the erotic energy that it both masks and releases. "Woman alive," he tells her, "it's what any man might think the way ye're—" (129). Rosaleen herself cannot admit her physical desire. With Kevin, talk replaced and released desire; the two of them sparred joyfully: "for more than a year they had tried to get the best of each other in the talk, and sometimes it was one and sometimes another, but a gay easy time and such a bubble of joy" (115). In the rich verbal relations with Kevin, Rosaleen's maternal longing and erotic energy found an outlet.

Throughout Porter's tale, Rosaleen peers into her looking glass, seeking confirming images of herself as young, beautiful, not without hope. She looks first in the glass after Kevin's departure; again after a disturbing exchange with her wild, virile neighbor, Guy Richards; and yet again at the close as she almost yields to but finally resists Richards's dangerously attractive appeal. Each time she hopes to see the young, sensual Rosaleen she feels inside; each time what looks back at her is a face broken into fragments, "leaping into shapes fit to scare you" (133). For Rosaleen hope ends with her unsuccessful trip to Boston. She set out with twin goals, to find her sister Honora and to purchase a new looking glass, one without a crack. She seeks, in other words, to regain her self-image as a woman still rich in physical potential while at the same time keeping her relation to her honor. But the story tells us this is all a fantasy. Romantic love is the illusion with which Rosaleen stuffs herself before the silver screen of *The Lover King,* and sexual self-expression appears in the grim reality of Hugh Sullivan's grasping seduction. The two are thoroughly opposed: against dreams of honor and love Rosaleen cannot set child or lover—only shame and disillusionment. At the close of "The Cracked Looking Glass," this lesson is repeated when Rosaleen, hearing Guy Richards's sensual song out on the highway, momentarily leaps to her feet only to realize that she cannot follow that appeal and retain her self-image as an honorable woman. "It flashed through her mind that a woman would have a ruined life with such a man, it was courting death and danger to let him set foot over the threshold" (134).

The looking glass reflects not only Rosaleen's unfulfilled womanhood but also, disturbingly, her imperfection as a woman artist. As Porter's 1932 letter to the editor of *Scribner's Magazine* makes evident, in her mind the looking glass represented art; she drew on Joyce's description of the art of Ireland as "the cracked looking glass of a servant." When Rosaleen looks in her glass, what she sees frightens her. As she tells Dennis, the glass makes her "face look like a monster's" (122). For a feminist reader, the image richly resonates across the history of women's writing, linking Porter's gender-thinking with that of many women who wrote, in varying ways, of the monstrous self that is a thinking woman.[41] At the same time, the image of a woman as a monster connects to Porter's own gender-thinking on the problems of reconciling women's potential as creators and procreators. To quote yet again her words on St. Rose, "The body of woman is the repository of life, and when she destroys herself it is important. It is important because it is not natural, and woman is natural or she is a failure. . . . Therefore women saints, like women artists are monstrosities. . . . You might say that if they are saints or artists they are not women."[42] Unfulfilled as a mother, locked in her sterile marriage to wintry Dennis, Rosaleen uses her art, storytelling, as creative outlet. As Jane Krause DeMouy suggests, "Through language, Rosaleen is the creator she cannot be through her body."[43] Like Porter's bejeweled Princess, Rosaleen is a Scheherezade with her art, weaving work after work—her goal, the deflection of sexual energy from body to text.

In "The Cracked Looking Glass," Porter did not give her heroine any joyous compensations for her physical difference. Unlike the Miranda figure in "Holiday," this woman artist knows only her conventional past and the small sphere of her present, alone and unfulfilled, warming her husband's dinner and spreading a blanket across his knees. At the close of "The Cracked Looking Glass," we see Rosaleen accept her husband's dreary limitations. As he tells her about the mirror that gives her only a monstrous image of herself, "It's a good enough glass . . . without throwing away money" (122). Turning away from the door, away from the possible dangers and delights of Guy Richards's virile songs, this frustrated May sits down by the side of her wintry husband. Drawing again on Eliot's language of modern anguish and ennui, Porter connects Rosaleen, immobilized and unfulfilled, with her other wasteland heroines. The dream of romantic love is dead, and what remains for Rosaleen is a diminished thing:

> She was wondering what had become of her life; every day she had thought
> something great was going to happen, and it was all just straying from one terrible
> disappointment to another. Here in the lamplight sat Dennis and the cats, beyond
> in the darkness and snow lay Winston and New York and Boston, and beyond that
> were far off places full of life and gayety she'd never seen nor even heard of, and
> beyond everything like a green field with morning sun on it lay youth and Ireland
> as if they were something she had dreamed, or made up in a story. Ah, what was
> there to remember, or to look forward to now? (134)

The close of "The Cracked Looking Glass" is even more terrible than that of "Pale Horse, Pale Rider." There Miranda accepted her desolation and determined to face the world fully costumed, ready at least to cover her emptiness with art. Here Rosaleen, who has yet clung to her art, her revisions of the past and visions of the future, finally yields all to the sterile Dennis: her magical voice, her hopes for change, her individual authority, her maternal energy. Laying her head on the knee of her aging husband, she asks, "in an ordinary voice," "if anything happened to you, whatever would become of me in this world?" And she docilely accepts his answer, agreeing to close the doors of hope and imagination, promising always to anticipate his needs and put away her own. "Let's not think of it," advises Dennis; "Let's not, then," replies Rosaleen. "For I could cry if you crooked a finger at me" (134).

In Rosaleen's final self-abasement, Porter represents her own view of marriage's dangerous potential, which she described most fully in her 1951 essay "Marriage Is Belonging." Yielding to Dennis's authority, Rosaleen enters into a marriage of "possessing," which requires, according to Porter's definition, "surrendering gracefully with an air of pure disinterestedness as much of your living self as you can spare without incurring total extinction; in return for which you will, at least in theory, receive a more than compensatory share of another life, the life in fact presumably dearest to you, equally whittled down in your favor to the barest margin of survival."[44] Lives lived narrowly recur in Porter's portrayals of marriage. There is a clear downward path from the bickering couple of "Rope" to the terrors and delusions of the Hallorans in "A Day's Work." There, bitter and enraged by her disappointments, the terrible Mrs. Halloran savagely beats her weak-minded, alcoholic husband on the face with a knotted towel. All that remains of marriage's ideals in this story are Mr. Halloran's vaguely recalled attraction to Mrs. Halloran during their courtship, and Mrs. Halloran's shocking advice to her own daughter, now trapped as well in an abusive marriage: "If anything goes wrong with your married life it's your own fault. . . . Bear with the trouble God sends as [your] mother did before [you]."[45]

Many episodes in Porter's own life throughout the 1920s underlie her depiction of the dangers of possession—and dispossession—that accompany committed sexual relationships, including marriage. As she wrote of the decade, "These were the years in which only the unexpected happened . . . and almost always difficult unpleasant and wasteful things."[46] One that might stand for many is her unsuccessful relationship with Ernest Stock, ongoing at the time she began "The Cracked Looking Glass."[47] Joan Givner describes Stock as a "naïve, humorless, and indecisive man." The couple lived for a summer in Merryall, Connecticut, near several friends, including the writer Josephine Herbst. Before the summer's end, however, Porter felt "that the creative power in her was almost quenched and that she was strangled speechless." Again her art and her love affairs could not be reconciled; she "realized once again that she must free herself from the prison" of a sexual relationship. Porter's short story "Rope" depicts much of their affair, in particular, according to Givner, Porter's own "continuing disappointment at her inability to have a child."[48] In that story the young couple bicker over money and responsibility for routine housework. Beneath that bickering lie frustrations with their marriage, not just disappointment at their childlessness, but, especially for the young woman, feelings that her time and her work are not given sufficient recognition. Approximately eight years after the summer in Merryall, Josephine Herbst published "The Man of Steel," a short story that also depicted Stock and Porter's relationship. Here, as in "The Cracked Looking Glass," the failure to bear a child brings feelings of hopelessness and sterility:

> It sometimes seemed as if her stillborn baby that had never breathed was the realest of all to her. He had had arms and legs, a perfect thatch of hair, everything for living except life. Why hadn't he lived? Why had everything she loved withered and died to her touch? . . . The black cat mewed and stretched, arching his back as he came toward her. Even he had worms in spite of the eggs and olive oil and the vegetables that she pampered him with. She petted him now and he rubbed himself against her still mewing. If she had a dog it would get fits, a horse, it would break a leg, a bird, it would die of the pip. A kind of cursed black doom seemed on her like a mound.[49]

Later in the 1920s Porter wrote another story based on her relationship with Ernest Stock, or "deadly Ernest," as she came to refer to him. Meant to be comic, "The Spivvelton Mystery, or the Importance of Being Deadly Ernest," is a light and not entirely successful work of wish fulfillment; a better subtitle for it might be "How to Get Rid of an Unwanted Husband, but Keep His Useful Money, and Almost Get Away with It." It was rejected for publication and she filed it away for more than forty years. It finally saw the light in the glow of publicity that followed the publication of *Ship of Fools*. In this short tale, published in *Ladies' Home Journal* in 1971, the heroine Ida May discovers that she no longer adores her husband. His face "seemed to grow sillier and sillier every day," and she "began to brood on the prospect of spending her life in the same house with such a face."[50] Discovering a marvelous new fluid that completely dissolves flesh and bone, she douses Ernest with it in the bath and watches as he "dissolved rapidly and ran gurgling down the drain" (75). Ida May's hope is to wash away her irritating husband but retain the apartment, "the radio-tv, the silver cocktail shaker," and all of their other desirable material possessions. Divorce will not achieve her ends, for "she knew well that if they separated he would try to keep everything on the grounds that he had bought it all with his money. She knew men, she hoped. How? How? How to separate Ernest from the flat?" (75).

Unfortunately, Ernest proves ineradicable. Shortly after his watery demise, he returns as a shade, pleading for some clothing to wear in the land beyond. Ida May is caught burning his suits and raincoats in the furnace of their apartment building. In jail her spirit breaks, for she can only imagine an eternity with Ernest and his silly face when she joins him "on the Other Side" (101). The message of this blithe but unappealing tale is more than evident. Girls, Porter seems to be telling her readers, I know you wish to get rid of your silly husband and keep the cash, but you will not get away with it. Told from Ida May's point of view, "The Spivvelton Mystery" convinces us most that Ernest is a silly, fish-faced burden and Ida May a clever modern woman. The story sets aside the painful conflicts tied to marriage and money, vocation and romance, and treats with light mockery the swift shift of a marriage from infatuation to boredom and disgust. The story is a superficial contribution to Porter's thinking on the relations of gender and personal freedom, releasing antagonism toward men and their material privilege while containing that anger in a moralistic close.

Much of Katherine Anne Porter's writing that emerged out of and recorded the 1920s depicts a wasteland strewn with broken ideals and the bones of romantic love. Responding to what she saw and experienced during the decade, Porter followed several paths with her gender-thinking. She continued to probe the cultural barriers dividing the role of traditional woman from the sought identity of woman artist, and she exposed the fallacies of both sexual liberation and romantic love for modern women. The frustration and anger her writing communicates about the illusions and betrayals of love deepened in the years after the twenties. When she returned to the subject of love and the woman artist years later, in *Ship of Fools*, bitterness had replaced hope, and romantic relations are the enemy of creativity. But in the intervening years, all was not bleak. For some of Porter's compatriots, gender roles retained their inequities of power and freedom, but for others who had never found these roles credible, the twenties offered new avenues for social and sexual experimentation. In the early thirties Porter forged strong and lasting friendships with members of the gay literary establishment, and in their playful response to proscribed sexual identity—the comedic forms of camp, the freedoms of cross-dressing, the interplay of social class and sexuality—she found rich new directions for her gender-thinking.

CHAPTER EIGHT

GENDER AND COSTUME

As the Princess lies dead in the glimmering water, her protective costume slowly floats away: "the waves lipped back and forth over her heavy robes and the cold inert jewels . . . until softly, oh, softly they were loosened." Finally her body is uncovered, as it was before she undertook her sartorial arts. The people come to view her corpse, "naked and glistening" in the water, and find her satisfyingly diminished. "'Ah, do you see!' cried one of the women, in a voice cold with spite. 'She was not so mysterious! She was like the rest of us, simply a woman, after all!'"[1] Without her art, the self-creation of her bejeweled armor, the Princess is neither a heretic nor an enchantress, merely a woman. Costume allowed the Princess, for a time, to fend off traditional female roles, giving her freedom hitherto unknown to the women in her culture. However, this final image of her dead and naked suggests that her womanhood, although briefly avoidable, was always fundamental—an inescapable fact of body, not a flexible medium of action or dress.

This interest in the relations of costume and sexual identity, and accompanying inquiry into gender as performance versus fact, appears elsewhere in Katherine Anne Porter's fiction and joins her to many of her contemporaries who investigated similar subject matter. In two of her lengthier works from the 1930s, "Hacienda" and "Pale Horse, Pale Rider," and in several of her essays, both published and unpublished, Porter's gender-thinking engages in questions of the relations of tradition and social order to artistic and sexual experimentation, questions central to other modernist writers. As many critics have made evident, a "crisis in gender identification underlies much modernist literature." Clothing, or costume, was a central sign in this discourse.[2] Sandra Gilbert, for example, concludes in an early essay, "Costumes of the Mind: Transvestism as Metaphor in Modern Literature," that male modernists "oppose[d] costume (seen as false or artificial) to nakedness (which is true, 'natural').")[3] Connecting social disorder and decay to the breakdown of traditional heterosexual roles, they represented their anxieties in imagery of bodily corruption, "perverse" sexuality, or transvestism. By contrast, as Gilbert argues in a later study coauthored with Susan Gubar, "The feminist counterparts of these men . . . not only regarded all clothing as costume, they also defined all costume as problematic. In fact, to most of these writers the supposedly fundamental sexual self was itself merely another costume."[4] Although Porter's gender-thinking reveals no such clear-cut division of thought, she did actively explore questions of social disorder and sexuality, particularly homosexuality, and joined her contemporaries in drawing on costume as a key metaphor for analyzing questions of gender as performance or reality. Is gender "a stable identity or locus of agency" or, drawing here on the arguments of Judith Butler, "an identity constituted in time . . . through a *stylized repetition of acts*"?[5] As recent gender theory demonstrates, gay or "queer" cultural practices continue to provide an avenue for exploring the construction of sexual identity, as they did for Porter. Butler, for example, asserts, "*In imitating gender, drag implicitly reveals the imitative structure of gender* itself."[6] In her inquiries, Porter often held opposing viewpoints in tension or moved from one to another in different written works. At times she was intensely homophobic, yet in her revised "Hacienda" she briefly presents female homosexuality as a potential means of liberation from heterosexual confines. In her criticism and letters, she several times attacked individual gay and lesbian writers, presenting their sexual preferences as both symptom and symbol of disorder, and in general her views on sexual roles grew more conservative and hard edged as she left the twenties and thirties behind. Yet from the 1930s almost until her death, she sustained a close friendship with the literary couple Glenway Wescott and Monroe Wheeler and clearly enjoyed their ironic play with gender identity. Through them she met the gay photographer George Platt Lynes, for whom she posed numerous times in grand, arguably campy style. In short, her creative exploration of sexual identity, especially through the then common metaphors of costume and performance, reveals gender-thinking that is wide ranging and contradictory.

Attention to sexual identity and costume recurs in Porter's literary criticism. Her unpublished papers include brief critical attacks on writers and texts others acclaim but, she privately admits, she cannot celebrate. In several of these rather vituperative jottings, the writer's sexuality provides Porter with a sufficient explanation for his or her ultimate failure.[7] Hence she swiftly dismisses Whitman, writing of him, "Walt Whitman, I suppose, is the purest example of a man whose human experience, based on homosexuality, was as abnormal and irresponsible as could well be. . . . If normal commonplace experience is necessary to the production of great literature, on what do we base our admiration of Walt Whitman?"[8] Most notorious of all Porter's attacks on a contemporary homosexual writer is her published 1947 essay on Gertrude Stein, reprinted in her *Collected Essays* under the title "The Wooden Umbrella," the final portion of a series titled "Gertrude Stein: Three Views."[9] In this essay Porter constructs an equation in which Stein's physical appearance, her sexual orientation, her intellectual character, and her texts are all versions of the same thing, each an expression of the same core disorder. Thus Stein's female appearance when she was "youngish" represented "an envelope" that "was a tricky disguise of Nature." Inside this costume were only negations of recognized sexual identity: "She was of the company of Amazons . . . not-men, not-women, answerable to no function in either sex." This invalidity or absence at Stein's sexual core expressed itself in clothing that lacked shape, and this costume expressed—in Porter's view—mental and physical chaos. Thus Stein wears "thick no-colored shapeless woolen clothes" that correspond to her "shapeless and undisciplined" mind; and when Stein writes, she creates a "slow swarm of words, out of the long drone and mutter and stammer of her lifetime monologue." Stein's thoughts rest on "the void of pure unreason," wrote Porter; she possesses an "ambiguous mind."[10]

Porter's attack on Stein aligns her vision much more with the male modernists who, as Gilbert and Gubar summarize in *Sexchanges*, "often opposed false costumes—which they saw as unsexed or wrongly sexed—to true, properly sexed, clothing and, by doing so . . . suggested that [the sociopolitical world] should be founded upon gender distinctions, since the ultimate reality was in their view the truth of gender."[11] Following the logic of Porter's imagery, the breakdown of gender distinction—Stein's "no function in either sex"—finds embodiment in her "monk's robe, her poll clipped, her granite front" and expression in texts that have no form. Thus Porter describes a Stein poem: "form, matter and style" go "stuttering and stammering and wallowing together with the agitated harmony of roiling entrails."[12] In this late 1940s portrait of Gertrude Stein, we find Porter's gender-thinking on sex roles at its most conservative. Here a break in sexual order results in textual disorder, the erasure of necessary distinctions, and ultimately, complete chaos at every level.

Porter's gender-thinking on the interrelatedness of sexual and social disorder reappears elsewhere in her critical writing. In a 1957 appreciation of Willa Cather, about whose sexuality she seems unaware, she describes the 1920s as chaos, a time when traditions no longer held and homosexuality became, to her mind, more prevalent. It was a terrible time for her, she wrote about thirty years after the decade, because "very literally everything in the world was being pulled apart, torn up, turned wrong side out and upside down; almost no frontiers left unattacked . . . even the very sexes seemed to be changing back and forth and multiplying weird, unclassifiable genders."[13] In this essay Cather's texts represent a steady thread of reason and tradition to which Porter clung as she struggled through the decade's chaos. Amid disorder, she is steadied by Cather's "level, well-tempered voice saying very good, sensible right things with complete authority."[14]

Porter's most lengthy critical discussion of social/sexual disorder occurs in an unpublished essay already discussed in this study, her response to Malcolm Cowley's 1934 *Exile's Return*.[15] Titled "The Twenties," the essay represents an urgent effort on Porter's part to articulate her own view of that turbulent decade. Besides exploring her feelings of homelessness and repeated romantic disappointments, Porter builds a cultural analysis in the essay that focuses on experimentation in the arts. Many of the artists of that period lived lives unfixed from traditional roles and values; hence, she argues, they produced debased art that violated natural categories of order. Here she explicitly connects the decade's general breakdown of order to sexual disorder, her comments revealing that at this point in her gender-thinking she drew on the assumption that sex roles and desires are grounded in biological difference and that fixed gender identity is necessary to cultural order of all kinds. Thus the decade involved misuse of objects at every level, manifesting a fundamental confusion about the basic appropriateness of form and function. Consider trends in interior decoration: "I noticed things being put to uses for which they were not intended . . . Queen Anne marrow scoops for cocktail muddlers; winebottles and water jugs for lamp bases, milking stools for ash tray holders." Homosexuality is a central manifestation of this disorder, as her freely written draft continues: "At that time too I began to notice a cult of sexual perversion—the blind Bow boy whose symbol is the dungfork came into the open most belligerently. . . . and I saw the connection between the misuse of things, etc." Her reference to "the blind Bow boy" is likely an allusion to Carl Van Vechten's 1923 novel with that phrase as its title.

Not just in the material and social cultures of daily life in the twenties, but also and more terribly in the arts, Porter saw things meant to be kept apart perversely brought together. In her retrospective writing about the decade, Porter's descriptions of artistic experimentation employ language of startling anger. She calls such experimentation "perversely trivial, stupid, or malignant-dwarfish tricks: fur-lined cups as sculpture, symphonies written for kitchen batteries, experiments on language very similar to the later Nazi surgical experiments of cutting and uniting human nerve ends never meant to touch each other." In the violence of Porter's comparison of artistic experimentation to Nazi experimental surgery, one can read how deeply threatening at this particular point in her gender-thinking she found the sexual and textual freedoms of the postwar years.

However, if we turn from Porter's published and unpublished critical essays to her fiction and trace there her depiction of gender roles and sexual identity, we find far more complex and ambivalent, potentially liberal gender-thinking. Two stories from the 1930s, "Hacienda" (1932, 1934) and "Pale Horse, Pale Rider" (1938), employ costume as the central image in their examination of the social control of sex roles and gender performance. As we have seen, "Pale Horse, Pale Rider" originated in Porter's near-death influenza infection during World War I. "Hacienda" takes its setting and subjects from a 1930 visit she made to the Mexican Hacienda Tetlapayac, where the Russian experimental film director Sergei Eisenstein was setting his film *¡Que Viva Mexico!*

Porter wrote "Hacienda" twice, first as a highly subjective piece of reportage, chronicling her immersion in the sickly world and disturbing events of the hacienda. This she published in *Virginia Quarterly Review* in 1932.[16] She then rewrote the text, fleshing it fully into a work of fiction. It is in this second, richer version that she explores gender issues and draws on the metaphorical resources of costume and performance to think about social control and sexual identity. Throughout, the second version of "Hacienda" sustains close parallels between the theatrical and the real—shooting script and shooting people. Everybody in the story is a performer. In their activities at the hacienda, the producer and his entourage play out parts in a life lived as spectacle. All pass the day gazing at the "landscape of patterned field and mountain" while being photographed in patterned poses: "with a nursling burro, with Indian babies; at the fountain . . . before the closed chapel door."[17]

Not only does the film crew constantly stage itself, but also all the residents at the hacienda employ costume to achieve identity. They form a chaotic group, for rather than sharing common bonds, each plays out a fantasy of identity imitated from another experiential context. Thus, for example, Betancourt, who aspires to direct a film, wears "well-cut riding trousers and puttees, not because he ever mounted a horse . . . but he had learned in California, in 1921, that this was the correct costume for a moving-picture director." During the filming "he always added a green cork-lined helmet, which completed some precious illusion he cherished about himself." Likewise, Stepanov wears the costume of his proudest achievements, rather than one appropriate to the present: "a champion at tennis and polo, [he] wore flannel tennis slacks and polo shirt" for his evening attire. Doña Julia, wife of the hacienda's owner, is "a figure from a Hollywood comedy, in black satin pajamas" (154). Her flirtation with Stepanov is entirely a theatrical experience. To the narrator she appears an "absurd little figure strayed out of a marionette theater," but in her own mind Doña Julia is a Hollywood star, and she slants at Stepanov "the glittering eye of a femme fatale in any Hollywood film" (161). As a sign of her authenticity, the narrator alone feels unsure of her clothing. Unlike her companions, she sought to dress for an external occasion, not an internal fantasy. Her flexible "knitted garment" is, unfortunately, "the kind which always appears suitable for any other than the occasion on which it is being worn" (154).

In the narrator's eyes, the famous film director, "the celebrated Uspensky," is no more admirable than his costumed companions. The characterization she developed suggests that Porter disapproved of Sergei Eisenstein, finding his experimental film another debased 1920s art form. In "Hacienda," she describes him as an imitator and a fool, his clothing expressive of his superficial, inauthentic self. He wore "his monkey-suit of striped overalls, his face like a superhumanly enlightened monkey's. . . . He had a monkey attitude towards life" (153). Resembling the self-proclaimed artists that she denigrates in her essays on the 1920s, Uspensky enjoys the "bump-and-grind" burlesque of debased art; "he amused himself at the low theaters in the capital, flattering the Mexicans by declaring they really were the most obscene" (153). And like the "motion picture comedians" who receive her ire in those essays, Uspensky enjoys "staging old Russian country comedies" in which he plays the loudest and most tasteless parts, shouting "his lines broadly . . . prodding the rear of a patient burro, accustomed to grief and indignity, with a phallus-shaped gourd" (153).

As in her highly critical writing about the 1920s, Porter employs homosexuality in "Hacienda" as a sign of social disorder, hinting at a homosexual relationship between Betancourt, an adviser from the Mexican government, and his "sleek and slim-waisted" assistant (168). However, at the center of her revised version of the story is a more complexly imagined affair between an actress, Lolita, and Doña Julia, wife of the owner of the hacienda. Porter's depiction of this lesbian relationship is fascinating because she plays it from both sides. On the one hand, the relationship emphasizes the general corruption of these very modern filmmakers and their hangers-on. Like the incestuous relationship between the local actor Justino and his sister, also developed in her story, and the intermixing of art and life that severs human relations from human feeling among the filmmakers and the performers, Lolita and Doña Julia are one more example of things that, because they are much alike, should be kept apart. On the other hand, Porter uses the lesbian relationship to undermine and even mock the patriarchal assumptions that have governed women's lives at this hacienda for generations.

When she revised "Hacienda" and wove her gender-thinking into the text, Porter carefully linked Doña Julia with the milky pulque, that river of corruption that flows through the whole culture. While the first version of the story described the "apartments of Don J—and his lady" as simply "next to the vat rooms,"[18] in the revision the apartments become Doña Julia's alone and are permeated with the stench of pulque. In the evening the narrator walks through them: "Doña Julia and I passed through her apartment, a long shallow room between the billiard and the vat-room. It was puffy with silk and down, glossy with bright new polished wood and wide mirrors, restless with small ornaments, boxes of sweets, French dolls in ruffled skirts and white wigs. The air was thick with perfume which fought with another heavier smell" (161). Every image in this passage suggests Doña Julia's superficiality and corruption, from the location of her bedroom near the vats of stinking, fermenting liquid to the room's ornaments, "restless," narcissistic, and perfumed. The apartment defines Doña Julia herself, her painted feminine surface and hidden corruption. Linked with the white liquor that keeps the Indians enslaved, drowning memory and desire in forgetfulness, Doña Julia's sexuality is one of Porter's symbols of modern Mexico. This costumed woman and her high-speed husband, along with their shared actress lover, represent the complete breakdown of traditional human relations Porter had located at the core of the 1920s.

Yet true to the more rich and complex gender-thinking of her fiction, Porter could not resist depicting the ways in which Lolita and Doña Julia's love affair entirely undermines male authority in "Hacienda," particularly the patriarchal Genaro family that has held Hacienda Tetlapayac for generations. Faced with the women's very public affection, Don Genaro is thrown into confusion; he "has no precedent whatever for a husband's conduct in such a situation" (145). His upbringing has taught him that there are degrees of women, more or less sexually available to men, but sexual relations between women lies outside of his education and the assumptions on which it is based. In marrying Doña Julia he felt himself modern enough; he has gone far beyond his gentlemanly grandfather "who had always known how to judge, grade, and separate women into their proper categories at a glance" and who viewed Doña Julia as appropriate only to a "temporary association" (153). Don Genaro might rebel against social class constraints, but a break in heterosexual convention is far too unsettling. The sight of Lolita cooing at Doña Julia in a "deep throaty voice," and then swinging "her leg over the saddle" is clearly unprecedented (144).

In Porter's comic portrayal of male confusion, as well as the theatrical quality of the relationship between the costumed women, her gender-thinking comes the closest it ever does to that of her feminist contemporaries who saw gender not as a biological, natural fact but as an entirely arbitrary construct. Lolita and Doña Julia, arm in arm, one in her Chinese silk pajamas, "made by a Hollywood costumer," the other "in the stiff elegance of 1898," could easily have strolled from the pages of Djuna Barnes's *Nightwood*, or Virginia Woolf's *Orlando*. As much as Porter employs these two women to represent the corruption of the modern world, just as her male contemporaries might do, she also joins several of her female contemporaries, who used the figure of the lesbian to protest patriarchal tradition. As Carroll Smith-Rosenberg suggests of feminist modernists like Woolf and Barnes, they used the "'Mannish Lesbian'—the woman who stood between and thus outside of conventional sexual categories," to represent their "repudiation of conventional gender distinctions and restrictions."[19]

In "Pale Horse, Pale Rider," Porter continued her exploration of social order and sexual identity, and, as in "Hacienda," costume serves as a central image in her analysis of the regulation of social roles. Here she looks closely at the tightened, even stifling, gender constraints with which American culture responded to World War I.[20] The most memorable costuming in the story comes at the close, when Miranda calls for garments with which to cover her skeletal body. This dramatic—and much discussed—closing gesture does not stand alone but is, in fact, the climax of the narrative's discourse about costume, one that connects "Pale Horse, Pale Rider" even more firmly to Porter's gender-thinking during the post–World War I decades.

Descriptions of dress and dressing, putting on makeup, and removing or not removing hats appear throughout "Pale Horse, Pale Rider." Scenes are set in cloakrooms and theaters, places where costumes are donned. Like "Hacienda," "Pale Horse, Pale Rider" employs theater to suggest that identity has been reduced to a performance. Miranda works as a theater critic, and in her illness she sees death as a shadow play or ritualized dance projected through a screen, suggesting as in "Hacienda" the ways in which death can be reduced to just part of the show in a decadent modern world. Miranda as theater critic also corresponds to Miranda as social critic, pointing to a central concern in the story—the way in which the theater of war controls the roles of the players on the home front. Many of the characters in "Pale Horse, Pale Rider" act the part and feel inauthentic (except for the authentic and ideal Adam, who is "all the way through, flawless, complete" and who cannot survive into the inauthentic postwar world).[21] Individuals respond to powerful social pressures by parroting patriotic speeches, making the right loyal or ironic gestures, and dressing appropriately, displaying their gender in the ways that best meet the needs of the state. In this last, Porter shows with clear and cutting honesty how, especially in a war period, the personal becomes political: control of sexuality is one manifestation of a general tightening of social control over the individual.

During the war, women in particular must be controlled, for with a large portion of the male population absent, female independence becomes increasingly possible. Although cultural historians have argued that the war years allowed women a wider variety of public and professional opportunities, Porter's story argues otherwise. The young single women in Denver, "wallowing in good works" for the war effort, are strongly encouraged to bring their "brightly tinted faces to cheer the brave boys" ill with influenza in the hospitals—"boys who already, you might very well say, had fallen in defense of their country" (275). Miranda joins them, likewise donning the mask of gay feminine cheer; putting on "fresh make-up . . . she went out to join a group of young women fresh from the country club dances" (275). Social pressure is so powerful that these young women fear resisting the requisite bedside flirtations with the troops. Complaints are quickly suppressed; the women are "cautious" and keep their bright masks in place. In her thoughts, however, Miranda unmasks the war effort as a way to control potentially disruptive female energy not channeled into heterosexual relations with the men off fighting the war. To her mind, the bandage rolling, peach pit accumulation, and hospital flirtation are but ploys to keep the products of women's labor "on the altar of their country": "It keeps them busy and makes them feel useful, and all these women running wild with the men away are dangerous, if they aren't given something to keep their little minds out of mischief. So rows of young girls, the intact cradles of the future, with their pure serious faces framed becomingly in Red Cross wimples, roll cock-eyed bandages that will never reach a base hospital." Miranda concludes with bitter irony, "Keeping still and quiet will win the war" (290). Behind the war effort is a geared up, barely masked effort to control female sexuality, keep it channeled into married, heterosexual relations that will serve the state. As in her earlier story "Holiday," Porter's gender-thinking in "Pale Horse, Pale Rider" reveals her view that male authority and affluence depend on keeping women under patriarchal control, regulating both their offspring and the products of their labor.

At one point in "Pale Horse, Pale Rider," Miranda and a fellow female reporter together resist the ever more oppressive social control. Towney, whom Miranda meets in the cloakroom at work, is the only woman who unmasks herself in front of Miranda. As her androgynous name suggests, Towney refuses to play the feminine role fully. Part of this is her refusal to turn all of her labor over to serve the war effort. Towney sits "knitting on something rose-colored," and when Miranda asks her if it is for a soldier, she responds with a tough honesty: "'Like hell, . . . I'm making this for myself. That's that'" (274–75). Both Towney and Miranda hold nontraditional jobs, for both have become reporters, an occupation generally held by men. However, their job status is vulnerable and quickly disappears when they exhibit solidarity with other women rather than with male authority. Thus when they together refuse to write the story of a young woman who had eloped and then not married, they are demoted. Both women had powerfully identified with "the recaptured girl" and refused to join in the socially proscribed punishment she should receive for violating the unwritten law that women's sexuality must be contained within the marital bond. "Miranda and Towney had then taken their punishment together, and had been degraded publicly to routine female jobs, one to the theaters, the other to society" (275).

In "Pale Horse, Pale Rider," Porter extends her gender-thinking to an analysis of the enforcement of masculinity, making it clear that she recognized how, during wartime, the social control of gender roles becomes more intense for men as well. While "young girls, the intact cradles of the future," are taught to keep quiet and be obedient, only occasionally allowed to flirt with light and innocent gaiety during mass hospital visitations, young men endure correspondingly narrow definitions of appropriate masculinity. Chuck, another of Miranda's fellow reporters, suffers within these confines. Because the appropriate male behavior is now enlistment, Chuck feels publicly emasculated, for a bad lung keeps him from service. He is sensitive to any potential slight to his masculinity, and costumes himself carefully to announce his manly heterosexuality, self-conscious, for example, about "the hobnailed tan boots which he hoped would help to disguise the fact that he had a bad lung and didn't care for sports." Sports are Chuck's assignment at the newspaper. Although he would rather be the theater critic, his sex bars him from the job assignment: "he didn't give a damn about sports . . . preferred shows and didn't see why women always had the job" (287–88). Not only is he forced into an exaggerated, self-conscious masculinity by the emphasis on socially acceptable gender performance during the war, but Chuck is also denied interests that do not fall within the narrowly defined arena of appropriate male activity.

Adam, too, feels constrained by the increasing conventions surrounding masculinity. Unlike Chuck, however, Adam is muscular, handsome, and enlisted, and thus these conventions provide him with rewards, which make their limitations less constraining. Still Adam's body itself is tightly bound by the state: he is "infinitely buttoned, strapped, harnessed into a uniform as tough and unyielding in cut as a strait jacket" (279). Resistance is impossible, the image suggests; to fight against the militarization of the state and each individual within it is only to invite a more complete bondage, as a straitjacket tightens about a resisting body. That the trappings of appropriate masculinity are themselves social rather than natural constructs, Porter makes evident in one telling detail—Adam's wristwatch. Like the other young soldiers, he is self-conscious about the watch because, like them, he grew up believing "that only sissies wore wrist watches. 'I'll slap you on the wrist-watch,' one vaudeville comedian would simper to another, and it was always a good joke, never stale" (279). In this small detail we see Porter's awareness that male sexuality can be controlled by homophobia, which responds to all behavior not conventionally masculine with ridicule, opprobrium, and ultimately violence. In Adam's youth the wristwatch had functioned as a sign within this system of gender definition—as have countless other arbitrary aspects of costume and gesture throughout cultural history. His self-consciousness arises from the uncomfortable moment when one of these signs shifts meaning. During the war a watch facilitates the regimentation of individuals necessary to mass military activity. Thus it becomes part of the "strait jacket" of the uniform and now denotes loyalty to the heterosexual norm desired by the state. Unfortunately, for Adam and many of the other soldiers, the watch's earlier function, to signal a lack of heterosexual masculinity, still holds denotative force.

Throughout "Pale Horse, Pale Rider," Porter nicely uses dress to point out the tight social control of individual activity, particularly gender activity. Hats, gloves—bodily accessories—come to stand for attitudes toward the war and thus toward all the social controls it brings into heightened status. Gloves provide a wonderful sequence of images. Miranda knows from her job that obeying conventional rules of judgment and activity will bring approbation and remuneration. As Chuck the consummate costumer advises her, to be a successful theater critic, she need only please Rypinsky, a local power broker in the theater scene. This will "please the advertising department, please them and you'll get a raise. Hand-in-glove, my poor dumb child" (289). Most of the time, Miranda does keep her "hand-in-glove," hiding her true opinions from all the people she interacts with daily. Signaling the honesty of their relationship, Adam tries to unglove Miranda, first pulling "a little at the tips of her gloves" (283), and finally "carefully and seriously" pulling one glove off. Adam's effort to be honest with Miranda requires stripping away the costume that their culture constructs around the relationship of a man and a woman. His perfection as a romantic lover is apparent in his unfamiliarity with the words of love. Unlike the debased modern lovers who change the language of love into "mush," Adam is "shy . . . of the word *love*, he seemed never to have spoken it before" (302). Fresh minted as a lover, Adam is nevertheless not at all free of convention. When Miranda, in her illness, breaks the rules that govern gender and language and tells him that he is "beautiful," he needs a bit of defensive laughter in order to receive praise embodied in a word culturally assigned to women (301).

The war, and the influenza that kills the young soldiers even more efficiently, "simply knocks you into a cocked hat," Miranda thinks. That is, war knocks you into an attitude displayed by costume. Stripped of the possibility of romantic love with this near-perfect man, stripped of ideals and hopes, stripped even of her desire for life, Miranda, at the close of "Pale Horse, Pale Rider," becomes the ultimate self-costumer. As she prepares to enter the postwar world, she carefully lists the makeup and clothes she will need to sustain the illusion that she is a living woman: "One lipstick, medium, one ounce flask Bois D'Hiver perfume, one pair of gray suède gauntlets without straps" (316). Better than any of her contemporaries, she now knows what is needed for performance in the daily theater. She plans to visit other survivors and "help them dress" (317).

In her biography, Joan Givner identifies Porter's near-death influenza bout as marking the point where she decided to pursue a writing career. According to Givner, Porter saw the experience "as a crucial episode in her life and as the moment in which her desire to be a good writer and a good artist crystallized." She quotes Porter's own retrospective view from a 1963 interview: "It just divided my life, cut across it like that. So that everything before that was just getting ready, and after that I was in some strange way altered, ready."[22] When Porter depicts this turning point in "Pale Horse, Pale Rider," she describes her fictional counterpart first preparing for a new life by ordering the materials of female dress: "one lipstick, medium, one ounce flask Bois d'Hiver perfume." The "medium" lipstick suggests a wish to achieve the average, to appear most normal, yet the perfume—winter woods—suggests a continued sense of deathliness or sterility. (One thinks of the unfinished story "Season of Fear.") As Towney notes to Miranda, each piece of clothing she orders is "without something"—gloves "without straps," stockings "without clocks." Even costumed as a woman, with makeup and perfume, Miranda will remain marked by an absence; she is incomplete, external lack pointing to internal lack. Overall the costume chosen by Porter's fictional counterpart suggests that when Porter herself transformed this time in her life into fiction, she saw it as a period when female identity became a matter of careful costume, an "art" rather than a physical fact. As Miranda tells Towney in the story, "No one need pity this corpse if we look properly to the art of the thing" (316).

It is intriguing that at this key fictional moment—one that corresponds to an actual period of vocational dedication—Porter dressed her fictional counterpart in the costume of the 1920s women who most rebelled against gender conventions. Miranda does not just want stockings and gloves in "Pale Horse, Pale Rider," she jokingly calls for a "top hat and stick," and plans to carry "a walking stick of silvery wood with a silver knob" (316). In such garb she would resemble the transvestite women painted by Romaine Brooks, who display the gloves, walking sticks, and top hats of the nineteenth-century dandy, the delightful and foppish figure that became one cultural role and potential stereotype for homosexuals. Miranda's clothing holds in tension the image of a woman costumed as a woman with lipstick and perfume, and the image of a woman costumed as a man with top hat and cane. When set against Porter's own sense of self-transformation at the start of the twenties, Miranda's costume suggests that Porter saw herself moving into a precarious, undefined sexual location as she moved toward her vocation. The word she chose—"altered"—in the 1963 interview Givner cites—"after that I was in some strange way altered, ready"—suggests the unsexing she viewed as part of becoming "ready" to claim her place among the women who had taken on the unwomanly ambition of being an artist.[23]

If we turn from Porter's essays and fiction to her personal life, we find yet another, even less scrutable, response to homosexuality. While her literary criticism is predominantly homophobic, and her fiction is keenly aware of hegemonic heterosexuality and intrigued by gender performativity, her personal life presents a complex and contradictory message. On the one hand, she enjoyed a warm and intimate relationship with a group of gay men who had significant influence on the arts community of her time. This friendship rested in part on shared pleasure in costume and gender play. On the other hand, she experienced episodes of intense homophobia. Two well-recorded events provide sufficient evidence of her fiercely negative responses to active homosexuality, one with poet Hart Crane, the other with the young woman writer Carson McCullers.[24]

In Mexico in 1931, Porter was Hart Crane's neighbor and friend. However, their initially warm relations broke down in the face of what she viewed as his entirely unacceptable behavior. She wrote several times about the incidents that led to their estrangement, describing Crane's passionate outbursts: "drunk, he would weep and shout, shaking his fist, 'I am Baudelaire, I am Whitman, I am Christopher Marlowe, I am Christ,' but never once did I hear him say that he was Hart Crane." In her retrospective thoughts on Crane, Porter became especially concerned with the connections Crane's admirers tended to make between his genius as an artist, his alcoholism, his sexuality, and his mental condition. As she wrote in a much-drafted letter to Crane's biographer, Philip Horton, "I wish you would not be deceived by the romantic assumption that the artist is a monstrous growth on the brow of society, that his ways are inexplicable and that his feet take hold on hell." Most important to Porter is her conclusion: "I do not in the least believe in the romantic interpretation of Hart's drunkenness and sexual perverseness as being necessary to his life as a poet."[25]

Another encounter further evidences Porter's gender-thinking about the artist's sexuality and achievement, and the relations of social order and heterosexuality. At Yaddo in 1940, Carson McCullers developed an ardent crush on Porter and even lay across the threshold of the older woman's bedroom, hoping in vain for some attention. Porter responded with outrage. On June 23, 1940, she composed a theory of universal harmony in which homosexuality becomes a "perversion of natural law": "When the tension between opposites, which maintains a balance between them making for form and order, is set up between like forces, and the stresses that should exist between opposites is artificially set up between like and like, the result is a perversion of natural law, nothing can go well until the balance is restored." In 1951, just over a decade later, she scrawled in the margin of these notes, "These generalizations are particulars, really, of the nuisances that Carson McCullers and Rebecca Pitts made of themselves to me at Yaddo—Dreadful Creatures!"[26]

Intriguing in Porter's 1940 thoughts on homosexuality and "natural law" is her struggle to understand why she feels such rage toward lesbians and yet enjoys the company of gay men. As she writes in these private musings, "This is a little curious: I can like with deep friendship and understanding a homosexual man. . . . But no quality, no mental gifts, no talents, and no amount of beauty can make a Lesbian, or perverted woman, anything but repellant to me." Her only conclusion is that a gay man has no unspoken intentions and hence, "I can be at my ease."[27] In the more complex and generous vision of her fiction, Porter recognized the radical potential and play of modernist lesbian culture, but in her own life she was adamantly closed toward this community, writing terrible private notes about Djuna Barnes's classic *Nightwood* and turning away from even her closest friends when they expressed same-sex desire.[28]

Yet, despite her strongly expressed homophobia—especially toward lesbians—from 1932 until her death, Porter enjoyed a rich and generally supportive friendship with Glenway Wescott and his partner Monroe Wheeler, as well as their friend the photographer George Platt Lynes.[29] The friendship formed in Paris and, buoyed by the affluence of Barbara Harrison, Wescott's sister-in-law and the publisher with Monroe Wheeler of fine edition texts, proved fruitful and enduring. In two years Harrison of Paris published both a collection of French songs translated by Porter and her revised "Hacienda."[30] Glenway Wescott was an established novelist, poet, and essayist, and Monroe Wheeler was an editor and litterateur later to become the director of publications at the Museum of Modern Art. The two men met in 1918 and formed a sixty-eight-year-long relationship. In 1927, just a few years before they met Porter, Wescott and Wheeler became close friends with George Platt Lynes, a successful fashion photographer remembered now for the visual record he created of the American Ballet Company under Kirstein and Balanchine and most recently recognized for his photographic images of the male nude. Wescott, Wheeler, and Lynes were influential members of a well-connected, extraordinarily creative early-twentieth-century gay community.

For years Porter enjoyed warm and congenial friendships with these men, in particular Wescott. Her comments on this friendship in an interview with Enrique Lopez confirm her pleasure in relations free from heterosexual tensions. As Lopez quotes Porter in his *Conversations*, she enjoyed a "most comfortable alliance" with Lynes, Wescott, and Wheeler: "It was so nice to relax with that kind of man, to enjoy his delightfully malicious wit and intelligence, without having to worry about bruising his male ego, his machismo, and having to deal with all that ritualized wrestling around at the end of an otherwise cheerful evening."[31] In the letters Porter sent to gay friends, she is open and even playful about their sexuality. Consider comments on Auden to Wescott in Baton Rouge, 1939: "Auden had with him a young boy who looked like a combination young satyr and newly made eunuch, who sat with a blind self-conscious, sullen stare on his face, jolly well knowing he was simply irresistible in that pose"; or to Lynes, again in 1939: "We've had a rehearsal already with Auden, and his young friend Kollman. . . . It was really gay, having them, so think how much gayer to have you."[32] Porter's use of "gay" here—a rare word in her vocabulary—likely represents a playful allusion to Auden's and Lyne's sexuality and reveals her familiarity with 1920s and 1930s homosexual culture. According to one source, "in the 1920s and 1930s the word GAY surfaced in the underground homosexual subculture as a term of identification among homosexual men. Expressions such as 'You're looking gay tonight,' or 'That's a gay tie you have there' were used to establish mutual identity in social situations."[33]

Porter's friendships with Wheeler, Wescott, and Lynes are recorded in a notably rich and lengthy correspondence. As Janis Stout describes it, "All together, the Harrison-Wescott-Wheeler files (along with the George Platt Lynes . . . files, representing friendships that arose out of her acquaintance with Wescott et al.) are among the most voluminous in the Porter papers." Stout terms the letters exchanged with Wescott "scintillating."[34] Overall, the friendships had a very positive effect on Porter's writing, both epistolary and fiction. It is intriguing to realize that both "Hacienda" and "Pale Horse, Pale Rider" were first composed or fully revised at the beginning of the Porter, Wescott, Wheeler, Lynes friendships. As noted, "Hacienda" first came out in 1932 in the *Virginia Quarterly Review* but was published again, much expanded, in 1934 by Harrison of Paris. The outlines of "Pale Horse, Pale Rider" were certainly in Porter's mind by the early 1930s, and at the same time that she was writing the story she was posing for a series of very stagy photographic portraits by Lynes. The first set of Lynes's portraits was shot in 1936, and the story, finished late in 1937, was immediately celebrated in a letter to Wescott.

A look at the Lynes portraits of Porter makes it no surprise that both "Hacienda" and "Pale Horse, Pale Rider" employ clothing and theater as metaphors in their complex treatment of gender. In these highly artificial formal photographs, Porter—dramatic, moody, elegantly and expensively dressed—is an over-the-top representative of self-absorbed female beauty. The photographs attest to Lynes's public work as a fashion photographer. But they also are involved in his extensive work with the male nude (work unacknowledged until long after his death). Only recently have we begun to understand Lynes's significant role in shaping a gay aesthetic, and it is intriguing now to consider how much Porter was aware of these complex and sensual images—many created during the time of their friendship.

Renewed interest in Lynes's work began in the early 1990s. Since then his photographs have been displayed in several large shows and explored by numerous critics, the attention spurred by the recognition of his significant homoerotic work with the male nude, part of a tradition brought to public attention most recently through the controversy surrounding Robert Mapplethorpe. As a historian of photography comments in a 1994 *Art Journal* review of Lynes's achievement, "Lynes's nude photographs. . . . helped to establish the 'code,' which is the aestheticized, youthful, muscular, posed, and depersonalized male body as a symbol for gay specular desire."[35] Lynes's work on the male nude spanned his entire career, from the late 1920s to his death in 1955. During his lifetime, however, he was publicly known as a portraitist and fashion photographer. His career began with an early trip to Europe in 1925, where he met Glenway Wescott and Monroe Wheeler, beginning the friendship that connected him also to Porter, and, more significant for his style, where he was exposed to and much inspired by surrealist artists. Lynes helped bring the surrealist aesthetic to fashion photography; his influence on images in glossies such as *Vogue, Harper's Bazaar,* and *Town and Country* remains evident today. "The model in Lynes's fashion photographs tended to be placed in stark, hauntingly lit spaces, either mock landscapes or architectonic interiors, where she—or rather, the dress she wore—was elevated to the status of apparition."[36] In the 1930s at his New York studio, and in the early 1940s as *Vogue* photographer in Hollywood, Lynes was enormously successful. He was the documentary photographer for the American Ballet Company, a leading fashion photographer, and an in-demand portraitist, particularly of the wealthy and celebrated. Lynes's photographs defined glamour for his contemporaries, and Porter was flattered to pose for him as she did many times, always elaborately costumed.

Recent critical attention to Lynes's achievement provides several viewpoints on his portraits of Porter—these viewpoints are likewise useful for understanding her gender-thinking. German culture critic Günther Metken, for example, in commenting on the rise of highly stylized fashion photography, notes its relation to post–World War I culture:

> Photography, too, is a part of the complete work of art known as decoration, with which the pleasure-seeking society ever since the Art Deco Exhibition of 1925 has been surrounding itself in order to repress the effects of the first World War and in hopes of warding off the swiftly approaching second World War. This society elevated mannequins and rich representatives of the world of fashion to the level of aesthetic sensualist super-existence that is hermetically sealed to keep reality from seeping in.[37]

Gloved, gowned, jeweled, coiffed, elaborately staged, stagily lit, elegantly dreaming—the Katherine Anne Porter of Lynes's photographs inhabits a perfected, unchanging aestheticized landscape, one that is wealthy, cultured, and self-contemplating. That these images of Porter appeared in *Vogue* and *Town and Country* underlines the fact that she served (and perhaps for some still serves?) as a kind of cultural fantasy. That fantasy, as the next chapter will explore, forms a thick undercurrent to her own life and work, a current that rises up in efforts to establish elegant homes, evoke a mythical past, find a perfect love. It is easy to move from these photographs to the beautiful Aunt Amy and Cousin Isabel of *Old Mortality*. Easy too to connect Adam from "Pale Horse, Pale Rider": "his uniforms made by the best tailor he could find"; his "extraordinary face, smooth and fine and golden in the shabby light"; he is "flawless, complete" (279, 295). Adam is a perfected order poised before the chaos and death of war. Like the glossy and elegant images of Porter, he is the offspring of modern nostalgia and anxiety.

Historians and critics of photography have viewed negatively Lynes's portraits of Porter. In a *Contemporary Photography* overview of Lynes, for example, Elmer Borklund rejects the "melodramatically over-lit, kitsch portraits of . . . Katherine Anne Porter" as "malicious parodies of Hollywood publicity shots."[38] However, recent work on gay style in general, and on the homoerotic work of Lynes in particular, opens up other intriguing ways of viewing the parodic or "kitsch" style of these images. Lynes often played with his subject matter, creating a tension between high seriousness and staginess that makes his photographs ironic, or—to employ a term richly debated in gay studies—camp. In his study, *The Queening of America: Gay Culture and Straight Society*, David Van Leer describes camp as "the best-known gay linguistic style" and defines it as follows: "a complex of loosely defined theatricalisms, camp imitates the hyperbole of musicals and popular movies as well as other visual extravagances like overstated decor and fashion, and especially cross-dressing."[39] Lynes's portraits of Porter have the hyperbole of camp; they are so clearly artificial, stagy, posed, and theatrical.[40] The crucial question is to what extent Porter was aware of, even participating in, this "camping." In discussions of his photography, Lynes is repeatedly praised for his ability to capture the true character of his subject; his theatrical settings often use "'accessories in the manner of symbolic badges.'"[41] The central props in these portraits are elaborate gowns and expensive jewelry. Are they pure fantasy, an indulgence in social class aspiration and extreme femininity? Or does their artificiality call their meanings into question, expose them as constructs of costume and performance? Is Lynes critical of his subject, ironic? Is Porter?

Lynes's portrait of Porter holding the detached head of a doll offers one lo-

Porter holding a doll's head.

Photograph by George Platt Lynes. University of Maryland Libraries
Special Collections, Box 53, no. 2463. Courtesy of the University of
Maryland Libraries and the estate of George Platt Lynes.

cation for confronting such questions. The portrait is one in a series of such images presenting Porter either in the full, striped satin skirt pictured here or, even more elegantly, in black lace with short black gloves and clustered rhinestone jewelry. But only in this one shot does she hold the disjoined head. Face turned away, eyes closed, Porter appears remote, beautiful, and sensual in the photograph, but her pose is countered by the doll's fixed bright gaze in the opposite direction. Ayer and Brown's popular song "Oh, You Beautiful Doll" comes inescapably to mind. The image undermines all of the other portraits, for the doll's head highlights their artificiality. Porter is not a real woman here but a construct, an object, even a plaything, dressed up for show. That the doll is disjoined, decapitated, suggests the deathliness of such heightened femininity, frozen out of time and change, but the image, at least initially, feels more absurd than serious, so staged and dramatic that it mocks its own pretentious glamour and unhinges cultural notions of beauty.

On a deeper level, more personal to Porter's life, the image is quite disturbing—the severed head evoking with horrible irony her real or deeply imagined stillbirth and failed maternity. Holding the head, Porter clearly is playing along with some of George Platt Lynes's queering of gender roles; she is camping glamour. But it is unclear how many of the image's complex and disturbing implications she intends.

Another portrait by Lynes, this one of Katherine Anne Porter and Jane Gray, only deepens the ambiguity. Consider the two women, lost in aesthetic bliss, gracefully arranged around a reproduction of Raphael's fresco *Fire in the Borgo*. The allusion to Raphael confirms the women's cultural status; up through the nineteenth and into the twentieth century, he was considered *the* great artist of the big three: Leonardo Da Vinci, Michelangelo, and Raphael.[42] It is not difficult at all to read from this 1930s photograph to Porter's Doña Julia and Lolita in "Hacienda," "affectionately entwined," dressed in "cinema Chinese" and "the stiff elegance of 1898." The two women lounge "on the edge of the fountain, whispering together, arms lying at ease about each other's waists" (144). Intriguingly, the image on Porter's lap, with its muscular, entwined male nudes reproduced in black and white, calls to mind Lynes's own portraits of male nudes. Is he alluding to his private work within a more public portrait? Or does the reference reverberate back to its context? Porter appears to have swooned away in the photograph. Is she overcome by the aesthetic moment, or, as the allusion to Lynes's erotic homosexual nudes might suggest, is she overcome by the proximity of Jane Gray? Is Jane looking at the book or at Porter's bosom?

Porter with Jane Gray.

Photograph by George Platt Lynes from Conversations with Katherine Anne Porter: Refugee from Indian Creek *by Enrique Hank Lopez (Boston: Little, Brown, 1981). Courtesy of the estate of George Platt Lynes.*

Delightful questions abound, both serious and silly, and any answers must be tentative at best. Some evidence suggests that Porter had two responses to her portraits by Lynes. She found them deeply satisfying and wish fulfilling, frequently gave them to friends, was delighted when they appeared in magazines, and was enraged when other, less flattering images of her were reproduced. At the same time, however, she was aware that they were stagy, melodramatic, even funny, as her private comments make fully evident. The photo with Jane Gray is "one of the terribly posey pictures which George liked to take," she wrote on the back of a copy. To her niece in a letter in which a particularly spectacular image was enclosed, she wrote, "You must have one, even if only for a good joke; you'll never see me, you never did see me in Fifty-Eight Thousand dollars worth of high class trash, and it is a sight."[43] Dressing up for Lynes, Porter could simultaneously fulfill and laugh at her own desires, play the grand lady and parody her. It is easy to view the photos as examples of Porter's ability to "cross-dress" in social class codes—she wears "high class trash" in full dramatic style, simultaneously loving and laughing at the performance. Yet questions of heterosexual and homosexual identity and desire remain unanswered; it is unclear how much the highly posed Porter of Lynes's portraits is herself addressing one of camp's central subjects—gender as performance, a matter of costume, not fixed and fundamental biological fact.

Perhaps the performative quality of camp set Porter free to create these melodramatic and extravagant images with Lynes. Perhaps the pleasure she found in freedom from rigid sexual codes sustained her lifelong friendships with gay men, despite her expressed homophobia. One of the most interesting sets of photographs for such questions are those of Porter and Lynes himself, acting out *Romeo and Juliet* in 1940s Hollywood. Here is Lynes, as golden and perfect as the fictional Adam, clad only in shorts, and Porter, gowned and white gloved, a figure of pure, yet remote, femininity. He yearns toward her; she is frozen in passionate waiting; he gazes longingly upward; she looks dreamily away. As the two reproduce one of the primary texts of Western heterosexuality, what are their intentions? At this time, Porter is fifty-seven years old, Lynes just turning forty. In charge of the *Vogue* studios in Hollywood, he is privately producing some of his most powerful, erotic images of the male nude; she has just left behind a short stint in screen writing to focus on *Ship of Fools*. Joan Givner suggests that Porter "tried to make [Lynes] her lover in spite of her knowledge that he was a homosexual." However, despite his lack of interest, she outwardly "remained close friends with him," a surprisingly common

Porter and George Platt Lynes playing Romeo and Juliet.
University of Maryland Libraries Special Collections, Box 15,
no. 2110. Courtesy of the University of Maryland Libraries and the
estate of George Platt Lynes.

outcome for her failed relationships with men, gay or straight.[44] In their roles as Romeo and Juliet, the two create a complex performance of opposites: she is older, he younger; she is heterosexual, he homosexual; she is fully dressed, he nearly naked; she is remote, elevated; beneath her, he yearns. The two are clearly enjoying themselves, playing great, tragic heterosexual roles, yet neither suiting the part. Through this parodic play with Lynes, and more generally through her friendships with gay men, in particular Monroe Wheeler and Glenway Wescott, Porter could make light of the romantic ideals of love that plagued her throughout her life. As her friend Allen Tate described her in a private letter to a friend, "she is trapped in a cycle of romantic emotions that repeat themselves about every five years."[45] Yet with her gay friends she could make light of what otherwise was often a painful burden, tossing about the language and poses of love with exaggerated and campy freedom.

Katherine Anne Porter's rich friendships with Lynes, Wheeler, and Wescott likely encouraged some of her most complex and courageous gender-thinking, thinking that bore fruit in the portraits of remarkable fictional women. Wielding top hat and stick, Miranda as Romaine Brooks, can step out of the deathly world of "Pale Horse, Pale Rider" into the "dazed silence that follows the ceasing of the heavy guns" (317). Embracing in their Hollywood garb, Lolita and Doña Julia can become "oblivious to the summons from the embattled males" (144). In the patriarchal worlds of war and a Mexican hacienda, these "thoroughly outrageous" (144) costumed women strike out in new directions, their clothing and feisty attitudes calling into question the assumptions of male power and privilege that sustained the old order. Through her cross-dressing women, Porter brings some hope, and even some comic relief, to the wasteland of the 1920s depicted in these stories. In the freedom of gay style and comradeship, she probably found similar relief and humor, a safe place to play with those gender roles and costumes that were elsewhere—like the Princess's biting jewels—both painful and constraining.

CHAPTER NINE

SOUTHERN BELLE
SOUTHERN LADY

Elaborately dressed and bejeweled, never stepping out of her role as the visionary virgin artist, the Princess becomes a living legend. Soon the people of her kingdom forget her past and see only her presence. As Porter writes, "She became even as she lived among them, a legend. There were many who professed that they could not remember her face."[1] The transformation of a woman from human to symbolic status fascinated Katherine Anne Porter, as we have seen in her stories of women as artists' models, explored in chapter 3. In the 1930s, fueled by new friendships with members of the Agrarian/Fugitive writers group, Porter returned again to questions of performance and identity from a new direction, scrutinizing the popular roles of white southern womanhood—the Belle, the Lady. Her portraits of southern women, especially Aunt Amy and young Miranda Gay, contain some of her most complex and interesting gender-thinking, for she sees both power gained and lost for women who achieve a symbolic social status by embodying cultural fantasies. It is fascinating to discover that while Porter was composing these stories, she was also drawing on family stories passed down by her paternal grandmother, Catherine Ann Skaggs Porter, to construct a personal legend of genteel southern womanhood for herself. Becoming a professional southerner, performing southernness for her readers and her friends, eventually Porter (like her Princess) became herself a living legend; in her final years neither she nor her audience could recall Katherine Anne before she claimed her affiliation with that "white-pillar crowd."[2]

Southern gentility came as much through invention as through inheritance to Katherine Anne Porter, born Callie Porter in Texas poverty. Janis Stout, one of Porter's biographers, aptly terms Porter a "borderlands writer," one whose work and identity have been deeply divided by life experienced on the edges of differing cultures, for Porter not just Texas and Mexico, Stout argues, but also the American South and Southwest.[3] Two interacting forces moved Porter toward her self-presentation as a product of southern gentility in regretful decline: the first her increasingly close ties with the Agrarian fellowship and their influential, ideologically drenched version of the South, past and present, the second her own deep and painful ambivalence about her family and her childhood.

The origins and intellectual attitudes of the Agrarians need little rehearsing here. Their published work in the 1930s represents the most sophisticated articulation of the ideological cluster that sustains popular versions of antebellum white southern life. The Agrarian response to the modernization and moral upheaval accompanying World War I was a retreat to "the past," as Richard King argues, a "yearning for an organic, hierarchical order such as allegedly existed in the ante-bellum South."[4] Their ideal society represents a solidly patriarchal construct; it reverences the white southern family, identifies the landed gentry as inherently superior by virtue of birth, enthrones the white man, and sets the white woman up on a pedestal. It is a vision of family stability and class privilege that appealed deeply to Porter. As Stout also argues in her discussion of Porter as a self-made southerner, "Especially after she became closely acquainted with such (white) pillars of Southern letters as Allen Tate, Caroline Gordon, and Andrew Lytle, Porter constructed herself as an heiress of the Confederacy, 'the grandchild of a lost war,' a southern woman of distinction, elegance, and agrarian roots sprung from aristocratic, even if not moneyed, origins."[5] Through the 1930s Porter composed autobiographical fiction that drew on family stories to construct her own family myth while simultaneously deconstructing idealizations of southern womanhood. Her gender-inflected version of the Agrarian pursuit proved difficult on two fronts, however. First of all, she was keenly aware of the sexual repression and anxiety that accompanied the idealization of young white women in the South. Second, like other southern women writers, she had to contend with the sexist assumptions of those very Agrarian writers she admired and sought as compatriots in the creation of a regional social identity and literature. Although men like Allen Tate and Andrew Lytle sought to liberate southern letters, they were not equally ready to liberate southern women. Porter's ties with the Agrarian group were long and intimate. In the late 1920s she moved into a Greenwich Village apartment building also housing Caroline Gordon. Through Gordon she met Tate, Robert Penn Warren, and his wife Eleanor Clark, and through them, ten years later, her last husband Albert Erskine, editor of the *Southern Review*. Porter found these fellow southerners highly congenial and joined them in giving a regional definition to her generation's post–World War I experience of historical and cultural dislocation. Her ties to this group were very strong throughout the 1930s, and she was often a guest at Benfolly, the Gordon-Tate's home, and at one point contemplated forming a residential writing community in Virginia with them.[6] During these years she labored to construct her own southern identity on several fronts, composing the autobiographical fiction that wove together southern legend, family story, and personal memory while at the same time inscribing in letters, memoir, and performance a genteel family past that sustained the self she wished to be in the present. The ties between Porter's writing and that of the Agrarians are most apparent in the influential April 11, 1935, number of the *Virginia Quarterly Review*, where Porter's remarkable story "The Grave" appeared in the company of Allen Tate's influential essay "The Profession of Letters in the South."

In "The Profession of Letters," Tate laments the South's failure to produce great writers: "We lack a tradition in the arts," he complains; "more to the point, we lack a literary tradition. We lack even a literature." There have been southern writers, Tate acknowledges, but they have been of the wrong sort: romantic, sentimental, soft minded, cut off from the soil, their writing an "unreal union of formless revery and correct sentiment." There needs to be a general toughening up of tone, he proclaims: "If there is such a person as a Southern writer, if there could be such a profession as letters in the South, the profession would require the speaking of unpleasant words and the violation of good literary manners."[7] In her analysis of the racial and sexual underpinnings of the Agrarian movement, Susan Donaldson persuasively argues that Tate's call for a new kind of southern writer is deeply gendered: "Coded into Tate's own unpleasant words was the conviction that modern southern letters should dissociate itself from the successful women writers of the nineteenth century."[8] Donaldson and others establish, in fact, that by arguing for a literature composed by white men, Tate continues an enduring southern tradition, one whose extent Anne Goodwyn Jones mapped in her book *Tomorrow Is Another Day: The Woman Writer in the South, 1859–1936*. This is a tradition Porter and her peers knew well. Indeed, it is disturbing to note how fully an 1867 denunciation of women writers, quoted by Donaldson, echoes Porter's own view of the woman artist as a monster. According to the editor of the early Baltimore-based *Southern Review*, a woman writer is "*une femme incomprise*—a woman out of her sphere, an anomaly, an imperfection."[9]

Recent critical attention has turned to the impact on southern women writers of the decidedly masculine bias of the influential male Agrarian/Fugitive critics, teachers, and writers. How did their chauvinism affect the highly talented women who were their students and friends, their fellow advocates of a reconstructed southern tradition? If Caroline Gordon could write to Porter of then *Kenyon Review* editor John Crowe Ransom, "He can't bear for women to be serious about their art," how did she and her literary southern sisters respond?[10] Katherine Hemple Prown has looked most closely at the work of Flannery O'Connor, mentored by Andrew Lytle, her teacher at the Iowa Writers' Workshop, as well as by John Crowe Ransom and Caroline Gordon. According to Prown, O'Connor consciously crafted her fiction "to ally herself with a masculinist literary and cultural tradition," choosing violence and misogyny as her way to separate herself from the genteel female fiction Tate excoriates.[11] Obeying Tate's directive for the serious southern writer, O'Connor wrote fiction that deliberately speaks "unpleasant truths" and violates "good literary manners" in its portraits of the maimed, deluded, and disagreeable. As Prown summarizes, "Banishing female characters, silencing female voices, and redirecting her satirical gaze from men to women, O'Connor reshaped her work to appeal to a literary and critical community built on gender-based and racial hierarchies that had traditionally characterized southern culture."[12] It seems that like the 1867 editor of the *Southern Review*, or like Porter, born in 1890 and her senior by thirty-five years, O'Connor also perceived the woman writer as going against sexual norms, at best celibate, perhaps unnatural. As she wrote to her intimate friend "A," "There is a great deal that has to either be given up or taken away from you if you are going to succeed in writing a body of work. There seem to be other conditions in life that demand celibacy besides the priesthood."[13] Not just in the fiction she wrote, but also in the life she chose, O'Connor worked to conform, at least publicly, to the edicts of southern ladyhood. Her choices, both enabled and justified by her illness, Prown suggests, allowed her to stay at home, the publicly dutiful daughter and quiet invalid who was simultaneously free enough from both domestic labor and social responsibility to dedicate herself to her art.

Porter chose another route to acceptance by her Agrarian/Fugitive peers than did O'Connor. She found in the Agrarian community not just the joys of intellectual companionship and literary community (and, albeit briefly, a young husband) but also deeply appealing visions of the past, of family, and of social class, potential balm to soothe and cover over the painful fractures of her own impoverished west Texas childhood and reconnect her to the more lustrous family past of her grandmother's stories. Where O'Connor may have assumed the role of reclusive invalid, dutiful daughter, and admiring mentee, Porter embraced the role of southern Lady. As Joan Givner revealed after Porter's death, "In the place of Callie Porter, raised in poverty and obscurity, she created Katherine Anne Porter, an aristocratic daughter of the Old South and the descendant of a long line of distinguished statesmen."[14] Initially her Agrarian colleagues were entranced. Allen Tate confided to Andrew Lytle in 1928, "If I would have three wives, and were privileged to take them, they would be Carolyn [Gordon], Katherine Anne [Porter] and Leonie [Adams]."[15] About four years later Lytle wrote Tate asking if he had "seen that beautiful, soft-talking tiger-wandering woman, Katherine Anne."[16]

From the 1920s through the 1940s, as her Agrarian admirers were working to constitute a southern literary tradition, Porter was working to constitute herself as a southerner rooted in the cultural mythology they celebrated. Her description of herself in a *Paris Review* interview in 1963 as "a Southerner by tradition and inheritance" and a member "of that guilt-ridden white-pillar crowd"[17] represents, in the words of Janis Stout, the culmination of "a long process of identity construction."[18] Crucial to that process was the interweaving of her life and her family's stories with the life and legends of her fictional counterpart Miranda Gay. Throughout Porter's texts, the fictive "she" is always a hairbreadth away from the "I." But this is particularly true in the case of her Miranda stories, which constitute crucial texts for understanding Porter's own self-transformation. In some of Porter's unpublished papers, "I" and "Miranda" alternately identify the same subject on the same page. These papers also reveal that the Miranda stories, including the short novel *Old Mortality* and the sketches that make up *The Old Order*, find their origins in work on *Many Redeemers*, a novel Porter was hard at work on while living in Paris in 1932.[19] This is a year that also witnessed her first draft of "Noon Wine," a story more true to her Texas roots. Allen Tate and Caroline Gordon visited her during this fruitful year, a time when Porter was revisiting and reconstructing childhood memories. As Tate wrote Lytle from Paris that Christmas, "Katherine Anne is a plumb flurry of sentiment." He signed himself "Katherine Anne's Knight [but a 'hind-titter' too]."[20] The work Porter undertook in Paris is indeed full of "sentiment," for it mingles personal desire, family stories, and historical record, fiction and fact, or—to use Porter's terms—"legend and memory." "Legend and memory" became Porter's name for a theory of autobiographical fiction she formulated as she drafted *Many Redeemers*. It argues that all memory inevitably becomes legend, and that all legend becomes truth. In the light of this theory, Porter could perceive her revisionary family history as her true heritage.

Never completed as a single unified text, *Many Redeemers* represented an extraordinarily ambitious plan to retell the Porter family history in fictional form. It would cover "from about 1700 to 1918," Porter decided, moving from European roots to the present. Through the novel Porter hoped to place her own life within a historical context that would give it both order and meaning. In a brief outline of *Many Redeemers*, she aligns her personal alienation from her historical present with a version of southern history; like her Agrarian compeers, she is caught in the final throes of a dying South, thrown from the land, the old ties of place and family broken. As she wrote in notes outlining the novel:

> Then my own generation, born on the edge of another break-up, for the real break-up did not occur immediately after the war, but with the death of my grandmother, an old woman who almost single-handedly held the thing together until her last day. . . . I belong to the generation left stripped and homeless . . . not my father's generation . . . because they still had the land and they still had the tradition. . . . Stop with my generation on the edge of life, facing all that we did face.[21]

Following the Agrarian drama, Porter created a personal history in which she represented the disinherited descendent of "an aristocratic and organic order cemented by ties of family, status, [and] tradition."[22] Her published autobiographical essays, such as "Portrait: Old South" or "Noon Wine: The Sources," ring with phrases like "good old family," "nobly unreconstructed," or "blood-knowledge"—the chimes of the Agrarian nostalgia.

For Porter, the need to construct a "never-never land" of peaceful affluence and meaningful order was perhaps more acute than for her contemporaries. Her actual childhood left her with particularly painful memories, which gave her recurring unhappiness throughout her life.[23] It is disturbing to read her autobiographical notes from the years when she worked on *Many Redeemers*, for moments of reverie, where imagination creates a past replete with order and affluence, are repeatedly ruptured by recollected unhappiness and violence. Family ties simultaneously sustain and strangle. For example, an unpublished fragment of autobiography titled "Pull Dick—Pull Devil" moves between recollections of a disorderly, increasingly impoverished childhood and rhapsodies of orderly living. Porter describes her family life as emotionally chaotic; between "successive uproars, we were beaten and lectured and prayed over. . . . I realize now that all of us, from my grandmother down, were neurotics, they all seemed to live in a hornet's nest of disorder." Yet then, in the space of a sentence, she yields to imagination, to happy memories of "lavender scented bed linen and thin old silver . . . Negroes singing in the cotton field." As in Porter's public reminiscences or interviews, especially later in her life, these "memories" characteristically contain the three elements Francis Pendleton Gaines long ago designated as central to the plantation legend: a landed aristocracy, black servants, and a world resembling a golden age—the people more beautiful, life more leisurely and pastoral.[24] However, except for a few family heirlooms and her grandmother's stories of former prestige and security, Porter's childhood offered scant real material for the depiction of home and family that appears in either her fiction or her later fictive reminiscences. In her first year of life, Porter lived in a two-room log house in Indian Creek, Texas; neighbors lived in sod huts.[25] Whatever backbone he possessed, her father, Harrison Boone Porter, lost soon after Porter's mother died of an illness complicated by repeated pregnancies. Porter was then about a year and a half old. Her family crowded into Porter's grandmother's house in Kyle, Texas, until her grandmother's death when Porter was eleven. Then, uprooted, they left the Texas countryside for a series of homes in San Antonio.

Reconstructing her past represented Porter's response to the instability and unhappiness of her childhood. The pattern of "Pull Dick—Pull Devil," alternating lovely fictive memory and painful recollection, reappears in many forms in her drafts as she labored to cover over actual memory and confirm her ties to a more salutary inheritance. *The Old Order* and *Old Mortality*, fiction that came out of work on *Many Redeemers*, present family and place as essential to identity and fill the Gay family homes with heirlooms, ritual, and a wealth of tradition, while at the same time their central heroine, Miranda, rages against and resists family ties. Before her final resolution to know her own story at the close of *Old Mortality*, Miranda chants a litany of rejection: "She did not want any more ties with this house, she was going to leave it"; "she would have no more bonds that smothered her in love and hatred"; "I hate love, she thought, as if this were the answer, I hate loving and being loved, I hate it."[26] Miranda's rage against family ties echoes Porter's own, recorded many times in journals and letters. Although in the abstract she might embrace the Agrarian idealization of familial traditions and imagine another better past to sustain herself in the present, actual childhood experience, including her early disastrous marriage at age sixteen, left a legacy of pain. "The truth is, I can hardly bear to think," confess some scribbled notes, dated Mexico 1921. "And when I do, I go blind with simple anxiety and the suffering of remembrance."[27] On June 12, 1928, she wrote her sister Gay Porter Holloway that "I have no happy memories at all to bring me there [to Texas], the first part of my life that I can bear to remember begins after I left . . . the South and went to Denver." And again she wrote to her sister on August 8, 1949, "Very sincerely I date the beginning of my strange bad fortune since I came back from Europe, to my returning to Texas in 1936. . . . The murderous old hex of the family which I had just beaten off by main strength and had fled for fifteen years, just reached out and took me by the throat and started strangling again, just like the good old times." The past may sustain, if it can be transformed into the "good old times" of the Old South. However, "the deathly bear trap"—as Porter once described her family—would not yield easily to any form of idealization.[28] It took years for Porter to rewrite her own story.

On the most basic physical level, Porter tried repeatedly and unsuccessfully to create homes that reproduced her imagined heritage; in part this explains the fact that she bought antiques and then claimed them as cherished family heirlooms.[29] Of more importance is the theory of "legend and memory" that she formulated as she labored to link her life and her autobiographical fiction. *Many Redeemers* represented the self-confirming text for Porter, reconstructing her heritage as an articulation of the Agrarian ideal. Believing that appearance, intellect, and ability—in short, identity—originate in and are indelibly stamped by lineage, she undertook genealogical research, which she then wove into her work on *Many Redeemers*, trying to construct a line of descent that would connect her family back through pioneer ancestors to aristocratic European forebears, following the southern apologists in her attention to the purity and potency of inherited blood. The emphasis on "blood," an integral part of the southern myth, probably appealed to Porter for reasons other than the obsession with racial purity that marked post–Civil War ideology. She imagined that her "blood" connected her to ancestors more admirable than her immediate family. As she once wrote her sister, describing her response to her father's lack of motivation and personal failure, "Sometimes I have such a horror of having had such a father it almost cripples me. Then I have to remember that I have hundreds of years of other ancestors too, really brave and firm, and I rely on them."[30]

Constructing her bloodlines, Porter was less concerned with proof of descent than with prestige, as Joan Givner has shown, and chose the most illustrious from among the Porters and Boones of history.[31] She wrote Caroline Gordon that her guide in *Many Redeemers* was a truth deeper than fact; as she reconstructs history, she will "depend precisely on what I know in my blood, and in my memory, and on something that is deeper than knowledge."[32] These sources are most fully defined in a speech she gave to the American Women's Club of Paris in 1935. Describing her work on *Many Redeemers*, the speech anatomizes the material she drew on while attempting to write "my own past retold in the history of my family": "I have for this only legend, those things I have been told or that I read as a child . . . and my own memory of events taking place around me at the same time. And there is a third facet: my present memory and explanation to myself of my then personal life, the life of a child, which is in itself a mystery, while being living and legendary to that same child grown up."[33] Porter's three sources can be viewed as an interactive continuum. At the farthest end lies legend, representing the past transformed and perfected into fiction. Memory extends from legend up to the present, becoming increasingly muddled as it is more immediate. The present continually seeks to explain and so order memory, gradually transforming the farthest events into legend. Thus "the life of a child" becomes legendary "to that same child grown up."

Yet Porter's autobiographical fiction is not a simple transformation of memory into legend; it is instead a conglomerate of extant legend, personally transformed memory, and present desire. None is simple or singular. As Porter lays out her theory of "legend and memory": "No legend is ever true . . . the legend is that work of art which goes on in the human mind, adding to and arranging, harmonizing and rounding out, making larger or smaller than life, and holding the entire finished product in a good light and asking you to believe it. And it is true. No memory is really faithful. It has too far to go, too many changing landscapes of the human mind and heart, to bear any sort of really trustworthy witness, except in part. So the truth in art is got by change."[34] Truth comes not from autobiographical fact but from transformation. The remade life—that is, the life as it is transformed into fiction—is the true story. As Porter wrote Eudora Welty, "By the organic process of creation, the scattered and seemingly random events remembered through many years become fiction, that is—not a lie, really as I think you call it—but symbolic truth."[35]

The legend Porter formulated as she researched ancestors, delved into her own memory, and recalled stories of her family's past tells of well-established, even aristocratic ancestors who endured life in a log cabin only as a temporary interim between more settled periods when their lives reproduced the world of the Old South. It is a legend shaped by the Agrarian imagination. To draw a representative selection from among the scattered, undated notes throughout her unpublished papers:

It was simply true that my ancestors, crossing the Cumberland gap and going through the wilderness had carried their Latin and Greek grammars, old books of music, a piece or two of rosewood or mahogany, even an occasional tall gilded harp. They wore coonskin caps and moccasins and lived in log cabins, but only so long as they had to: their goal was land, a landed estate, with a house as much like the one they had left in Virginia or Pennsylvania as they could manage: which in turn had been as much like the one they had left in England.[36]

The gilded harp in the log cabin is both a grand flight of fancy and an image overwhelmingly vulnerable to ridicule. Like many others in Porter's published and unpublished memoirs, the passage above has close companions in the Agrarian manifestos. One might compare it to John Crowe Ransom's description of the southern gentry in the lead essay of *I'll Take My Stand*: "They too were the heirs of impatient pioneers who endured the hard labor of settlement in order to bring about as quickly as possible material comfort sufficient for aesthetic pursuits. Their true inheritance is not labor but leisure." As he writes of this first generation's descendants, "They have elected to live their comparatively easy and routine lives in accordance with the tradition which they inherited, and they have consequently enjoyed a leisure, a security, and an intellectual freedom that were never the portion of pioneers."[37]

Through the process of transforming her family's history, Porter transformed herself: memory moved from legend to truth. Although she never finished *Many Redeemers*, she did create a self-embracing legend that, from this point on, progressively influenced her public identity. Increasingly, Porter took on the role of aristocratic Southern Lady of Letters, presenting herself as blood inheritor of the Old South. If in the 1920s and 1930s she could camp high-class femininity with her gay friends George Platt Lynes and Glenway Wescott, in later years the role play became less playful and more sustained, accompanied by the hardening of her views on gender and sexual identity evident in the 1940s essays on Gertrude Stein or the extensive unpublished responses to Cowley's *Exile's Return* discussed in chapter 8. The role of southern lady deeply appealed to Porter, for it offered a revised past to cover over her unwanted origins, a social status she found very appealing, and, crucially, a highly feminine public identity, one that completely negated any charges that her independence and commitment to a literary career were unwomanly.

Porter's role as southern lady resembles the dramatic roles played by other modernist women such as Edna St. Vincent Millay and Elinor Wylie. Unlike the "mannish" lesbian, these women did not refute heterosexual arrangements.

Instead, they heightened their femininity to the level of performance. Sandra Gilbert and Susan Gubar briefly suggest in *Sexchanges* that such "extravagantly feminine artists as Edna St. Vincent Millay, H.D., Elinor Wylie . . . wore their glamorous garb so ironically that they could in some sense be considered female female impersonators."[38] How much Porter, especially later in her career (or for that matter Millay), was actually ironic or consciously impersonating is open to debate. Certainly, however, hyperfemininity provided armor against many accusations. Whether it is Porter's big hats, pearls, and massive emerald, or Hellman's Blackgama furs, or Millay's "flowing robe, aquamarine velvet, with a train"—her costume for a 1928 reading at the University of Chicago—the elegant and expensive trappings of successful femininity defend a woman artist against accusations of unnatural sexuality.[39] Porter, like Millay or other elaborately feminine modernist women, used feminine display to achieve freedom and gain her own ends in a male-dominated world. By developing a public identity that overlapped with and was enhanced by her texts, she brought her art and self into a union of textuality and sexuality that many readers found very attractive. The recent comments of Harold Bloom are sufficient testimony to her success: "A beautiful lyricist and a beautiful woman necessarily celebrate their own beauty, and Porter surpassingly was both. Even her stories' titles haunt me, just as photographs depicting her hold on in the memory."[40]

As Porter became increasingly committed to her public identity, she assumed it at every level, from dress and speech mannerism to publicly presented values. Janis Stout nicely connects Porter's grand public performances to her early years in theater, noting that she "was helping support her family as early as her fifteenth year by teaching skills of the theater, elocution and dancing." As Stout sums up, "Porter . . . was known for bravura performances on the stage of her life. Through quasi-theatrical means of self-presentation, she engaged in the construction of a glamorous and feminized persona, with an assemblage of domestic possessions functioning as stage props."[41] The combination of gender, class, and region performance that make up the role of southern lady eventually permeated all aspects of Porter's life; her houses, which she decorated with great care, provided stage sets. Reading Barbara Thompson's 1963 description of Porter in her home, as the two settle over minted iced tea for the *Paris Review* interview, one cannot help but imagine a refined, aged, but still charming belle. Writes Thompson, "The parlor to which a maid admits the caller is an elegant mélange of several aspects of the past, both American and European. High-ceiling, dim and cool. . . . Finally, a voice in the upper hallway: its tone that of someone talking to a bird, or coquetting with an old beau."[42] Particularly after *Ship of Fools,* when she finally achieved financial security, Porter played the Southern Lady to the hilt and seemed to believe herself the embodiment and confirmation of that cherished American role.

If Porter, like her Princess, eventually became inseparable from her own myth, she was at first more productively distanced. In the fiction she crafted during the 1930s when she was formulating her southern family history, we find complex and critical gender-thinking about southern womanhood. In fact, Porter's responses to idealizations of white southern life are sufficiently ironic and acute that they made her Agrarian friends uncomfortable. Her short novel, *Old Mortality,* seems to have infuriated Allen Tate. His letter to John Peale Bishop, detailing a visit to Porter in Paris in 1941 and recording his response to Porter's portrayal of three generations of southern women, merits extensive quotation because it reveals so much about the challenges for women writers in the Agrarian community. If in the 1930s Tate was enchanted when Porter exhibited "a plumb flurry of sentiment," ten years later he was less charmed by an older, more successful woman. As he wrote to Bishop:

> There has been a wonderful change in her since I first knew her, even since about 1932, and I don't think it means anything good. She has become a great Person- age, and my experience of this sort of transformation convinces me that it signals, in her as in others, a weakening of the creative powers. It is easy to see how she has drifted into this state of mind: she has few of the ordinary human satisfac- tions—she can't live in the world, she can't have a deep emotional relationship with anybody. . . . When the human personality suffers repeated failures in a fundamental objective experience, it recoils into self-worship, or at best a refined egoism; and women usually achieve only the former. She has got so she can't dis- tinguish between admiration of her work and admiration of herself; and the one feeds the other—which I need not say is a very dangerous situation. Look at the end of Old Mortality: all the rich life of those people is swept away with a callow judgment by MIRANDA (significant name); look at Pale Horse, Pale Rider, whose heroine's emotions are commonplace but whose personality is handled with a solemnity that comes very near being sentimentality. This is a distinct defect in K. A.'s work.[43]

A successful Katherine Anne seems less appealing to Tate. No longer a fantasy third wife, she is now an egotistical grand dame. It is not surprising to read that, like the work of the women who preceded her in southern letters, Porter's writing now also bears the fatal weight of sentiment that, according to Tate, impeded the profession of letters in the South. Yet one cannot help but wonder if it is Tate himself who is sentimental about "the rich life of those people" whose choices Miranda, a modern young woman, calls acutely into question at the close of *Old Mortality*. Likewise, in 1941 Andrew Lytle was less enthusiastic about the work of that "beautiful, soft-talking tiger-wandering woman, Katherine Anne" he had so thoroughly admired in 1932. As he wrote Tate from New Orleans, "I've been looking into Flowering Judas recently. As fine as it is, it is not as tough as Caroline [Gordon's] work. There is a certain female impurity which Caroline lacks, and I believe this is the thing a woman writer will naturally find the greatest hazard."[44] According to these two Agrarian men, women writers travel a perilous path; between the Scylla of "self-worship" and the Charybdis of "impurity," few of their sex succeed. By 1950, in fact, even Porter's friend Glenway Wescott, who delighted in role play himself, complained in his journal, "K.A. is giving a reception for fifty people this Friday. . . . daffy creature that she has become, it signifies or symbolizes more than anything. The Southern sociability . . . in her; as it were a kind of malaria."[45]

If we turn now from the creation of Katherine Anne Porter, grand daughter of the Confederacy, to her other fictional creation Miranda Gay, we find that in the 1930s Porter produced a complex, gendered analysis of southern womanhood, contributing to the Agrarian call for more realistic, less sentimental southern letters. One of the central themes of this fiction is the role of memory. The Miranda stories that rose out of *Many Redeemers* present several characters who are sustained and even ennobled by their own legends of the past. In one of the published fragments of the novel, titled *The Old Order*, Porter represented her theory of "legend and memory" through the image of quilt making. Just as Grandmother and Nannie stitch together fragments of fabric from the past, they stitch together their memories, creating a beautiful and sturdy truth by which they can explain their present lives. Perhaps Porter's most heroic characters, Grandmother and Nannie, seem more than human, possessing unwavering self-knowledge, strength, and authority. Their shared, self-made legend underlies their strong sense of identity, describing who and what and where they are from what they and their forebears have been. Although the world that surrounds Grandmother and Nannie has changed, they remain stable, suffering no dislocation.

The self-confirming power of a personal fiction returns as a central theme in *Old Mortality*. Although this short novel records only a fragment of the *Many Redeemers* project, it stands as the summation and minor accomplishment of Porter's fictional family history. Initially Amy represents the "perfect" achievement of womanhood, the family's symbol of its own past possession of perfection against which the present is measured and diminished. An "angel" or "singing angel," Amy sits forever posed in memory against the "bright blank heavenly blue sky" of family legend.[46] Among Porter's papers gathered under the title *Old Mortality* is a typescript containing her own brief analysis of the story. It includes a discussion of the photograph with which the story opens:

> It is an imperfect photograph—doesn't really give her beauty. The children don't understand why she is thought so beautiful. Too imperfect, it doesn't give us a true picture . . . but it does give us an idea of the past. The people who had seen her and who had lived at that time had not seen her at all. The picture brought back their own youth and their own sense of reality. When they saw her as she was alive and moving and they were with her—brought back their own past and made their own lives seem real and vital.[47]

The passage is wonderfully suggestive. It emphasizes that the photograph is an "imperfect" record, not "true"; yet it gives "an idea" of the past. That "idea" seems to be the act of recollection, which invigorates the self in the present. Twice the passage equates remembering with achieved identity: to have youth "brought back" is to attain a "sense of reality"; to have the past "brought back" is to feel one's life suddenly "real and vital." Looking at the photograph or handling heirlooms, the older family members know who and where and what they are. Speaking of Amy, they become storytellers; like Grandmother and Nannie they possess a legend that explains and orders their present. As Porter states, Amy's family had never "seen her at all." The point of recollection is the self: memory creates legend, and legend creates personal identity.

Old Mortality also suggests that legends of the past need not be beautiful to be true; they must only be believed. Porter sets the story of Amy's perfection against another version of the past, Cousin Eva's. According to Eva, Amy was "too free" and flirtatious, insensitive, "sex-ridden," and diseased (215, 216). Porter's notes indicate that Eva's story is companion rather than corrective to the family legend: "Scene on the train. Legend not exploded because the legend was true as the one who loved it told it, true as Miss Honey told it, who hated it, and true as Eva told it." Eva's version of Amy's legend represents another "symbolic truth," to use Porter's term in her letter to Eudora Welty. It arises from the wedding of legend and memory and confirms Eva's present identity: it is her ordering fiction. In her conversation with Miranda, Eva repeatedly juxtaposes herself, "I," against Amy, "she," finding herself in the opposition: "she" was ill at home; "I was sent to the hospital"; she "died!"; "I came out"; "she was simply sex-ridden"; "I took to the soap box and platform when I was called upon" (215,

216). Eva finds pride and identity opposing herself to Amy; in her story she is the strong survivor, and Amy is the guilty victim of the decadent past.

Cousin Eva, like all of Miranda's elders, including Grandmother and Nannie, possesses a "truth," a legend of the past that sustains a present identity. At the close of Old Mortality, when Miranda watches her father and Eva sharing family history at the train station, she sees them become more perfect and complete through the act of storytelling. They take on the ease and security of people "who occupied by right their place in the world": "They were precisely themselves; their eyes cleared, their voices relaxed into perfect naturalness. . . . They sat back and went on talking steadily in their friendly family voices, talking about their dead" (219). From their communion, their easy identity and sense of place arising from a shared, idealized past, Miranda is excluded. Bitterly she realizes, "It is I who have no place. . . . Where are my people and my own time?" (219). Stubbornly closing her mind "against remembering, not the past but the legend of the past, other people's memory of the past," Miranda resolves to find "the truth about what happens to me." Yet as Porter's closing appraisal of her heroine suggests, such a resolution may represent a kind of "hopefulness," but it is also "ignorance" (221). The "truth" about the self is accessible only through legend.

The irony with which Porter surrounded Miranda's final words seems to have eluded Allen Tate. If Porter's young heroine does sweep away "all the rich life of those people . . . with a callow judgment," that does not mean her author necessarily endorses her action; she simply understands it, with sympathy and wisdom. Not Miranda's past, nor her father's, not her grandmother's, nor the Agrarians'—Allen Tate's, for that matter—can be known in full truth. It comes steeped in legend, drenched in memory with all of its partial repressions and unacknowledged desires. If Porter eventually came to claim herself a daughter of the Confederacy, earlier in her life she knew that the wish to know one's past as a simple and sustaining truth was full of "hopefulness and ignorance."

Tate seems to have missed as well Porter's witty and very unsentimental gender-thinking about his call in the "Profession of Letters" for writing that rejects the "formless revery and correct sentiment" that had hitherto burdened southern literature. Miranda's family loves romantic stories, and dashing Amy Gay, now long dead, epitomizes their favorite subject matter. Like Edgar Allen Poe, Miranda's parents and grandparents find no subject matter more beautiful than the death of a beautiful woman. Thinks young Miranda in part one of Old Mortality:

Their Aunt Amy belonged to the world of poetry. The romance of Uncle Gabriel's long, unrewarded love for her, her early death, was such a story as one found in old books: unworldly books, but true, such as the . . . poems by Edgar Allen Poe. "Her tantalizing spirit now blandly reposes, Forgetting or never regretting its roses. . . . " Their father read that to them, and said, "He was our greatest poet," and they knew that "our" meant he was Southern. (178)

Responding to such sentiments, the Agrarian/Fugitive poets—Tate and Ransom in particular—wrote poems that spoke "unpleasant words" about popular poetic topics such as the death of young children, or of women in childbirth, both common themes in the work of nineteenth-century female poets. And, like their student Flannery O'Connor, they sought to violate the "good literary manners" of southern letters. Observing the influence of the "anti-Poe" position on her subject, the O'Connor scholar Katherine Hemple Prown writes, "As far as Tate and the other Fugitives were concerned. . . . In making such topics [bluntly unsentimental even violent depictions of female experience] the subject of their poetry, Tate and his associates no doubt understood that their local audience, conditioned by years of reading verses like Poe's 'The Raven' and 'Annabel Lee,' would recognize The Fugitive as an affront to their aesthetic expectations and tastes. O'Connor's own fascination with the death of female bodies owes much to the dissemination of an aesthetic in which the unsentimental depiction of the death of a woman is understood as the very antithesis . . . of southern writing that O'Connor so studiously attempted to avoid."[48]

In *Old Mortality* it is thoroughly modern Eva who articulates the Agrarian/Fugitive antisentimental style when describing a woman's demise. "It was just sex," Eva tells Miranda of the force that drove young Amy Gay, "it was all smothered under pretty names, but that's all it was, sex." Not delicacy but abortion, suicide, or disease—any one of these—did away with the Southern Belle. Amy and her lovely friends "simply festered inside," Eva rages. And momentarily Miranda, as seduced by this blunt tale of horrors as she is by gilded legend, imagines "a long procession of living corpses," brides heading for the "charnel house" of love. But she sheds the vision easily, thinking to herself, "This is no more true than what I was told before, it's every bit as romantic" (216).

Porter joined with the Agrarians in advocating antisentimentalism, although she never went as far as the young Allen Tate, who described a woman dead in childbirth in the following bleak terms: "you were twenty-six / And died giving us an homunculus with bald head."[49] She is adamant, however, that she stands apart from the sentimental tradition in southern letters. In 1940 she wrote Lodwick Hartley a letter in response to his criticism of some of her stories, noting to him, "Your mild accusation of sentimentality in certain stories, or passages perhaps, struck me rather sharply. Of course, we know that sentimentality is a fighting word, like romantic, or whatever it is one doesn't want to be or be called. Myself I think half the evils of human relationships are rooted in sentimentality."[50] Porter provides her own gender-inflected version of the Agrarian push for realism when she delineates the simultaneous idealization and control of female sexuality that shape the cultural ideal of the Southern Belle. In the late nineteenth century, popular plantation fiction and its companion, a social ideology of white racial supremacy, used the image of the white Southern Belle as a discursive sign. The Belle's beauty and gaiety, and most of all her virginity, confirmed the beauty, gaiety, and racial purity of the white, southern aristocracy. In this mythology, white women's sexuality was the sign of white southern manhood and thus the focal point of a complex, repressive ideology, which rigidly defined women's place and function.[51] Porter's stories from Many Redeemers are fractured by violent images of female sexuality, which tear through the smoothly woven texts of legend and memory. Beneath the surface of the smiling Belle, she saw women oppressed and destroyed by an ideology that enforced obedience to men and endorsed repeated childbearing while simultaneously denying women's sexuality. The Miranda stories share a violent imagery of defloration, suggesting Porter's recognition that for the Belle sexual intercourse represents a kind of social death.

"The Grave," another published fragment from Many Redeemers, succinctly juxtaposes the idealization against the actuality of women's sexual experience in the nineteenth-century South. In the story, Miranda is just on the verge of puberty. She fantasizes about assuming the role of Belle and, for a moment, longs to "take a good cold bath, dust herself with plenty of Maria's violet talcum powder . . . put on the thinnest, most becoming dress she owned, with a big sash, and sit in a wicker chair under the trees."[52] But as she lingers, caught up in this fantasy, her brother shoots and then cuts open a pregnant rabbit, exposing in a "bloody heap" the rabbit's womb and the dead babies within. It is a violent lesson in the facts of womanhood for Miranda, a moment marked with the bloodshed that accompanies menstruation, defloration, and childbirth.

The same trail of blood runs through Old Mortality. If superficially Amy Gay represents the perfection of the virginal, light-spirited Belle, the blood that stains her handkerchiefs when she coughs suggests the physical facts of sexuality that she and her admirers would deny. Although she may drink "lemon and salt to stop her periods," she can never escape the bloodshed that is both symbolically fatal to her status as a Belle and potentially fatal to her as a woman.[53] Amy's "greensickness," or chlorosis, and that of her mother before her, may be read as a further expression of her efforts to resist her culturally mandated decline from virginal Belle to sexual womanhood and maternity. As Lorraine DiCicco establishes through her research on the prevalence of chlorosis in the late nineteenth and early twentieth century, "Girls at this particular juncture in American history learned to sicken their bodies as a way of passively rebelling against the very destiny to which their bodies fated them."[54] For a woman, the price of winning is blood: Amy hemorrhages after "dancing all night three times in one week" (191), and Miss Lucy, Uncle Gabriel's horse, has "thick red rivulets" covering her "tender mouth and chin" after her triumph at the races (199).

A bride is a doomed woman in *Old Mortality*. Amy insists on wearing a gray wedding gown marked by a bloody splash of red feathers: "It is my funeral," she informs her mother; "I shall wear mourning if I like" (182). The story's imaging of the symbolic as well as the potential death accompanying marriage climaxes in Miranda's quickly rejected, horrific vision of "a long procession of living corpses, festering women stepping daily towards the charnel house . . . their dead faces lifted smiling" (216). The women are brides, "their corruption concealed under laces and flowers" (216). With the gay yet obedient step of the Belle, they march toward their graves. The association of the female body with death and decomposition that infects Eva's imagination and here gains a momentary hold on Miranda recurs throughout the work of male Agrarian/Fugitive writers. Prown identifies it as an aspect of their efforts to masculinize southern letters: "Fetishizing the death of women and linking female sexuality to decay functioned as a means of easing latent anxieties regarding the femininization of Southern literary culture."[55] Miranda, likely expressing her creator's gender-thinking, acknowledges the power of this counter version of southern womanhood but acutely perceives it as equally sentimental, or in Miranda's words, "every bit as romantic"—the reversal of a reflection rather than a new vision.

Although the published fiction that emerged from Porter's work on *Many Redeemers* contains clear, critical gender-thinking about the traditional roles of genteel white southern womanhood, Porter herself increasingly endorsed the myths of antebellum white southern life consolidated by the mid-twentieth century. She repressed her painful memories of childhood, layering over them a fantasy of stability and privilege. And as the years passed, she moved closer and closer to her male Agrarian counterparts, publicly embracing a view of womanhood entirely at odds with her own experience. Perhaps the most extreme example of her transformation appears in a 1956 essay titled "The Gift of Woman." Here she mandates the passive performative female role whose sadomasochistic manifestations the gender-thinking of her 1920s fiction had delineated with unflinching clarity. Writing for *Woman's Home Companion* in 1956, Porter pronounces of her sex: "The nature and genius of woman is for love and giving gladly. . . . Her arts are decorative and interpretive, and her gift is for being pleasing. . . . it is man that woman wishes to please when she sets out to please. She is bride and mother; that is her destiny and things go much better if everybody accepts it without too much uproar."[56] Perhaps as she aged, questions of sexuality became less personally threatening to Porter. For whatever reason, she eventually embraced without hesitation her public identity as a daughter of the Old South. Memory sank ever more deeply into legend, and her early conflicts slowly disappeared below the surface. The role of Southern Lady grew to be Porter's own, enthusiastically endorsed by her admirers. Joan Givner's biography provides ample illustrations of her dramatic self-presentation. Interviewers enjoyed describing her big hats, ropes of pearls, and gushing southern speech. Her appearance became the confirmation of a cherished American myth, and in her last years she grew to be a sort of public treasure. If publicly Katherine Anne Porter increasingly performed the part of the Southern Lady, with its established postures of class, gender, and region, the texts that emerged at the start of this self-transformation radically question such a role. But as she grew into the past she had written for herself, she not only raised fewer questions about the sexual ideology that accompanied her heritage, she also grew defensive about the mingling of legend and memory on which her identity was grounded. Late in life, the possession of a secure identity rooted in the South became one of her most triumphant themes. In 1969, when an interviewer asked her, "Are you sustained by your own legend?" she made clear that the word legend had become an anathema to her. "I am sustained by my past—" she responded, "it's not a myth, it's history; we have the records and I know who my ancestors were and I know what they did and believed. So that this late anguish of the search for identity—of people who have no roots or no roots that they wish to acknowledge—but I know who I am and where I am and what I'm doing."[57] Almost fifty years after her first trip to

Europe, Porter forcefully denied that legend and memory form the source of a secure and sustaining identity in the present. Possessed by the legend she had labored to create throughout the thirties, she had become—from a Miranda's point of view—as blind as Nannie and Grandmother or all the storytellers in *Old Mortality* whose "hearts and imaginations [were] captivated by their past" (175).

CHAPTER TEN

NO SAFE HARBOR

Conversations between the Princess and the young acolyte follow a distinct pattern. He expresses his desire for her love; she responds with visionary decrees and another layer of glittering razor-sharp armor. Sexual obsession alternates with physical and emotional wounds. Brief, unconsummated, the marriage ends with her death, leaving a poet singing about "his faithful love, and her unrelenting cruelty."[1] Somewhere near forty years after she wrote "The Princess," Katherine Anne Porter published a novel that recalls but far surpasses her early tale in its depiction of love, obsession, and sexual violence. *Ship of Fools* contains some of her most startling representations of gender identity and most disturbing portrayals of sexual relations. It is a novel about love's terrible consequences, its setting a ship full of lonely and fearful human beings whose yearning to lose themselves leads them to unworthy and debased lovers. Desire leads to shame; hate repeatedly swallows love; sexual and social nausea manifest themselves in bodily deformity, sickness, and violence. Like "Pale Horse, Pale Rider," *Ship of Fools* employs illness as metaphor for all manner of wrongs. When the ship first reaches "High Sea" at the start of part 2, the novel's center, it is literally awash in vomit: "Hundreds of people, men and women . . . wallowing on the floor, being sick." Like "The Princess," as well, *Ship of Fools* portrays a young woman artist, less alienated perhaps than Porter's early heroine, but no less unhappy, still struggling against a hostile, predatory world that refuses to recognize the union of two roles: woman and artist. Many readers view Jenny Brown of *Ship of Fools* as an autobiographical character, based on Porter at the age of forty-one, when she traveled to Europe by ship from Mexico in the company of Eugene Pressly.[2] As a self-portrait, Jenny is troubling, for to this young woman Porter gave all the inner afflictions and outer adversities that had impeded her own long career.

Perhaps because the novel offers so little good cheer, most scholars have focused their attention on its lengthy, sporadic composition or debated its overall quality rather than paying close attention to individual characters or scenes. The novel was long awaited and critical response was extensive, although mixed; since then readers have been progressively less enthusiastic. In 1992 Thomas Walsh called *Ship of Fools* "the mediocre work of a writer of short fiction" and described its contents as Porter's "revenge against the world that denied her the love and happiness for which she yearned all her life."[3] Author of an intellectual biography of Porter, Janis Stout concurs with Walsh's views, and there are few strong dissenting opinions. The novel's formal qualities have challenged readers, for it works in short vignettes, shuffling through a thick deck of characters, depicting their interactions in brief, acute, and often distasteful scenes. Critics have attributed its choppy structure and thematic periodicity to Porter's affinity for the short story; however, it is just as likely that the novel's iterations are intended to reinforce its central theme. As Porter described it in a detailed letter to Caroline Gordon approximately sixteen years before the book finally reached publication: "My book is about the constant endless collusion between good and evil; I believe that human beings are capable of total evil, but no one has ever been totally good: and this gives the edge to evil. I don't offer any solution, I just want to show this principle at work, and why none of us has any real alibi in this world."[4] "Endless collusion" finds formal expression in repetition; like riders seated on a Ferris wheel, the characters of *Ship of Fools* rotate before our eyes, moving in and out of the harsh light of Porter's vision.

In his illuminating analysis of Porter's evolving intellectual thought, *Katherine Anne Porter's Artistic Development: Primitivism, Traditionalism, and Totalitarianism*, Robert Brinkmeyer describes the intense conservatism that increasingly characterized her writing from the late forties through the sixties. This "radical hardening and harshening of Porter's views resulting from her obsession with totalitarianism," he persuasively argues, underlies the racial and ethnic stereotyping of *Ship of Fools* and fuels the novel's repetitive demonstration of the human capacity for evil.[5] Brinkmeyer finds the novel atonal: "In the grip of her single-minded ideas that dwelled on the hidden evil within the heart of humanity and its visible manifestations in tyrannical politics and interpersonal relations, Porter in *Ship of Fools* reworked many of the themes and concerns of her previous fiction . . . with a single-minded monologism."[6] Although he attributes Porter's narrowing thought to an antitotalitarianism that originated in political ideologies that grew out of World War II and into the cold war, the "aristocratic elitism" he notes, with its attendant class and race prejudices, found equally rich soil in the regional identity she emphasized as the years progressed. As she donned the mantle of southern ladyhood, Porter grew as rigid and single-minded in her political views as the body of her glittering, armored Princess.

Yet *Ship of Fools* has defenders, and readers have consistently acknowledged the epigrammatic brilliance of its scenes. Noteworthy fans include Jon Spence, whose 1974 essay provides the most eloquent analysis of both the novel's animal imagery and its debt to the techniques and perspectives of eighteenth-century satire. In her 1985 book, Darlene Harbour Unrue also provides a close, positive reading of the novel, generously attributing personal growth to both Jenny and Dr. Schumann, and thereby countering views that characterization in the novel is essentially static. Both Spence and Unrue see the novel as a multistranded analysis of the kinds of human self-absorption and illusion that lead to the failure of community and love.[7] Their focus on love opens up a fruitful avenue for approaching Porter's final opus. Although in the most embracing terms the novel is about good and evil, its central vehicles are relationships, primarily between men and women, although Porter is also interested in parents and children and even pets. Porter's fascination with the cultural construction of masculinity and femininity continues, and the subject matter of much of her earlier writing reappears. We see once again her interest in women as media for the male imagination, with the corresponding concern for women's attraction to their own objectification, and she confronts yet again the recurring conflicts women artists face between romantic relationships and their vocation. But in *Ship of Fools* she seems particularly interested in the expression of sexual desire and—again and again—the seemingly uncontrollable choice of a debased, unworthy object for that desire. The novel contains some of her most brilliant depictions of gender identity and sexual relations, but it works primarily through repetition and accumulation; the complexity and contradiction that accompanied gender representations in her short fiction are largely missing.

Three pairs of women and men merit examination for both the imaging and patterning of their relations in the novel. The three women—Jenny Brown, Mrs. Treadwell, and La Condesa—have strong autobiographical roots; the shape of their lives and their current appearance or desires often evoke Porter's own story.[8] The three men—David Scott, William Denny, and Dr. Schumann—are linked as well, most notably through their contempt for women. Denny, an unpleasant character whose mind is a wallow of ugly prejudices and predatory lusts, has moments when he hates "women—all women, the whole dirty mess of them."[9] Dr. Schumann and David, socially more agreeable, have similar thoughts but keep them to themselves. Judgmental, fastidious, puritanical, these two men share a rigidity of mind, aquiline noses, and the neat, lean bodies Porter assigns her attractive men. Both men are, in David's words, "sick of things all runny at the edges" (363), but runniness, unfortunately, characterizes women in the novel. Dr. Schumann experiences the horrified fascination of a Swiftian voyeur peeping in Celia's closet when he enters La Condesa's cabin: the air "thick with Turkish cigarette smoke, a mixture of heavy scents, and ether . . . badly worn luggage . . . spread about open, with . . . wrinkled soiled fine gloves, and pale-colored unbotanical flowers of crumpled silk and shattered velvet tumbling out" (118). David, repeatedly tagged with the characterizing term "cold," suffers bouts of hot sexual nausea in which "his mind was a reek of spermy violent images and sensations which he loathed for the pleasure they gave him" (376). For all three men—in fact for every character on this *Ship of Fools*—shame and self-loss accompany enacted desire; rigidity shatters, fluidity breaks through. This imagery appears in innumerable forms. Beyond the stiff rails of the ship's upper-class deck is the shifting ocean on one side, the stench and confusion of steerage on the other. The illicit, whether it be alcohol, dancing, or sex, leads characters up to these ever-present brinks. Lawlessness—often represented by Ric and Rac—can throw things over the edges. So too can alcohol, bringing nausea, and so too can desire, unleashed by alcohol, memory, and imagination.

One scene with Dr. Schumann illuminates this recurring image cluster of rigidity, passionate action, and risk of bodily dissolution. Early in the novel Dr. Schumann rescues a cat about to be drowned at the hands of Ric and Rac, horrific figures of anarchy on the ship—unruled, "instinctive," incestuous (i.e., disobeying sexual taboos)—their faces alike "except for the mysterious stigmata of sex" (112). The rescue brings Dr. Schumann, who suffers from a heart condition, near his own death. As the twins flee he sits still, fingers on his pulse, waiting for his heart to burst or grow calm. As he sits, he reflects on the incident: "He smiled inwardly, with a composed face, at the thought of the cat, that supposedly most astute and self-possessed of all animals, being seduced within an inch of his life by a tickling of his nerve endings. . . . Nothing in his celebrated instincts had warned him that those stroking hands were willing to give him a moment of his private pleasure so that they might the more easily seize him by the scruff for their own satisfaction" (113). So too love, he broods. He has spent his life "patching up" those damaged by love, "the deceived, the foolhardy, the willfully blinded, the lover of suffering; and the most deadly of all, the one who knew what he was doing . . . and yet could not for anything resist one more fling at his favorite hot thrill of the flesh . . . though it might be his own death" (113). "His own death, or my own death," Dr. Schumann concludes and, after briefly closing his eyes in prayer, opens them to the sight of the mad Condesa, stroking her breasts and thighs as she corners a young sailor. It is La Condesa who will arouse, repeatedly, the "astute" and "self-possessed" doctor, causing his pulse to race dangerously with repressed excitement.

The cat controlled by the scruff of the neck while yielding to a dangerous caress finds disturbing reflection in a later scene where Freytag holds Jenny, drunk in his arms, while David Scott crouches in the shadows, watching. Freytag completely controls Jenny's half-conscious, yielding body: "spreading one hand upon her hair, he held her head back, turned her face up to his, studied it with quiet interest for a few seconds, then kissed her deliberately with the utmost luxury on the mouth" (452). In response, Jenny passes into unconsciousness. Freytag cares little for Jenny, considering her "a teasing bitch," and this moment is shameful and abusive for the young woman, yet it is also what she desires. From her first meeting with her seducer she had hoped to have sex and hence lose consciousness with him—the two are one in her mind: "If we could sleep together without too much trouble," she thinks, "and lose ourselves together for a little while, I'd be easy again" (92).

Other scenes provide other mixtures of the same elements: desire, violence, shame, loss of consciousness. While Jenny finds release in alcohol and sex, Dr. Schumann offers La Condesa the bliss of oblivion again and again in the novel, replacing her solitary ether addiction with the jabs of his *piqûre*. When she provocatively smashes bottles and taunts him in her close cabin, he quickly drugs her: "Dr. Schumann did not wait for La Condesa to get back in bed, but seizing her by the upper arm as she passed plunged the needle abruptly into the soft muscle. She shuddered deeply with pleasure, her eyes closed, and she reached up to breathe in his ear warmly: 'What a bad-tempered man you are, and what shall I do without you?'" (236–37). Slaps, jabs, bruises, wrestling—violence walks hand in hand with lust throughout this novel: Pepe arouses Amparo with "a blow of his fist" (224); the Huttens grapple "together like frogs" and roll "in a savage wrestling match" (323). Frau Ritterdorf enjoys a "positive thrill of sensual excitement," imagining "what would have happened if ever she had, no matter how playfully, attempted to strangle her Otto" (155).

The relationship between Mrs. Treadwell and William Denny differs from that of Dr. Schumann and La Condesa or Jenny Brown and David Scott, for it is neither intimate nor prolonged. But the two are bound together. The scene in which Mrs. Treadwell beats Denny's face with the heel of her gold slipper is one of the most powerful and disturbing in the novel. It is a climactic moment of female rage that deeply satisfies not just Mrs. Treadwell but also Jenny (and, likely, Porter herself).[10] The two women share a delicious moment of "light laughter . . . quite blithe and ruthless" at Denny's expense. It is not the first time that Porter has depicted a woman beating the face of an unconscious man. In her 1940 story "A Day's Work," Mrs. Halloran releases her built-up anger at her drunken ne'er-do-well husband by repeatedly striking him in the face with the "good hard knots" she has made in a wet dishtowel.[11] Like Mrs. Treadwell, she avenges disappointed hopes for love, her own and her daughter's. Mrs. Treadwell's name bespeaks both affirmation of her act—she has "tread well" with her sharp spiked heel—and the fact that for her, as for Mrs. Halloran (as, in fact, for Porter, herself), the path of romantic disillusionment is well trodden.

Mrs. Treadwell's disappointment in love recalls that of other heroines in Porter's fiction, from Miranda, who thinks of her marriage as "an illness she might one day hope to recover from" (213), to Rosaleen, to Granny Weath-erall, to the grandmother of *The Old Order*, who ended life with a "deeply grounded contempt for men" (337). Oddly enough, however, the imagery of Mrs. Treadwell's encounter with Denny most recalls "Virgin Violeta." Like a "convent-bred girl," Mrs. Treadwell sleeps in a demure white nightgown, her brushed hair held back "with a white ribbon, in the Alice in Wonderland style she has worn in bed since she was four or five" (205–6). As a child she was full of romantic illusions. Where Violeta felt sure that "everything beautiful and unexpected would happen later on,"[12] Mrs. Treadwell once believed she "was always going to be gay and free, later, when she was rid of nurses and school was over, and there was always to be love—always love" (208). But where Violeta's innocence was erased by Carlos's rapacious kiss, Mrs. Treadwell's disappeared in an early marriage to a man who "preferred sleeping with any chance slut" and yet was "so jealous he beat [her] until [she] bled at the nose" (141, 208).

In the earlier story, discussed at length in chapter 3, Violeta is first astonished by the predatory gleam she finds in Carlos's eyes, and then terrified as his words and gaze transform her from "adorable angel" to "little whore" or from virgin to "violated" seductress.[13] Older, and fully aware of the performative displays that communicate female sexual status, Mrs. Treadwell will consciously transform herself from a beribboned Alice in Wonderful innocent to a painted whore, manipulating gender codes for her own means. But despite her mastery of her culture's gender codes, she remains, emotionally, in their grip. Men like William Denny, "shambling" (18), uncouth and unkempt, deeply threaten Mrs. Treadwell, for she flees her own disorders: "ten years of divorce, shady, shabby, lonely, transient" (210); the bruising and cruel pinch of beggar women; the eyes of predatory men like Denny running "like a hand to her ears, her neck, over her breasts, down her thighs" (61). She seeks, instead, romantic fantasies in the arms of men who appear safe, like the ship's young officers, all "in immaculate white," all wearing "plain red-gold engagement rings on their left hands" (46). But even here she encounters betrayal. She chooses a ship's officer as blank as possible, with "a smooth fair face with no expression at all . . . as sleek, neat, immaculately correct and inhuman-looking as if he were poured into a mold" (434), and in the arms of this sexless automaton she feels sufficiently safe to slip into the romantic dreams of her childhood, enjoying "the pleasant male near-ness, no weight and no burden, but only a presence . . . this wraith who guided her with light fingers at waist and palm, the lover who had danced with her in her daydreams long before she had danced with any man" (434). But when Mrs. Treadwell briefly opens her eyes, she glimpses "a peculiar intentness" in her officer's gaze, "a goatish gleam" akin to the gleam in Carlos's "macaw eyes" that terrifies Violeta. Her young officer never leers, like Denny, "with such abandon his face went all out of shape," yet threatening sexual disorder still lies beneath his rigid surface. He will not allow her to sustain her fantasy of innocence. In a scene that replicates "Virgin Violeta," the officer first kisses Mrs. Treadwell, "violently on her mouth," a kiss that gives her the peculiar and revolting "sensation of being bitten, of the blood being drawn by suction to her mouth," and then accuses her of leading him on: "Why did you come with me, why did you encourage me to kiss you?" (460–61).

But after this moment in which Porter's two texts—written at least twenty years apart—come closest together, they immediately divide. For Violeta flees Carlos in terror, whereas Mrs. Treadwell laughs, "with a somewhat extreme amusement," and then begins a series of complex, private responses. Returning to her cabin, she carefully paints on her face a sensual mask with "a large, deep scarlet glistening mouth, with square corners, a shape of unsurpassed savagery and sensuality" (462). Mrs. Treadwell's face, with the great red lips and heavy powder "a thick clown white" (462), inevitably recalls another early story, "The Circus," where a young Miranda takes her first steps into adult experience. Looking under the bleachers, she encounters the gaze of young men who gather there to peer under women's skirts, their "bold grinning stare without any kind of friendliness in it," a gaze akin to that of Carlos or Mrs. Treadwell's officer. The circus clown, blowing "sneering kisses" from its "long scarlet mouth," sends Miranda into a frenzy of terror; it is her first glimpse from innocence into experience, a world where laughter expresses "savage delight" at another's endangerment, smiles mask suffering, and kisses come from "cruel mouths."[14] But Mrs. Treadwell is not the watching child, she is the performer. A painted lady, she imagines herself "one of the zarzuela company—Amparo perhaps" (462). Unlike Miranda, she does not fear adult experience; she knows it well, hates, endures, and seeks to elude it daily. It seems at first that in putting on the face of the scarlet woman, Mrs. Treadwell is amusing herself by manipulating the images she imagines men, like the young officer, have of her in their minds, images of a sexually available, experienced older woman. But as she sits on her bed, she begins to wonder if the mask reveals "something sinister in the depths of her character . . . unpleasant traits," perhaps she is indeed a seductress, perhaps "savagery and sensuality" lurk under her restraint, beneath her pretty "white satin gown with the bishop sleeves" (466).

Denny's drunken appearance at her door allows Mrs. Treadwell to release her savagery and sensuality through assault. She is full of rage at men, rage for the destruction of her childhood innocence, rage for her disappointed romantic hopes, and rage at the sexual desires she carries, which men awaken. She fears and hates the shame, disorder, and potential self-loss that attend sexuality as much as Dr. Schumann or David Scott, likely more. She answers Denny's assault with one equally violent, feeling "furious pleasure" as her "sharp, metal-capped high heels" break into his face and, afterward, full of delight, kissing "her bloodstained sandal" (465–66). And then, in a remarkable transformation, she costumes herself again, this time in her more familiar virginal garb. She feels purged and invigorated, as if in beating Denny she has beaten out of her own self all that he represents, the ugly prejudices, the messiness, and the lust. After "lavishly" washing, "blissfully" humming while she ties her hair ribbon, she folds "herself into bed like a good little girl who has finished her prayers" (466).

Unlike Miranda in "The Circus" or virginal Violeta, Mrs. Treadwell can manipulate the most powerful and enduring cultural gender identities assigned to Western women. She can perform the whore and the virgin with equal ability; "slapping on warm water, anointing," she washes off Ampora and emerges as Alice in Wonderland. But despite all of her labor, her daily rituals and restraints, she cannot entirely control how the men around her assign meaning to her body. And like the other travelers on *The Ship of Fools*, alcohol, unhappiness, and repressed desire constantly erode her barricaded self. More disturbing is the fact that she seems unable to imagine any other roles, any other gender possibilities she might act out beyond these two extremes. Like La Condesa and Jenny Brown, Dr. Schumann, David Scott, and William Denny, she is caught in the grip of her culture's monsters, full of the hatred, fear, and nausea that accompany performing her proscribed gender identity.

Love is a battle in *Ship of Fools*—Porter portrays use and abuse, predation, violence, hatred expressed and hidden. Except for the silent, entwined honeymooners, who exist in a world entirely their own, the men and women on the *Vera* daily enact the battle of sexes, many as stoutly as Thurber's famous middle-class warriors did in 1949. The book leaves the reader feeling that these battles are endlessly to be fought and endlessly to be lost; there is little light and only bitter laughter as the characters gear up for one more round. The individual battles among the men and women in this novel express deep-seated and generally accepted misogyny and misanthropy.[15] At their very core, men distrust and even hate women, and women return the same. All, like Denny, who seeks a stereotype in which to pocket every person whose difference might threaten his fragile self-acceptance, find relief when they can reduce another to type. A moment in David's mind serves as sufficient example: "With relief he saw Jenny, that so-special creature, the woman like no other woman, merged into the nameless, faceless, cureless pestilence of man's existence, the chattering grievance-bearing accusing female Higher Primate" (397). As Thomas Walsh succinctly sums up his view of sexual relations in *Ship of Fools*: "The novel conclusively proves Porter's contention, first learned from her father, that men and women do not like each other, no matter what their sexual attraction at any given moment. In fact sexual attraction itself seems the source and expression of their hatred."[16]

The view of romantic love in *Ship of Fools* represents the culmination of a long process of narrowing and hardening in Porter's gender-thinking particularly evident in the nonfiction that, except for excerpts from the novel in progress, was her primary published new writing between 1941 and 1962. As the thirties receded, so too did the playful experimentation and productive work on memory that had fueled her writing, replaced by the darkness of a world war and the fact, for Porter, of her own aging. As she moved into and through her fifties, her thoughts on romantic love grew both more complex and bitter. She turned her attention from the pure gold dreams of early infatuation to the less tractable realities of marriage. While writing the novel she also wrote two lengthy essays on gender relations, both focusing on the issues she was at the same time exploring in *Ship of Fools*. The first, titled "Love and Hate," was published in *Mademoiselle* magazine in 1948; the second, "Marriage Is Belonging," appeared in *Mademoiselle* three years later.[17] "Love and Hate" is an utterly unromantic essay, suggesting that readers replace the fantasy of love with the actuality of hate. The essay begins with an ideal modern couple: "one of those gay, good-looking young pairs who ornament this modern scene rather more in profusion than ever before in our history." They both have their eyes wide open, assured that they can continue, in marriage and parenting, to "work at things that interest them." "Nothing romantic mind you; their feet are on the ground." Soon enough, however, despite her avowed clarity of mind, the "frank, charming, fresh-hearted young woman who married for love" is startled to discover that "she is capable of hating her husband" (182). For this Porter provides an analysis and explanation: the ideal of Romantic Love, being impossible, misleads, misrepresents, betrays, and finally, inevitably brings about its cruel counterpart, hate. She proclaims, "If it is not perfect, it is not love, and if it is not love, it is bound to be hate sooner or later" (184).

Of the two emotions, Porter argues, hate is the more believable, for it is based in human nature. Whereas love is a work of art, hatred is pure instinct. For the young woman, therefore, her hatred carries more validity; it is not something she has been taught to recognize or create. Writes Porter, "Her hatred is real as her love is real, but her hatred has the advantage at present because it works on a blind instinctual level, it is lawless; and her love is subjected to a code of ideal conditions, impossible by their very nature of fulfillment" (186). In the course of "Love and Hate," Porter does not reject completely the ideal of Romantic Love that complicated her own struggles for autonomous art and committed relationships. She allows the vision some appeal: "To a Western romantic such as I," she tells her reader, "though my views have been much modified by painful experience, it still seems to me a charming work of the human imagination." Rather than a full rejection of that "charming" fiction, love, Porter rather half-heartedly concludes that somewhere between the extremes of romantic idealism and "total depravity" lies human nature; this, acknowledged, allows us to achieve some imperfect "fragments of happiness" (185). However, despite her faintly platitudinous reconciliation, what remains most memorable in the essay is her dramatic and often reprinted statement on the impact and perceived veracity of the language of love and hate:

> Love. We are early taught to say it. I love you. We are trained to the thought of it as if there were nothing else, or nothing else worth having without it, or nothing worth having which it could not bring with it. Love is taught, always by precept, sometimes by example. Then hate, which no one meant to teach us, comes of itself. It is true that if we say I love you, it may be received with doubt, for there are times when it is hard to believe. Say I hate you, and the one spoken to believes it instantly, once for all. (183–84)

In its structure, "Marriage Is Belonging" also works with two opposing views. Porter initially holds in tension two contradictory positions on love—that it is an ideal achievement and that it is self-destroying. At first the essay defines marriage "as the art of belonging," but this definition slips swiftly into the language of warfare: "all too often the art, or perhaps only the strategy, and a risky one, of surrendering gracefully . . . as much of your living self as you can spare without incurring total extinction." The complex phrasing here does not mask the fact that she is defining marriage—a word that for her "instantly translates into 'love'"—as a dangerous battle in which the very real risk is the complete loss of self (187). Sexual desire is if anything even more dangerous; she defines it as "ecstatic reciprocal cannibalism . . . (Boy Eats Girl and vice versa)" (188). (The gluttonous lovers of her early fiction—Braggioni and Rubén—come to mind here.) To love is to surrender, be devoured, risk extinction, it is to invite violence against one's body and one's self. Yet this extraordinary essay goes on to movingly extol the Brownings for their ideal love, a love that Porter claims is "*very* old style" and yet also the "very newest thing, every day renewed in an endless series of . . . fortunate people" (192). Romantic love like that of the Brownings, she suggests, is traditional and perpetual. Porter makes no effort to reconcile the two views of love her essay presents. One thinks of the honeymoon couple moonily wandering the *Vera's* decks, untouched by the world that surrounds them.

In "Love and Hate," Porter had commented, somewhat bleakly, "There does exist a possibility for reconciliation between our desires for impossible satisfactions and the simple unalterable fact that we also desire to be unhappy and that we create our own sufferings; and out of those sufferings we salvage our fragments of happiness" (185). Her words leave no room for happiness except out of pain. The satisfactions we seek are "impossible"; our quest for unhappiness, however, is a "simple unalterable fact." The same thinking appears in *Ship of Fools*. A woman's desires are her enemies, the novel repeatedly demonstrates. Hatred and unhappiness are both inevitable and real, and both are often the outcome of desire. Love in the novel appears as a kind of hunger that cannot be controlled, like the "ecstatic reciprocal cannibalism . . . (Boy Eats Girl and vice versa)" of "Marriage Is Belonging." Jenny Brown, for example, repeatedly feels "gaunt and empty and famished," "starved and frozen out" by David Scott's self-absorption, a solitary "starved animal sitting by feeding on the wind of a daydream" (91–93). As Thomas Walsh effectively details in his discussion of the novel, metaphors suitable to cannibals and vampires recur throughout, "characters countering hatred with hatred in fear of being devoured by the other."[18]

Knowing all this, why do the women in *Ship of Fools* seek love, not once but again and again, moving in a seemingly endless, repetitive round of abject affection, rage, hatred, and separation and yet again reunion? David aptly describes his relationship with Jenny as "a terrible treadmill they mounted together and tramped round and round until they were wearied out or in despair" (43). There seems to be no simple answer, and the cycle of love and hatred that characterizes relationships in the novel seems terribly close to that of Porter's own experience. The descriptions of an "indwelling enemy," the images of famine or of a self slowly consumed by lovers, the exhausting circle of need and defensive flight appear for decades in Porter's papers. One might compare Jenny's feelings at one moment on her emotional seesaw: "She retreated at once, trying to turn her attention away from him, chilled with the familiar famished hollow in her midriff, suffused with the kind of suffering, so blind, so senseless she despised herself for it" (327), to Porter's notes on a love affair some time in the early 1920s: "Love affects me as a great sickness of the heart, a crushing nostalgia that withers me up, that leaves me fruitless and without hope."[19]

Or compare Mrs. Treadwell's reflections on her early marriage to autobiographical scraps Porter filed under "Writers and Writing." Mrs. Treadwell entered marriage full of romantic hope, living in "one soft shimmer" and dreaming of "the happiness she had expected, had been taught to expect, in first love." What she found were violence and disillusionment—"the long nightmare had set in"—and afterward years of recovery—she became "shady, shabby, lonely[,] transient" (210). Porter, too, found love debilitating. As she confessed in personal notes: "If I have said nothing of love it is because I really have nothing to say. . . . what it really did mean for me was a course, more or less prolonged, of fever and chills between us, and for myself, a slow wasting recovery. Every experience of love and marriage I had weakened me physically, depleted me materially, but above all worked some damage to the spirit, debased my natural belief in human love."[20] Consider also Miranda's thoughts on her marriage in *Old Mortality*: "the only feeling she could rouse in herself about it was an immense weariness as if it were an illness that she might one day hope to recover from."[21]

If we turn now from the general landscape of sexual relationships in *Ship of Fools* to its specific portrayal of a woman artist, it is not surprising to find Porter leaving no doubt what first and foremost impedes that woman's career: it is her relationship with a man. Eager to love and be loved, caught in seemingly endless vacillations of security and loss, Jenny allows her partner to influence all that she does, from her dress to her creative style, and David takes full advantage of her insecurity, relentlessly eroding her confidence as he seeks to diminish and contain her talent. In a moment of unpleasant self-congratulation, he thinks of his slow success: "Jenny, who had been brilliant as a macaw when he first fell in love with her, wearing for her own delight high, cool colors. . . . Little by little he had succeeded in undermining her confidence in this nonsensical way of painting. Her palette lowered in tone" (77). As is characteristic of Porter's portrayal of women artists, Jenny's body is as much her medium as is her canvas. Like the Princess, she wears—essentially embodies—her art. Thus aesthetic and physical attacks unite; as Jenny's confidence sinks, her colors darken and grow lifeless. "Gradually, too," David thinks approvingly, "she had taken to dressing in muted colors or black and white . . . and she was not painting much, but working almost altogether in charcoal or India ink" (77). *Ship of Fools* provides a simple, blunt answer to the question of David's antipathy toward Jenny's lively colors and freely expressive style. Like John Crowe Ransom, who, in Caroline Gordon's words, "can't bear for women to be serious about their art," David feels the phrase "woman artist" forms an unnatural union.[22] Although he professes to love Jenny, his unspoken thoughts reveal, repeatedly, that he loves her vocational choice not at all. "Deeply he hoped she would give it up altogether—there had never been a really good woman painter, nothing better than some superior disciple of a great man; it disturbed him to see a woman so out of place; and he did not believe in her talent for a moment" (77).

As a woman artist, it seems that Jenny is no more free to focus on her own subject matter than the women Porter wrote of in her 1925 review of the "Sex and Civilization" symposium. There she lamented that acting seemed a woman's greatest talent and hence she always serves as the "plastic medium for the expression of some one else's idea. She is creative only in so far as she can conceive this idea, add to it her own essential quality and bring forth from the thought germ a full born interpretation."[23] Jenny may not be a disciple, the only role David sees possible for a woman artist, but the work that brings her bread and butter is no less derivative. Rather than being fully free to paint as she likes, she must spend her time and talent as an illustrator, a necessity she bitterly resents. As she complains to David, "Even in Paris, if I ever get there, I'll still have to do those silly drawings for somebody's foul little stories" (53). Yet in *Ship of Fools*, Porter presents an even more bitter vision of the artist's venues. If she manages to avoid a role as medium for another's vision, she still sells herself. The marketplace prostitutes the artist's private life. It is David, in the face of Jenny's protesting idealism, who puts forth this grim interpretation of artistic success. When she proclaims, "I'm going to paint for myself." He responds, "I know, I know . . . and hope that somebody else likes it too, likes it well enough to buy it and take it home to live with" (55).

More disturbing than the dedication of the female artist's talents to the "expression of someone else's idea" is the view of her whole human self as a "plastic medium" for the male imagination. In the unfinished "The Lovely Legend," one of Porter's early stories of male artists and their models and inspirations discussed in chapter 3, Amado used and then discarded the gaunt prostitute Rosita, never loving his model but only "some fancy [he] had of her."[24] Likewise, David creates and re-creates a mercurial Jenny according to his own notions and desires: "he made her up out of odds and ends of stuff from his own rag-bag of adolescent dreams and imaginings" (450). As they prepare to disembark from the *Vera*, momentarily united, he admits to himself, "This new creature before him was certainly one he had created for himself, as he had created the other, out of stray stuffs of his own desire" (488). The relationship nurtures neither of these young lovers. Jenny's colors fade, but David cannot paint at all in her presence, and hence while they are together he produces nothing except blame: "there was something in her whole nature that obstructed the workings of his own; where she was painting he could not" (77). And when he is angry, he punishes her by restraining himself: "he no longer sketched in company with her," leaving Jenny to wonder "how long he would hold out" (408). David repeatedly enjoys moments when Jenny suffers: "the sight of her weakness and defeat gave him pleasure like no other," he admits to himself on the novel's concluding page (497). And in his malicious disrespect for her he has kinship with Freytag, who thinks of Jenny as a "teasing bitch," or William Denny, who advises David at one point, "If that bitch belonged to me, I'd break every bone in her" (170, 438).

For Jenny, the young woman artist, and her lover, David, love and violence walk hand in hand. As her most powerful expression of the destructive rage incipient in their relationship, Porter gives to Jenny a scene she herself had witnessed in Taxco, Mexico, and recorded in a letter to Caroline Gordon in 1930. As she traveled by bus along a dusty hot road, she saw a man and a woman armed with "knives and stones," blood-covered, locked in violent battle.[25] In Jenny's account the moment becomes a paradigm for the eternal battle between men and women: "abstract, purified of rage and hatred in their one holy dedicated purpose to kill each other. Their flesh swayed together and clung, their left arms were wound about each other's bodies as if in love" (144). Jenny revisits the scene repeatedly in dreams and, once, wakes in horror when the man's and woman's faces become "David's and her own" (145). Hatred and potential self-destruction lie at the heart of their relationship. For a woman who makes art, "spinning it out of [her] substance like a spider its web," as Porter once described her labors to her sister, love defeats rather than sustains creation, for it destroys the medium from which art draws its shape and substance.[26]

Responding to David's sexist assaults on Jenny's talent and his repeated denigration of her warm and changeable humanity, Darlene Harbour Unrue likens him to Gilbert Osmund from Henry James's *Portrait of a Lady*, the cold aesthete whom Isabel Archer belatedly realizes possesses the "faculty for making everything wither that he touched."[27] For Unrue, Jenny's recognition of David's rigid and hostile inner self represents one of the two crucial "affirmative" moments in Porter's otherwise bleak, "life-negating" novel.[28] Yet Jenny's recognition, albeit honest and painful, is also ineffectual and fleeting. It does not move her out of this self-destructive relationship; in fact, it draws her in. For as much as Jenny longs for independence, to make art for herself alone, to think and live freely, she longs equally powerfully to lose herself, to give in to others, to shed the painful burden of autonomy. Recalling her fantasy about Freytag—"If we could sleep together . . . and lose ourselves together for a little while, I'd be easy again" (92)—she experiences moments of reconciliation with David as a blurring of consciousness, times when her face wears "the gentle blinded look of abject tenderness" (148). In their final moment of concord, as the ship pulls into dock, Jenny snuggles "blissfully" against David and confesses, "David, darling, when you're like this, I could creep back inside and be your rib again!" (488). Longing to creep back into David, Jenny is longing to reverse her own creation, to escape the "burden" of her "self-hood." Such an escape lies at the core of her desires. She thinks of David, likewise, as seeking escape by returning to a kind of preexistence. Unlike her, however, he can literally retreat into her, sex providing a kind of return to the womb. There, she imagines, she will be burdened with him forever, "Like a petrified fetus for the rest of my life" (169). Regardless of the form love takes, whether she consumes her lover or subsumes herself in him, a sexual relationship diminishes rather than replenishes this young woman artist, diminishing her substantiality or implanting sterility at her creative core. At one point Jenny cries out to her lover, "Please, David, I can't help it. I'm just as much a prisoner in myself as you are in you" (432). But need repeatedly erodes knowledge throughout the long journey of *Ship of Fools*. Again and again this young woman artist forgets the pain and seeks the pleasure despite her plea to herself and God: "Oh, God, don't let me forget any more what really happened to me. Don't let me forget. Please help me!" (146).

So much works to damage and betray a woman artist, to distract her from her work and erode her courage, diminish her very being. Relationships with unsympathetic, predatory men, a marketplace that makes constant petty demands, and not least of all her own needy self, that insecure self that Porter painfully portrays as an indwelling enemy incurably hungry and cold. Jenny does have moments of startling self-recognition; there is no denying the pain of her self-awareness, but whether or not these lead her to personal change is fully debatable. In fact, Unrue's language is notably cautious when she concludes that Jenny makes "significant gains toward truth" in Porter's novel.[29] The world that surrounds the woman artist in *Ship of Fools* never nurtures recognition into action. Rather, it seems, unceasing need pulls awareness back into delusion. The woman artist may see and feel and know, but doing is impossible. Truth erodes, knowledge fades, and long-term personal goals are compromised again and again to satisfy immediate emotional hunger.

What can we make of this terrible portrait of the woman as a young artist? The intellectual energy that fueled Katherine Anne Porter's gender-thinking in her early years drained away over time, leaving only a bitter residue of anger and despair. *Ship of Fools* is an immense achievement, often brilliant, yet unremitting in its bitter view of human folly. We may all wish for a happier conclusion to Porter's long career, almost a century—from 1890 to 1980, from the cult of true womanhood to women's liberation, from rural west Texas to Paris, from Callie to Katherine Anne. Yet if we look once more at "The Princess," we must acknowledge that it is not just undeniably a remarkable and acute analysis of the relations of gender and art, it is also and equally undeniably an unhappy story. The Princess may resist her culture's dictates for ritual defloration, marriage, and childbearing, and she may produce intricate weaving and metalwork, following her own independent vision of beauty, but the price is physical pain and social alienation. In the end she commits suicide and her life story becomes the self-promoting property of a male poet. Porter's portrait of the artist as a young woman in "The Princess" confirms Wordsworth's grim prognosis: "We poets in our youth begin in gladness; but thereof comes in the end despondency and madness." However, Porter herself did not end in madness, although the monsters she grappled with throughout her long career gripped her life and work as the years passed and came to diminish her imagination of gender possibilities. Overall, Porter's life and work offer for our compassionate understanding and admiration a thinking woman's complex and ambivalent response to the changing discourses on sexuality and gender in American culture from the late nineteenth through the mid-twentieth century. If her long career did not end in gladness, it nevertheless represents an astonishing and significant achievement.

NOTES

INTRODUCTION

1. In *Uncollected Early Prose*, Alvarez and Walsh piece together Porter's typescript of "The Princess" (227–40), making this remarkable story available to Porter's readers.

2. Dinesen, *Last Tales*.

3. Wiegman, "Object Lessons," 368.

4. Wingrove, "Interpellating Sex," 869. One response to efforts such as Wingrove's to "pull down the pants" on feminist poststructuralism has been attention to the phenomenon of transsexuality. See, for example, essays in Epstein and Straub, *Body*.

5. Thompson, "Interview," 79.

6. Givner, *A Life*, 17.

7. Porter, "The Land That Is Nowhere," University of Maryland Libraries.

8. Porter, "Pull Dick—Pull Devil," University of Maryland Libraries.

9. Givner, *A Life*, 88.

10. Ibid., 106, 110.

11. The phrase "cult of domesticity" has been in common use since Barbara Welter's influential essay "The Cult of True Womanhood."

12. Porter, *Old Mortality*, 210.

13. Smith-Rosenberg, *Disorderly Conduct*, 253.

14. Simmons, "Women's Power," 171.

15. Simmons, "Companionate Marriage," 55–56. See also Simmons's essay "Modern Sexuality" and Jonathan Ned Katz's *Invention of Heterosexuality*, 79–81.

16. Smith-Rosenberg, *Disorderly Conduct*, 281. See also the chapter "Keeping Women Down" in Faderman, *Surpassing the Love of Men*, 332–40, and Faderman's more recent *To Believe in Women*, especially 160–64 and 308–16.

17. Ellis, *Studies*, 196.

18. Gilbert and Gubar, *No Man's Land*, 353.

19. Butler, "Performative Acts," 402.

20. Simpson, *Fable of the Southern Writer*, 157.

21. Ibid., 67.

22. Ibid., 92.

23. Porter, "The Life of St. Rose," University of Maryland Libraries.

24. "The First American Saint," in Porter, "*This Strange, Old World*," 113.

25. Braidotti, "Mothers, Monsters, and Machines," 65.

26. Gilbert and Gubar, *Madwoman in the Attic*, 51.

27. Barker, *Aesthetics and Gender*, 14.

28. When I coined this term I was not aware of Steven G. Smith's book titled with the same phrase, though not hyphenated: *Gender Thinking* (Philadelphia: Temple University Press, 1992). Although I applaud Smith for his "search for an adequate thought of gender" (xiii), I want to make clear that this book is in no way indebted to his efforts.

29. Stout, *Katherine Anne Porter*, 270, 289.

30. Brinkmeyer, *Artistic Development*, xi.

31. *El Heraldo*, December 14, 1920. Quoted in Walsh, *Katherine Anne Porter*, 20.

32. Hirsch, *Mother/Daughter Plot*, 95.

33. Wingrove, "Interpellating Sex," 878.

34. Givner, *A Life*, 4.

35. Thompson, "Interview," 83.

CHAPTER ONE. THE PRINCESS OF ART

1. As Nina Auerbach writes, "The wild magic of fairytales . . . seemed to license a new generation of writers . . . to be deviant, angry, even violent or satirical." *Forbidden Journeys*, 3.

2. Although the manuscript is undated, it was evidently composed sometime in the mid-twenties. As Joan Givner suggests, the story certainly is related to the other fairy tales Porter published in 1920, likewise tales of creative, self-transforming young women, two of them princesses as well (Givner, *A Life*, 144–45). However, "The Princess" was not written for a young audience. In fact, considering the story's content, it is unclear whether Porter intended it for publication at all. For an excellent, complementary analysis of this story, see Hait, "Gender and Creativity," 199–212.

3. This summary and analysis of "The Princess" is based primarily on the edited version provided by Alvarez and Walsh in *Uncollected Early Prose*. Subsequent page references will appear parenthetically in the text (here, 230). Working with a fragmented, much-edited typescript, these editors made excellent choices, patching together the most coherent narrative possible. However, at points alternate language or whole scenes from the typescripts are omitted in their version. Notes will be provided wherever I turn to materials from Porter's papers rather than the Alvarez and Walsh reconstruction of her unpublished work.

4. Willard, *City of the Sacred Well.*

5. Porter owned both the complete thirteen-volume set of Frazer's compendious work and the one-volume condensed version.

6. Frazer, *Golden Bough,* vii, viii. Quoted in Vickery, *Literary Impact,* 7. Vickery is an excellent resource for other texts addressing sexuality and religious ritual. Among the many studies more contemporary with Porter's story of the Princess, two are particularly fascinating resources: Sybille Yates's 1930 essay "Investigation of the Psychological Factors" and Clifford Howard's study *Sex Worship.*

7. Grosz, "Conclusion," 334.

8. Butler, *Gender Trouble,* 173.

9. Bloch and Ferguson, introduction to *Misogyny, Misandry, and Misanthropy,* viii.

10. Ibid., 249.

11. Ibid.

12. Gubar, "Blank Page," 250.

13. Gilbert and Gubar, *Madwoman in the Attic,* 79.

14. Ibid., 34.

15. Braidotti, "Mothers, Monsters, and Machines," 62.

16. This passage is drawn from the original typescript in the University of Maryland Libraries.

17. This conclusion of "The Princess" carries the same implications as the Eskimo people's cry near the close of "The Shattered Star," an earlier story discussed in chapter 2 that also presents a creative heroine who becomes a legend. There the glorious Northern Lights become a sign of Merah's, the male lover's, creative power, although they are solely the heroine Nayagta's creation.

18. Quoted in Rowe, "To Spin a Yarn," 60.

19. Ibid., 57. The tale of Philomela was a mainstay of nineteenth-century women writers. For a discussion of the image's recurring role, see Walker, *Nightingale's Burden.*

20. Rowe, "To Spin a Yarn," 57.

21. Katherine Anne Porter to Gay Porter Holloway, "All Soul's Eve," 1947, University of Maryland Libraries.

22. Rowe, "To Spin a Yarn," 58.

CHAPTER TWO. FAIRY TALES AND FOREIGNERS

1. Porter, *Uncollected Early Prose,* 231.

2. According to Alvarez and Walsh in *Uncollected Early Prose,* "Porter contracted to write children's stories derived from various sources"; hence the stories are "retold" (11). In private correspondence, Ruth Alvarez expressed her opinion of the originality of these earliest works: "I have no reason to believe that all three are not based on some original . . . although not Porter's own creative work, [these stories] contain

a significant amount of her own ideas, themes, obsessions, and stylistic signatures."
Letter of August 4, 1997.

3. Alvarez and Walsh, *Uncollected Early Prose*, 11.

4. Givner, *A Life*, 145.

5. Warner, *From the Beast*, xxiv.

6. Auerbach and Knoepflmacher, *Forbidden Journeys*, 3.

7. Canton, *Fairy Tale Revisited*, 13.

8. Zipes, *Fairy Tales*, 100.

9. Auerbach and Knoepflmacher, *Forbidden Journeys*, 13.

10. Swann Jones, *Fairy Tale*, 10.

11. Numerous studies record this fascination, best known among them, perhaps, Raymond Schwab's compendious *Oriental Renaissance* and Edward Said's influential *Orientalism*. For a discussion of the influence of Oriental narrative on American writers, see Luther S. Luedtke's introduction to *Nathaniel Hawthorne*, xv–xxiv.

12. Unless indicated otherwise, all quotations from these early tales will be from *Uncollected Early Prose* and will be cited by page number parenthetically. Here, 17.

13. "The Magic Ear Ring" significantly transforms "The Brave Princess," from Knowles, *Folk-Tales of Kashmir*, 197–202.

14. Swann Jones, *Fairy Tale*, 80.

15. Ibid., 13.

16. I am grateful here for the assistance of Professor Julie Cruikshank, University of British Columbia, who shared her knowledge of narrative traditions of subarctic peoples. Several book collections of folktales by far northern peoples were available during the early twentieth century, as well as stories collected by well-known scholars such as Franz Boas and Hans Rink and printed in studies such as the *Journal of American Folklore*. However, after extensive searching I have been unable to locate a tale that even resembles "The Shattered Star."

17. See chapter 4.

18. Givner, *A Life*, 145.

19. Porter, *Uncollected Early Prose*, 281. Subsequent page references will appear parenthetically in the text. The editors quote this passage and note that it "provides Porter's insight into her own character at a particular time in her life."

20. The editors of *Uncollected Early Prose* make a similar connection, p. 11.

21. Zonana, "Sultan and the Slave," 166. See also Perera, *Reaches of Empire*, especially chapter 4.

22. See Mieder and Dundes, *Wisdom of Many*.

23. *Webster's Seventh New Collegiate Dictionary* (Springfield, Mass.: G. and C. Merriam, 1965).

24. As Janis Stout has noted, "The unacknowledged children's stories Porter had published prior to 1922 had also developed the theme of a clever woman who outwits her rival." *Katherine Anne Porter*, 73.

25. In fact, as attentive readers have thoroughly demonstrated, the story is richly interwoven with Porter's own responses to the Mexican revolution and the fate of its indigenous people, both of which she wrote on eloquently after her own travels in Mexico between 1920 and 1922. My understanding of Porter's response to Mexico is indebted to the excellent scholarship of Ruth Alvarez and Thomas Walsh. Alvarez, "Royalty in Exile," 91–98; Walsh, *Katherine Anne Porter.*

26. See Coutts-Smith, "Some General Observations." As Marianna Torgovnik notes in her study *Gone Primitive*, "Primitivist discourse has affinities with the Orientalist discourse described by Said, [and] the Africanist discourse described by Miller" (252–53, n. 17).

27. See Brinkmeyer, *Artistic Development*, 57–59.

28. Torgovnik, *Gone Primitive*, 8.

29. Ibid., 18.

30. Porter, *Uncollected Early Prose*, 81.

31. For more extensive discussions of Porter and primitivism, see Stout, *Katherine Anne Porter*, especially chapter 4, and Brinkmeyer, *Artistic Development*, especially chapter 2.

32. Porter, *Uncollected Early Prose*, 79–80. Subsequent page references will appear parenthetically in the text.

33. Nance, *Katherine Anne Porter*, 15. In *Truth and Vision*, Darlene Unrue provides this summarizing observation: "'María Concepción' is about pure primitivism" (24).

34. Porter, *Collected Stories*, 3. Subsequent quotations from "María Concepción" will be from this edition, and page numbers will appear parenthetically in the text.

35. DeMouy, *Katherine Anne Porter's Women*, 21.

36. Alvarez, "Royalty in Exile," 95.

37. See, for example, DeMouy, *Katherine Anne Porter's Women*, 27, and Levy, *Fiction of the Home Place*, 135–36.

38. Tate "New Star," 352–53; Stout, *Katherine Anne Porter*, 311, n. 14.

39. Bartky, "Foucault," 28.

40. Marianna Torgovnik writes of several who sought alternatives in Africa. All were following their "desire to escape the limitations . . . which dictated that women define themselves through family, not work." *Primitive Passions*, 64.

CHAPTER THREE. BEAUTIFUL OBJECTS

1. Porter, *Uncollected Early Prose*, 231.

2. Betterton, *Looking On*, 204.

3. Porter, review of "Sex and Civilization." Page numbers will appear parenthetically in the text.

4. Pollock, *Vision and Difference*, 17.

5. Barker, *Aesthetics and Gender*, 14.

6. "The Evening," also briefly discussed in chapter 2, is included in Porter, *Uncollected Early Prose*, 218–26. All quotations from this story will be from this source unless otherwise indicated. Because the manuscript shifts about in point of view and is incomplete, it is not possible to state with any assurance Porter's final goals in "The Evening." But the text underscores her exploration of the sexual/sadistic bonds between passive women and controlling men, which rose out of her experiences in 1920s Mexico. In fact, among Alma's admirers, little Lino, who scrawls "obscene caricatures," is easily identified as Miguel Covarrubias, the young caricaturist who, with other members of Mexico's artist community, helped Porter organize an exhibition of Mexican folk art in 1922. The editors of *Uncollected Early Prose* have made an admirable effort to arrange the fragments into narrative order, and overall their decisions make sense. The text they create, however, establishes Gordito as the central character, setting aside fragments that focus more fully on Alma. Like them, I also feel the passages echoing T. S. Eliot's "The Love Song of J. Alfred Prufrock" belong near the end of the narrative.

7. Alvarez and Walsh include this passage in their "Notes on Texts," 281.

8. Berger, *Ways of Seeing*, 46–47.

9. Doane, "Film and the Masquerade," 184.

10. Kaplan, *Women and Film*, 26.

11. "The Evening," University of Maryland Libraries.

12. Ruth, *Issues in Feminism*, 90.

13. Porter, *Collected Stories*, 95, 97. All further quotations will be from this edition, unless otherwise indicated, and page numbers will appear parenthetically in the text.

14. DeMouy, *Katherine Anne Porter's Women*, 85–86.

15. In his study *Katherine Anne Porter and Mexico*, Thomas Walsh argues that Braggioni's sagging bulk "suggest[s] a repugnant picture of a woman in labor": "Braggioni's song and body work subliminally on Laura as a before-and-after object lesson of what could happen to her if she relaxed her vigilance. The pregnancy his body suggests does not give promise of new life, but only evidence of shameful, misshapen violation and danger of death in childbirth" (212). As we shall see, Porter inevitably associated childbirth with death, and thus imaged sexual relations as potentially murderous or self-destructive. Yet her simultaneous idealization of motherhood militates against a reading of a pregnant Braggioni. More likely he is a sexual threat; yet it is true that in covering over "the fullness of her breasts, like a nursing mother," Laura is covering over, or denying, her "natural" sexuality.

16. Bartky, "Foucault," 30.

17. Walsh, "Braggioni's Songs," 150.

18. Barthes, *Sade/Fourier/Loyola*, 31.

19. Lopez, *Conversations*, 75.

20. "The Collected Stories of Katherine Anne Porter—notes," University of Maryland Libraries.

21. De la Selva, "The Box of Sandalwood," in *Tropical Town*, 96.

22. "Notes on Mexico," University of Maryland Libraries.

23. "The Lovely Legend," University of Maryland Libraries.

24. Benstock and Ferris, introduction to *Footnotes*, 11. On barefoot dancing, see Janet Lyon's essay in this collection, "The Modern Foot," 272–81. Benstock and Ferris also include a version of Hans Christian Andersen's story "The Red Shoes," 305–10.

25. Porter, *Collected Stories*, 23. Subsequent page references will appear parenthetically in the text.

26. Likening Blanca to a blank page in a story about virginity and violation, I am invoking Isak Dinesen's feminist classic story "The Blank Page" discussed in an important reading by Susan Gubar, "'The Blank Page' and Issues of Female Creativity."

27. DeMouy, *Katherine Anne Porter's Women*, 32.

28. Ibid., 34.

29. Kaplan, *Women and Film*, 26.

30. Unrue, *Truth and Vision*, 115.

31. Porter, *Collected Stories*, 34. Subsequent page references will appear parenthetically in the text.

32. Unrue, *Truth and Vision*, 107.

33. The text of this drafted story, unpublished in Porter's lifetime, is pieced together in Porter, *Uncollected Early Prose*, 204–17. Unless otherwise indicated, quotations will be drawn from this version rather than Porter's typescripts, and subsequent page references will appear parenthetically in the text. Here, 207.

34. Porter, *Collected Essays*, 187.

35. "Mexico—notes," University of Maryland Libraries.

36. Ibid.

37. Porter, "The Life of St. Rose," University of Maryland Libraries.

CHAPTER FOUR. SEEKING THE MOTHER TONGUE

1. Porter, *Uncollected Early Prose*, 237.

2. Porter, "The Land That Is Nowhere," University of Maryland Libraries.

3. Ingman, *Women's Fiction*, 164.

4. My use of the phrase "bearing the word"—and indeed much of this chapter's theoretical grounding—is indebted to Margaret Homans's *Bearing the Word: Language and Female Experience in Nineteenth-Century Women's Writing*. Heather Ingman argues that drawing a connection between her mother's labors and her own allowed Virginia Woolf to affirm her choice to devote her life to her writing: "Finding a likeness between her mother and the artist in the act of creation freed the artist

in Woolf, helping her surmount her fear that writing was an act that unsexed her and isolated her from the world of women. It is precisely through creating that Woolf rejoins the mother" (*Women's Fiction*, 132).

5. Ingman, *Women's Fiction*, 164.

6. Porter, *Letters of Katherine Anne Porter*, 466–67.

7. Porter, *Collected Essays*, 71.

8. Homans, *Bearing the Word*, 142.

9. Porter, *Uncollected Early Prose*, 13.

10. Ibid., 15.

11. Homans, *Bearing the Word*, 18.

12. Ibid., 2.

13. Ibid., 7–9.

14. Porter, review of "Sex and Civilization." See chapter 3 of Porter, *This Strange, Old World*, for an extended discussion of this important review and its relation to central texts in Porter's gender-thinking. It is not surprising to find Porter engaged in psychoanalytic thinking about gender. Living from 1890 to 1980, she inhabited the same historical period as the "four 'founding mothers' of psychoanalysis": Helene Deutsch (1884–1982), Karen Horney (1885–1952), Anna Freud (1895–1982), and Mela- nie Klein (1882–1960). "In the inter-war period these female psychoanalysts were transforming Freud's patriarchal and phallocentric theories" (Ingman, *Women's Fiction*, 24).

15. University of Maryland Libraries.

16. Porter, "Here Is My Home," 3.

17. Portions of this typescript are also titled "Notes on a Decade" and overlap in content with another typescript titled "The Twenties." Also a response to Cowley's 1934 *Exiles Return*, "The Twenties" is dated in Porter's hand, "about 1942 or 43." As was characteristic of her writing on home, Porter follows her confession of rootless- ness with the claim that she did begin, in each and every place she settled, to put down roots, only to find the connection quickly destroyed. She writes, "Yet let me stand only an hour in one place, and when I lift my foot again you can hear the faint crackle of the tiny roots I had begun to thrust down, and except for the mystery of being which I cannot explain, it has seemed to me sometimes that I should have been rooted like a tree." Perpetually feeling that she has come home, perpetually feeling uprooted, Porter felt constantly homeless, torn up, unable to accept motion as her natural condition.

18. Shirley Scott, "Origins of Power," 47.

19. Porter, *Collected Essays*, 71.

20. Porter most fully defined her sources in a speech she gave to the American Women's Club of Paris in 1935. Describing her work on *Many Redeemers*, the speech anatomizes the material she drew upon while attempting to write "my own past re- told in the history of my family." Besides the material gathered from family anecdote

or historical records, she will draw on memory. During this period in her work, Porter saw memory as her central medium. This speech, much revised, was published under the title "Notes on Writing" in Porter's *Collected Essays*, 442–50.

21. Porter, *Collected Essays*, 449.

22. Italics Porter's. Katherine Anne Porter to Caroline Gordon, June 9, 1935, *Letters of Katherine Anne Porter*, 127.

23. Katherine Anne Porter to Welty, February 20, 1956, *Letters of Katherine Anne Porter*, 498.

24. Katherine Anne Porter to Robert Penn Warren, February 24, 1935, *Letters of Katherine Anne Porter*, 118.

25. "Go little Book . . ." dated preface to Porter, *Collected Stories*, v.

26. Porter, *The Old Order*, 327.

27. For provocative discussions of quilting and female creativity, see Showalter, "Piecing and Writing," and Ice, "Women's Aesthetics."

28. Kristeva, *Powers of Horror*, 54.

29. Ibid., 188–89.

30. Porter, "Notes on a Decade," University of Maryland Libraries.

31. Porter, *Collected Stories*, 175, 178.

32. Porter, *Collected Essays*, 489.

33. Porter, "Pull Dick—Pull Devil," University of Maryland Libraries.

34. "Notes, undated," University of Maryland Libraries.

35. Ibid.

36. Porter, "A Vision of Heaven," University of Maryland Libraries.

37. Givner, *A Life*, 37.

38. University of Maryland Libraries.

39. Katherine Anne Porter to Gay Porter Holloway, April 8, 1963, University of Maryland Libraries.

40. Porter, "Here Is My Home," 3.

41. Ibid.

42. Katherine Anne Porter to Glenway Wescott, January 23, 1941, *Letters of Katherine Anne Porter*, 190.

43. In the published version Porter omits this account of her perennial homelessness. Her draft indicates that originally she intended this passage to open the essay. University of Maryland Libraries.

44. Porter's notes are in the file titled "Anniversary in a Country Cemetery" in the University of Maryland Libraries collection. She mentions the visit to the grave and writing the poem there in letters to her sister Gay on October 28, 1950, and to an old family friend Cora Posey on February 28, 1956.

45. "Notes," undated, University of Maryland Libraries.

46. In her edited volume *Katherine Anne Porter's Poetry*, Darlene Harbour Unrue helpfully appends Porter's many revisions of this poem. See 154–55 and 170–72. Un-

rue also provides an insightful discussion of the poem's many revisions in relation to Porter's painful memories of her mother in her introductory essay.

47. Porter, *Collected Essays*, 489.

48. "Notes," Paris, 1932, University of Maryland Libraries.

49. In *Katherine Anne Porter's Poetry*, Unrue titles this poem "Time Has Heaped a Bitter Dust" and provides the following suggestion for a date, "written before 1936" (154).

50. Carter, "Prodigal Daughter," 89–90.

51. Ibid., 91.

52. Ibid., 88.

53. Hirsch, *Mother/Daughter Plot*, 35.

54. Carter, "Prodigal Daughter," 103.

55. Hirsch, *Mother/Daughter Plot*, 105.

56. Ibid., 36.

57. Porter, *Old Order*, 324. Subsequent page references will appear parenthetically in the text.

58. Porter, "Many Redeemers" folder, University of Maryland Libraries.

59. Shirley Scott convincingly links the image of the funeral in "The Fig Tree" to an event Porter vividly recalled from her own childhood. This recollection was, in Scott's words, "charged with the power of a submerged memory of her mother's death" ("Origins of Power," 49).

60. Shirley Scott's description of the mother's ordering presence suggests the goal of Miranda's rituals. By creating order herself, the child attempts to mitigate the confusion that follows her mother's death. Writes Scott, "The mother's presence is—for a time at least—an explanation of the world, an order and an ordering of reality. Her sudden absence could not but entail an early and almost overwhelming experience of loss and of the world's inexplicability" ("Origins of Power," 46–47).

61. Reprinted in Givner, *A Life*, 69.

62. Unrue, *Truth and Vision*, 52.

63. DeMouy, *Katherine Anne Porter's Women*, 140–43.

64. "Recent Southern Fiction: A Panel Discussion," Wesleyan College, October 28, 1960. In Givner, *Conversations*, 55.

65. Ruoff, "Katherine Anne Porter," 65.

66. Rooke and Wallis, "Myth and Epiphany," 68.

67. De Vries, *Dictionary*. See also Anthony S. Mercante, *The Facts on File Encyclopedia of World Mythology and Legend* (New York: Oxford University Press, 1988), and F. L. Cross, ed., *The Oxford Dictionary of the Christian Church*, 3rd. ed. (New York: Oxford University Press, 1997).

68. Bynum, *Gender and Religion*, 8.

69. Unrue, *Truth and Vision*, 151–52.

70. DeMouy, *Katherine Anne Porter's Women*, 144.

71. University of Maryland Libraries.

1. Porter, *Uncollected Early Prose*, 238. The editors print the final phrase here as "some of the people forgot themselves and argued with her [when] suddenly. . . ." However, Porter's typescript clearly indicates "laughed," not "argued."

2. Bakhtin, *Rabelais and His World*, 10.

3. Ibid., 34.

4. Russo, "Female Grotesques," 325.

5. Bakhtin, *Rabelais and His World*, 11.

6. Diane Price Herndl in "The Dilemmas of a Feminine Dialogic" further describes the complexity and inclusiveness of carnival laughter: "It is both festive and mocking; it is directed at everyone—those in power and those subjected to it . . . opposed to the 'official'" (9).

7. Russo, "Female Grotesques," 325.

8. Porter, *Uncollected Early Prose*, 238.

9. Core, "Holiday," 121.

10. Ibid., 124.

11. Unrue, *Truth and Vision*, 104.

12. Core, "Holiday," 120.

13. Unrue, *Truth and Vision*, 147.

14. Porter, *Collected Stories*, 428. Subsequent page references will appear parenthetically in the text.

15. Porter, "Holiday," University of Maryland Libraries.

16. Givner, *A Life*, 5.

17. Givner, *A Life*, 171, 434.

18. In the upcoming discussion of Porter's drafts of "Holiday," I am referring to the three typescripts of the story in the University of Texas collection. In the Porter collection at the University of Maryland Libraries, there are corrected galleys and a clean typescript of the final version.

19. Porter consistently identified the Koontzes as German, not Swiss—another way in which she expressed her antipathy for their patriarchal family structure. See Givner, *A Life*, 88.

20. Ibid., 96.

21. Ibid., 88–95.

22. Ibid., 98.

23. Porter, *The Old Order*, 337.

24. Brinkmeyer, *Artistic Development*, 208.

25. DeMouy, *Katherine Anne Porter's Women*, 169.

26. Ibid., 167.

27. Warren, *Katherine Anne Porter*, 11.

28. German was also the language of the Koontzes, whom Porter always viewed as German despite their Swiss descent. In "Holiday" the narrator's knowledge of

German is limited to sentimental clichés; wise now, she is aware that such knowledge, taken to heart, is "deadly." Most likely through her youthful marriage to John Koontz, Porter first confronted the disjunction between romantic language and actual experience.

29. Anne Goodwyn Jones, unpublished essay titled "Katherine Anne Porter's 'Holiday' and the Gender of Agrarianism." I am grateful to Anne Jones for generously sharing her paper with me.

30. Gilbert and Gubar, *Madwoman in the Attic*, 85.

31. Givner, *A Life*, 5.

32. DeMouy, *Katherine Anne Porter's Women*, 166.

33. Gilbert and Gubar, *Madwoman in the Attic*, 79.

34. DeMouy, *Katherine Anne Porter's Women*, 176.

35. It is interesting that women who have become mothers cannot hear this grief. As she heads toward the kitchen, the narrator sees Gretchen peacefully asleep, "curled up around her baby" (433).

36. Joan Givner, address at Katherine Anne Porter centennial conference, Georgia State University, Atlanta, 1990. I am grateful to Joan Givner for sending me a copy of her unpublished talk. In her preface to the revised edition of *Katherine Anne Porter: A Life*, Givner includes portions of this address.

37. Bakhtin, *Rabelais and His World*, 10.

38. Ibid., 34.

39. Ibid.

CHAPTER SIX. RUMORS AND REPRESENTATIONS

1. Porter, *Uncollected Early Prose*, 235.

2. Marcus, "Liberty, Sorority, Misogyny," 61.

3. Walsh, *Katherine Anne Porter*, 64. The rabbit's cut-open womb, an image linking pregnancy with death, expresses both Porter's own abortion and her more general fear of pregnancy, her fear that she, like her mother, would "die under torture." Porter's childlessness, whether due to a physical cause—as Joan Givner suggests—or to an insurmountable fear of childbirth, enhanced her feelings of homelessness and guilt.

4. From a different direction, Unrue also lightly approaches the interconnections between Porter's relationship to her mother, her personal hope for a child, and her art in her sensitive essay "Katherine Anne Porter's Birthdays."

5. The first draft in her papers is dated 1923 in her hand; however, she wrote this date in 1960. University of Maryland Libraries.

6. Quoted in Givner, *A Life*, 170. Porter's account to Schwartz is somewhat fanciful. Some of her notes for stories predating 1924 show that she was already considering Miranda as the name for an autobiographical character.

7. See Givner, A Life, 92, 170–76. It must be noted that other Porter scholars disagree with Givner and attest to the reality of the pregnancy.

8. University of Maryland Libraries.

9. Porter, Uncollected Early Prose, 235.

10. "Notes," October 20, 1954, University of Maryland Libraries. For a discussion of Porter's revelation and related correspondence, see Givner, A Life, 409–11.

11. Porter, "The Dark Forest," University of Maryland Libraries.

12. Porter, "Season of Fear," University of Maryland Libraries. All quotations from this unfinished story will be from this source.

13. University of Maryland Libraries.

14. Porter, Collected Stories, 269–70.

15. Porter, "Vision of Heaven," University of Maryland Libraries. All quotations from this unfinished story will be from this source.

16. Givner, A Life, 173.

CHAPTER SEVEN. ROMANTIC LOVE

1. Porter, Uncollected Early Prose, 233.

2. Duncan, My Life, 239.

3. Fishbein, Rebels in Bohemia, 199. For other discussions of cultural changes in views of sexuality, see Newton, "Mythic Mannish Lesbian"; Trimberger, "Feminism, Men and Modern Love"; Behling, Masculine Woman; and Franzen, Spinsters and Lesbians.

4. Newton, "Mythic Mannish Lesbian," 285.

5. Trimberger, "Feminism, Men and Modern Love," 143.

6. "Notes," University of Maryland Libraries.

7. Quoted in Rollyson, Lillian Hellman, 68.

8. Trimberger, "Feminism, Men and Modern Love," 143.

9. For an insightful discussion of these relationships, see ibid. Trimberger quotes lines from a play cowritten by husband and wife Hutchins Hapgood and Neith Boyce. Writing the heroine's lines, Boyce eloquently expresses the ways in which a woman artist sees her own achievements compromised by her male companion: "You have interfered with me, taken my time and strength, and prevented me from accomplishing great works for the good of humanity. . . . You have wanted to treat our relation, and me, as clay, and model it into the form you saw in your imagination" (141). Boyce's modern woman sounds remarkably like Katherine Anne Porter.

10. Nochlin, Women, Art and Power, 32.

11. Unrue, Katherine Anne Porter's Poetry, 85.

12. University of Maryland Libraries.

13. Ibid.

14. Porter, "The Land That Is Nowhere," University of Maryland Libraries.

15. Porter, *Collected Essays*, 30–31.

16. Ibid., 32.

17. Ibid., 34.

18. Cowley, *Exile's Return*, 291.

19. Porter, "The Twenties," University of Maryland Libraries.

20. Trimberger, "Feminism, Men and Modern Love," 141.

21. Porter, "Twenties."

22. "Notes," University of Maryland Libraries.

23. "The Art of Katherine Mansfield," University of Maryland Libraries.

24. "Quetzalcoatl" and "A Wreath for the Gamekeeper" in Porter, *Collected Essays*.

25. "Notes," University of Maryland Libraries.

26. "Mexico—notes," University of Maryland Libraries.

27. "Many Redeemers," University of Maryland Libraries.

28. Porter, *Uncollected Early Prose*, 226

29. Porter, *Collected Stories*, 97. Subsequent page references will appear parenthetically in the text.

30. West, "Katherine Anne Porter," 125.

31. University of Maryland Libraries.

32. Ibid.

33. Porter, *Collected Stories*, 59. Subsequent page references will appear parenthetically in the text.

34. Porter, *Collected Essays*, 153–54.

35. Porter, *Collected Stories*, 295. Subsequent page references will appear parenthetically in the text.

36. Givner, *A Life*, 129.

37. Ibid., 173.

38. Porter, *Letters of Katherine Anne Porter*, 71.

39. Porter, *Collected Stories*, 110. Subsequent page references will appear parenthetically in the text.

40. DeMouy, *Katherine Anne Porter's Women*, 66.

41. Examples abound. In *The Madwoman in the Attic*, Sandra Gilbert and Susan Gubar cleverly link Adrienne Rich's phrase "a thinking woman sleeps with monsters" ("Snapshots of a Daughter-in-Law"), echoed here, to the clustered images of domesticity and imprisonment, silence and mad or monstrous presence, that recur in nineteenth-century women's fiction (89).

42. Porter, "The Life of St. Rose," University of Maryland Libraries.

43. DeMouy, *Katherine Anne Porter's Women*, 69.

44. Porter, *Collected Essays*, 187.

45. Porter, *Collected Stories*, 392, 394.

46. University of Maryland Libraries.

47. Although Joan Givner states that Porter married Stock, there is no evidence that a legal union ever took place.

48. Givner, *A Life*, 174–75.

49. Quoted in ibid., 175.

50. Porter, "Spivvelton Mystery," 74. Subsequent page references will appear parenthetically in the text.

CHAPTER EIGHT. GENDER AND COSTUME

1. Porter, *Uncollected Early Prose*, 239–40.

2. Bonnie Kime Scott, introduction, 2.

3. Gilbert, "Costumes of the Mind," 393.

4. Gilbert and Gubar, *No Man's Land*, 331–32.

5. Butler, *Gender Trouble*, 179.

6. Ibid., 175.

7. As her longtime friend and admired fellow writer Glenway Wescott notes, writing in his journal, "Her attitude toward homosexual writers—Gide, Maugham, even Forster—becomes an expression of her (deadly) lonesomeness." *Continual Lessons*, 302.

8. "Criticism." University of Maryland Libraries.

9. Porter, *Collected Essays*, 251–70.

10. Ibid., 257–69.

11. Gilbert and Gubar, *No Man's Land*, 331.

12. Porter, *Collected Essays*, 265.

13. Porter, "Reflections on Willa Cather," in *Collected Essays*, 33–34. Given our current understanding of Cather's sexuality, there is, of course, an irony to Porter's adulation of this literary precursor, whom she describes, unlike Stein, as pure product of "provincial farming people . . . rock-based in character, a character shaped in an old school of good manners, good morals" (31).

14. Porter, *Collected Essays*, 37.

15. In the margin of the typescript, Porter noted "about 1942 or 3."

16. This early version is reprinted in Porter, *Uncollected Early Prose*, 256–71.

17. Porter, *Collected Stories*, 166. Subsequent page references will appear parenthetically in the text.

18. Porter, *Uncollected Early Prose*, 266.

19. Smith-Rosenberg, *Disorderly Conduct*, 288.

20. See the discussion in Jones, "Gender and the Great War."

21. Porter, *Collected Stories*, 295. Subsequent page references will appear parenthetically in the text.

22. Givner, *A Life*, 126. In her preface to the revised biography, Givner complicates this simple division of Porter's life into a before and after. With hitherto

unavailable material revealing Porter's extended hospitalization in 1916 and 1917 for tuberculosis, Givner writes, "New evidence convinces me that Porter substituted the more socially acceptable 'flu' for the devastating experience of her earlier years, which actually did constitute a divide in her life, and made her feel radically different from others" (2). Composing "Pale Horse, Pale Rider," Porter combined and condensed these several years of illness with imagery of the war into Miranda's intense and highly symbolic experience of near-death and transformation.

23. Another definition of "alter" is "Castrate, spay . . . to become different" (*Webster's Seventh New Collegiate Dictionary* [Springfield, Mass.: G. and C. Merriam, 1965]).

24. Porter's friend Glenway Wescott attributes her homophobia to incidents that occurred in the late 1940s in Hollywood. Writing in 1955 in his journal about a party he attended at Porter's, he notes, "Her nephew Paul was there, whom George [Platt Lynes] passingly seduced years ago. I fancy that may have been the start of her anti-homosexuality. It was when she was living with George for three or four months in Hollywood and felt some inclination to marry him. There are more plots in our lives than in our books" (*Continual Lessons*, 378). The events with McCullers and Crane, however, both predate Porter's stints as a Hollywood scriptwriter.

25. "Hart Crane," University of Maryland Libraries.

26. Ibid. The same feelings shaped her unpublished comments on Djuna Barnes's *Nightwood*. She read *Nightwood* with horrified interest and took the time to write about it privately, puzzling through her response.

27. Unpublished drafts and notes, University of Maryland Libraries.

28. Both Joan Givner, Porter's biographer, and Elinor Langer, biographer of Porter's longtime friend Josephine Herbst, suggest that Herbst may have expressed physical attraction for Porter, and that Porter responded very negatively and perhaps maliciously. See Givner's preface to the revised edition of *Katherine Anne Porter: A Life*, and Langer, *Josephine Herbst*.

29. Porter was especially close to Glenway Wescott, although their friendship was not without tension. Wescott's journals record his growing frustration with Porter over the years, noting in particular her garrulity, emotional neediness, and self-deception, particularly in matters of love and money. However, even when he found her character almost insufferable, Wescott continued to view Porter with great insight and, often, some humor.

30. Porter, *Katherine Anne Porter's French Song-Book* (New York: Harrison of Paris, 1933). Reprinted in *Katherine Anne Porter's Poetry*, ed. Darlene Harbour Unrue, 95–149 (Columbus: University of South Carolina Press, 1996).

31. Lopez, *Conversations*, 250.

32. Porter, *Letters of Katherine Anne Porter*, 169, 172.

33. Kramarae and Treichler, *Feminist Dictionary*, 173.

34. Stout, *Katherine Anne Porter*, 100–101.

35. Davis, "Personality versus Physique," 90.

36. Weiermair, *George Platt Lynes*, 10.

37. Quoted in ibid., 9.

38. Borklund, "George Platt Lynes," 623.

39. Van Leer, *Queening of America*, 20. For similar definitions, see also Bronski, *Culture Clash*, and Meyer, *Politics and Poetics of Camp*.

40. In *Gaiety Transfigured*, David Bergman lists "the elements of classic camping: 1) both the author and the reader wear disguises—the disguise of heterosexuality; 2) the masquerade enforces an intimacy even as it distances the participants in the masquerade; 3) it is maintained with a buoyant humor, the 'camp' laugh; 4) the entire affair is conducted in an elaborate style which, while seemingly superficial, reveals to the initiated an unspoken subtext" (111).

41. Quoted in Borklund, "George Platt Lynes," 623.

42. Thanks to colleague Matt Rohn.

43. Porter's marginalia on the photograph is reproduced in *Letters of Katherine Anne Porter*.

44. Givner, *A Life*, 358.

45. Young and Hindle, *Republic of Letters*, 172–73.

CHAPTER NINE. SOUTHERN BELLE, SOUTHERN LADY

1. Porter, *Uncollected Early Prose*, 237.

2. Thompson, "Interview," 83.

3. Stout, "Writing in the Borderlands."

4. King, *Southern Renaissance*, 51.

5. Stout, "On Stage," 33. Stout is quoting from Porter's *Collected Essays*, 160. See also Stout's extended discussion of Porter's ties to the Agrarians and to the South in *Katherine Anne Porter: A Sense of the Times*, 115–41.

6. For a detailed overview of Porter's relationship with the Agrarian/Fugitive circle, see Beck, *Fugitive Legacy*, 171–87.

7. Tate, "Profession of Letters," 520, 526, 530.

8. Donaldson, "Gender," 492.

9. "Woman Artists," *Southern Review* 5 (1867): 318. Quoted in Donaldson, "Gender," 494.

10. Waldron, *Close Connections*, 507.

11. Prown, *Revising Flannery O'Connor*, 2.

12. Ibid., 3.

13. Fitzgerald, *Habit of Being*, 176. Quoted in Prown, *Revising Flannery O'Connor*, 15.

14. Givner, *A Life*, 17.

15. Allen Tate to Andrew Lytle, December 21, 1928, in *Lytle-Tate Letters*, ed. Young and Jackson, 15.

16. Andrew Lytle to Allen Tate and Caroline Gordon, August 18, 1832, in ibid., 61.

17. Thompson, "Interview," 83.

18. Stout, "On Stage," 27.

19. Porter's unpublished papers in the University of Maryland Libraries include notes and outlines for *Many Redeemers* in several places. Most of the material connected with this project is in the files labeled "Legend and Memory" and "Many Redeemers"; however, references to the project and some manuscripts clearly connected to it are scattered throughout the Porter collection, several in the numerous files generically titled "Notes." Other titles she adopted at times for portions of the project include "Midway in This Mortal Life" and "Legend and Memory."

20. Allen Tate to Andrew Lytle, "Xmas Eve, 1932," in *Lytle-Tate Letters*, 77.

21. University of Maryland Libraries.

22. King, *Southern Renaissance*, 51.

23. Givner, *A Life*, 43, 45.

24. Gaines, *Southern Plantation*.

25. Givner, *A Life*, 36–37.

26. Porter, *Old Mortality*, 220–21.

27. University of Maryland Libraries.

28. Ibid. This passage from a letter to her sister invites further quotation: "Families are deathly bear traps. The very thought of falling into the hands of mine scares the pee out of me. . . . You'd better take steps to get a little free . . . before it is everlastingly too late. . . . I would have been dead twenty five years ago if I'd stayed on." Katherine Anne Porter to Gay Porter Holloway, December 13, 1945.

29. Givner, *A Life*, 20.

30. Katherine Anne Porter to Gay Porter Holloway, September 20, 1952, University of Maryland Libraries.

31. Givner, *A Life*, 26.

32. Katherine Anne Porter to Caroline Gordon, June 9, 1935, in *Letters of Katherine Anne Porter*.

33. I am quoting from the typescript titled "Legend and Memory" in the University of Maryland Libraries. A much-revised version appears in Porter's *Collected Essays* under the title "My First Speech."

34. Ibid.

35. February 20, 1956, in *Letters of Katherine Anne Porter*, 498.

36. University of Maryland Libraries.

37. Ransom, "Reconstructed but Unregenerate," 4.

38. Gilbert and Gubar, *No Man's Land*, 2:327.

39. Brittin, *Edna St. Vincent Millay*.

40. Bloom, introduction, 4.

41. Stout, "On Stage," 29, 30.

42. Thompson, "Interview," 78.

43. Young and Hindle, *Republic of Letters*, 172–73.

44. Andrew Lytle to Allen Tate, April 28, 1941, in *Lytle-Tate Letters*, 171.

45. Wescott, *Continual Lessons*, 275–76.

46. Porter, *Old Mortality*, 176, 181, 175. Subsequent page references will appear parenthetically in the text.

47. University of Maryland Libraries.

48. Prown, *Revising Flannery O'Connor*, 28.

49. Tate, "Elegy for Eugenesis," in *Collected Poems*, 178.

50. May 4, 1940, in Porter, *Letters of Katherine Anne Porter*, 176.

51. See the work of Anne Firor Scott, Louise Westling, Richard King, and others.

52. Porter, *Collected Stories*, 365.

53. DeMouy, *Katherine Anne Porter's Women*, 153. See also Lorraine DiCicco's fascinating essay on chlorosis or "greensickness" cited below.

54. DiCicco, "Dis-ease," 91.

55. Prown, *Revising Flannery O'Connor*, 32.

56. Porter, "Gift of Woman," 29, 32.

57. The typescript of this interview with Alice Denham, located in the University of Maryland Libraries, is undated. However, during the interview Porter expresses outrage about the footprints recently left on the moon. Her comments place the interview sometime shortly after July 21, 1969.

CHAPTER TEN. NO SAFE HARBOR

1. Porter, *Uncollected Early Prose*, 240.

2. The most thorough account of the novel's autobiographical material appears in Walsh, *Katherine Anne Porter*.

3. Ibid., 205, 229. See also Stout, *Katherine Anne Porter*, 215.

4. Katherine Anne Porter to Caroline Gordon, January 23, 1946, University of Maryland Libraries.

5. Brinkmeyer, *Artistic Development*, 219.

6. Ibid., 208.

7. Unrue, *Truth and Vision*; Spence, "Looking-Glass Reflections."

8. Joan Givner repeatedly draws these connections in *A Life*. For examples, see the following: La Condesa, 401–3; Mrs. Treadwell, 317; Jenny Brown, 246–47.

9. Porter, *Ship of Fools*, 313. Subsequent page references will appear parenthetically in the text.

10. For a discussion of Porter's response to critics who found Mrs. Treadwell's actions reprehensible, see Givner, *A Life*, 465–66.

11. Porter, *Collected Stories*, 405.

12. Ibid., 24.

13. The "angel"/"whore" phrases are from Porter's early unfinished story "The Evening" in *Uncollected Early Prose*.

14. Porter, *Collected Stories*, 344–45.

15. Darlene Harbour Unrue provides an excellent discussion of the novel's portrayal of sexism as one of the several systems through which human beings avoid truly knowing one another. See *Truth and Vision*, especially 190–91.

16. Walsh, *Katherine Anne Porter*, 224.

17. Both were reprinted in Porter, *Collected Essays*. "Love and Hate" appeared with a new title, "The Necessary Enemy." Subsequent page references will appear parenthetically in the text.

18. Walsh, *Katherine Anne Porter*, 212.

19. Scrap dated 1921 in file "Dove of Chapalco," University of Maryland Libraries.

20. University of Maryland Libraries. Internal evidence suggests a date after 1950.

21. Porter, *Collected Stories*, 213.

22. Waldron, *Close Connections*, 199.

23. Porter, review of "Sex and "Civilization," 23.

24. Porter, "Lovely Legend," in *Uncollected Early Prose*, 216–17.

25. Katherine Anne Porter to Caroline Gordon, August 13, 1930, University of Maryland Libraries.

26. Katherine Anne Porter to Gay Holloway, "All Souls Eve" 1947, University of Maryland Libraries.

27. Unrue, *Truth and Vision*, 203.

28. Ibid., 217.

29. Ibid., 216.

BIBLIOGRAPHY

WORKS BY KATHERINE ANNE PORTER

The Collected Essays and Occasional Writings of Katherine Anne Porter. New York: Delacorte, 1970.

The Collected Stories of Katherine Anne Porter. New York: Harcourt Brace, 1979.

"The Gift of Woman." *Woman's Home Companion.* December 1956, 29–32, 56.

"Here Is My Home." *Perfect Home.* November 1954, 3.

Katherine Anne Porter's Poetry. Edited with an introduction by Darlene Harbour Unrue. Columbia: University of South Carolina Press, 1996.

Letters of Katherine Anne Porter. Selected and edited by Isabel Bayley. New York: Atlantic, 1990.

Ship of Fools. Boston: Little, Brown, 1962.

"The Spivvleton Mystery." *Ladies Home Journal,* August 1971, 74–75, 101.

This Strange, Old World: And Other Book Reviews by Katherine Anne Porter. Edited by Darlene Harbour Unrue. Athens: University of Georgia Press, 1991.

Uncollected Early Prose of Katherine Anne Porter. Edited by Ruth Alvarez and Thomas Walsh. Austin: University of Texas Press, 1993.

OTHER WORKS

Adler, Cyril, and Allan Ramsey, trans. *Told in the Coffee House: Turkish Tales.* New York: Macmillan, 1898.

Alvarez, Ruth. "Royalty in Exile: Pre-Hispanic Art and Ritual in 'Maria Concepcion.'" In *Critical Essays on Katherine Anne Porter,* 91–98. New York: G. K. Hall, 1997.

Auerbach, Nina, and U. C. Knoepflmacher, eds. *Forbidden Journeys: Fairy Tales and Fantasies by Victorian Women Writers.* Chicago: University of Chicago Press, 1992.

Bakhtin, Mikhail. *Rabelais and His World.* Translated by Helene Iswolsky. Cambridge, Mass.: MIT Press, 1968.

Barker, Deborah. *Aesthetics and Gender in American Literature: Portraits of the Woman Artist*. London: Associated University Presses, 2000.

Barthes, Roland. *Sade/Fourier/Loyola*. Translated by Richard Miller. New York: Hill and Wang, 1976.

Bartky, Sandra Lee. "Foucault, Femininity and the Modernization of Patriarchal Power." In *The Politics of Women's Bodies: Sexuality, Appearance, and Behavior*, edited by Rose Weitz, 25–45. New York: Oxford University Press, 2003.

Beck, Charlotte. *The Fugitive Legacy: A Critical History*. Baton Rouge: Louisiana State University Press, 2001.

Behling, Laura. *The Masculine Woman in America, 1890–1935*. Chicago: University of Illinois Press, 2001.

Benstock, Shari, and Suzanne Ferris, eds. *Footnotes: On Shoes*. New Brunswick: Rutgers University Press, 2001.

Berger, John. *Ways of Seeing*. London: Penguin, 1987.

Bergman, David. *Gaiety Transfigured: Gay Self-Representation in American Literature*. Madison: University of Wisconsin Press, 1991.

Betterton, Rosemary. *Looking On: Images of Femininity in the Visual Arts and Media*. New York: Pandora, 1987.

Bloch, R. Howard, and Frances Ferguson. *Misogyny, Misandry, and Misanthropy*. Berkeley: University of California Press, 1989.

Bloom, Harold. Introduction to *Katherine Anne Porter: Modern Critical Views*. New York: Chelsea House, 1986.

Borklund, Elmer. "George Platt Lynes." In *Contemporary Photographers*. 2nd ed., 623. London: St. James Press, 1988.

Braidotti, Rosi. "Mothers, Monsters, and Machines." In *Writing on the Body: Female Embodiment and Feminist Theory*, edited by Katie Conboy, Nadia Medina, and Susan Stanbury, 59–79. New York: Columbia University Press, 1997.

Brinkmeyer, Robert. *Katherine Anne Porter's Artistic Development: Primitivism, Traditionalism, Totalitarianism*. Baton Rouge: Louisiana State University Press, 1993.

Brittin, Norman A. *Edna St. Vincent Millay*. Boston: Twayne, 1982.

Bronski, Michael. *Culture Clash: The Making of Gay Sensibility*. Boston: South End Press, 1984.

Butler, Judith. *Gender Trouble: Feminism and the Subversion of Identity*. New York: Routledge, 1999.

———. "Performative Acts and Gender Constitution: An Essay in Phenomenology and Feminist Theory." In *Writing on the Body: Female Embodiment and Feminist Theory*, edited by Katie Conboy, Nadia Medina, and Susan Stanbury, 401–17. New York: Columbia University Press, 1997.

Bynum, Caroline Walker, ed. *Gender and Religion: On the Complexity of Symbols*. Boston: Beacon Press, 1986.

Canton, Katia. *The Fairy Tale Revisited*. New York: Peter Lang, 1994.

Carter, Nancy Corson. "The Prodigal Daughter: A Parable Re-Visioned." *Soundings: An Interdisciplinary Journal* 68.1 (Spring 1985): 88–105.

Core, George. "'Holiday': A Version of Pastoral." In *Katherine Anne Porter: A Collection of Critical Essays,* edited by Warren, 117–25.

Coutts-Smith, Kenneth. "Some General Observations on the Problem of Cultural Colonialism." In *The Myth of Primitivism,* edited by Susan Hiller, 14–31. New York: Routledge, 1991.

Cowley, Malcolm. *Exile's Return: A Literary Odyssey of the 1920's.* New York: Viking, 1951.

Davis, Melody. "Personality versus Physique." Review of *George Platt Lynes: Photographs from the Kinsey Institute,* edited by James Crump. *Art Journal* 53.2 (Summer 1994): 88–92.

De la Selva, Salomon. *Tropical Town and Other Poems.* New York: John Lane, 1918.

DeMouy, Jane Krause. *Katherine Anne Porter's Women: The Eye of Her Fiction.* Austin: University of Texas Press, 1993.

De Vries, Ad. *Dictionary of Symbols and Imagery.* 2nd ed. Amsterdam: North Holland Publishing, 1976.

DiCicco, Lorraine. "The Dis-ease of Katherine Anne Porter's Greensick Girls in 'Old Mortality.'" *The Southern Literary Journal* 33.2 (Spring 2001): 80–93.

Dinesen, Isak. *Last Tales.* New York: Random House, 1957.

Doane, Mary Ann. "Film and the Masquerade: Theorizing the Female Spectator." In *Writing on the Body: Female Embodiment and Feminist Theory,* edited by Katie Conboy, Nadia Medina, and Susan Stanbury, 176–94. New York: Columbia University Press, 1997.

Donaldson, Susan V. "Gender, Race, and Allen Tate's Profession of Letters in the South." In *Haunted Bodies: Gender and Southern Texts,* 492–518. Charlottesville: University of Virginia Press, 1997.

Duncan, Isadora. *My Life.* Garden City, N.Y.: Horace Liveright, 1927.

Ellis, Havelock. *Studies in the Psychology of Sex.* Vol. 2. New York: Random House, 1936.

Epstein, Julia, and Kristina Straub, eds. *Body Guards: The Cultural Politics of Gender Ambiguity.* New York: Routledge, 1991.

Faderman, Lillian. *Surpassing the Love of Men: Romantic Friendship and Love between Women from the Renaissance to the Present.* New York: Morrow, 1981.

———. *To Believe in Women: What Lesbians Have Done for America: A History.* Boston: Houghton Mifflin, 1999.

Fishbein, Leslie. *Rebels in Bohemia: The Radicals of the Masses, 1911–1917.* Chapel Hill: University of North Carolina Press, 1982.

Fitzgerald, Sally, ed. *The Habit of Being: Letters of Flannery O'Connor.* New York: Random House, 1979.

Franzen, Trisha. *Spinsters and Lesbians: Independent Womanhood in the United States*. New York: New York University Press, 1996.

Frazer, *The Golden Bough*. 3rd ed. London: Macmillan, 1911.

Gaines, Francis Pendleton. *The Southern Plantation: A Study in the Development and the Accuracy of a Tradition*. Gloucester, Mass.: Peter Smith, 1962.

Gilbert, Sandra M. "Costumes of the Mind: Transvestism as Metaphor in Modern Literature." *Critical Inquiry* 7, no. 2 (Winter 1980): 391–417.

Gilbert, Sandra M., and Susan Gubar. *The Madwoman in the Attic: The Woman Writer and the Nineteenth-Century Literary Imagination*. New Haven: Yale University Press, 1984.

――. *No Man's Land: The Place of the Woman Writer in the Twentieth Century*. Vol. 2, *Sexchanges*. New Haven, Yale University Press, 1989.

Givner, Joan. *Katherine Anne Porter: A Life*. Rev. ed. Athens: University of Georgia Press, 1991.

――, ed. *Katherine Anne Porter: Conversations*. Jackson: University Press of Mississippi, 1987.

Grosz, Elizabeth. "Conclusion: A Note on Essentialism and Difference." In *Feminist Knowledge: Critique and Construct*, edited by Sneja Gunew, 332–44. New York: Routledge, 1990.

Gubar, Susan. "The Birth of the Artist as Heroine: (Re)production, the Kunstlerroman Tradition, and the Fiction of Katherine Mansfield." In *The Representation of Women in Fiction*. Selected Papers from the English Institute, 1981, New Series, no. 7, edited by Carolyn G. Heilbrun and Margaret R. Higonnet, 19–59. Baltimore: Johns Hopkins University Press, 1983.

――. "The Blank Page and the Issues of Female Creativity." *Critical Inquiry* 8 (Winter 1981): 243–63.

――. "Blessings in Disguise: Cross-dressing as Re-dressing for Female Modernists." *Massachusetts Review* 22 (Autumn 1981): 477–94.

Hait, Christine. "Gender and Creativity in Katherine Anne Porter's 'The Princess.'" In *From Texas to the World and Back: Essays on the Journeys of Katherine Anne Porter*, edited by Mark Busby, 199–212. Fort Worth: Texas Christian University Press, 2001.

Hendrick, Wilene, and George Hendrick. *Katherine Anne Porter*. Rev. ed. Boston: G. K. Hall, 1988.

Herndl, Diane Price. "The Dilemmas of a Feminine Dialogic." In *Feminism, Bakhtin, and the Dialogic*, edited by Dale Bauer and Susan Janet McKinstry, 7–24. Albany: SUNY Press, 1991.

Hirsch, Marianne. *The Mother/Daughter Plot: Narrative, Psychoanalysis, Feminism*. Bloomington: Indiana University Press, 1989.

Homans, Margaret. *Bearing the Word: Language and Female Experience in Nineteenth-Century Women's Writing*. Chicago: University of Chicago Press, 1986.

Howard, Clifford. *Sex Worship: An Exposition of the Phallic Origin of Religion.* Chicago: n.p., 1917.

Ice, Joyce. "Women's Aesthetics and the Quilting Process." In *Feminist Theory and the Study of Folklore*, edited by Susan Hollis, Linda Pershing, and M. Jane Young, 166–77. Urbana: University of Illinois Press, 1993.

Ingman, Heather. *Women's Fiction between the Wars: Mothers, Daughters and Writing.* New York: St. Martins, 1998.

Jones, Anne Goodwyn. "Gender and the Great War: The Case of Faulkner and Porter." *Women's Studies* 13 (1986): 135–48.

Kaplan, E. Ann. *Women and Film: Both Sides of the Camera.* London: Methuen, 1985.

Katz, Jonathan Ned. *The Invention of Heterosexuality.* New York: Plume, 1996.

King, Richard. *A Southern Renaissance: The Cultural Awakening of the American South, 1930–1955.* New York: Oxford University Press, 1980.

Knowles, J. Hinton. *Folk-Tales of Kashmir.* 2nd ed. London: Kegan Paul, Trench, Trubner, 1893.

Kramarae, Cheris, and Paula A. Treichler. *A Feminist Dictionary.* Boston: Pandora Press, 1985.

Kristeva, Julia. *Powers of Horror: An Essay on Abjection.* Translated by Leon S. Roudiez. New York: Columbia University Press, 1982.

Langer, Elinor. *Josephine Herbst.* Boston: Little, Brown, 1984.

Levy, Helen Fiddyment. *Fiction of the Home Place.* Jackson: University Press of Mississippi, 1992.

Lopez, Enrique Hank. *Conversations with Katherine Anne Porter: Refugee from Indian Creek.* Boston: Little, Brown, 1981.

Luedtke, Luther S. *Nathaniel Hawthorne and the Romance of the Orient.* Bloomington: Indiana University Press, 1989.

MacKenzie, Donald A. *Indian Myth and Legend.* London: Gresham, 1913.

Marcus, Jane. "Liberty, Sorority, Misogyny." In *The Representation of Women in Fiction: Selected Papers from the English Institute, 1981*, edited by Carolyn Heilbrun and Margaret Higonnet, 60–95. Baltimore: Johns Hopkins University Press, 1983.

Meyer, Moe, ed. *The Politics and Poetics of Camp.* New York: Routledge, 1994.

Mieder, Wolfgang, and Alan Dundes, eds. *The Wisdom of Many: Essays on the Proverb.* New York: Garland, 1981.

Nance, William. *Katherine Anne Porter and the Art of Rejection.* Chapel Hill: University of North Carolina Press, 1964.

Newton, Esther. "The Mythic Mannish Lesbian: Radclyfe Hall and the New Woman." In *Hidden from History: Reclaiming the Gay and Lesbian Past*, edited by Martin Bauml Duberman, Martha Vicinus, and George Chauncey, 281–93. New York: New American Library, 1989.

Nochlin, Linda. *Women, Art, and Power and Other Essays*. New York: Harper and Row, 1988.

Perera, Suvendrini. *Reaches of Empire: The English Novel from Edgeworth to Dickens*. New York: Columbia University Press, 1991.

Pohorilenko, Anatole, and James Crump. *When We Were Three: The Travel Albums of George Platt Lynes, Monroe Wheeler, and Glenway Wescott, 1925–1935*. Santa Fe: Arena Editions, 1998.

Pollock, Griselda. *Vision and Difference: Femininity, Feminism, and the Histories of Art*. London: Routledge, 1988.

Prown, Katherine Hemple. *Revising Flannery O'Connor: Southern Literary Culture and the Problem of Female Authorship*. Charlottesville: University Press of Virginia, 2001.

Ransom, John Crowe. "Reconstructed but Unregenerate." In *I'll Take My Stand: The South and the Agrarian Tradition, by Twelve Southerners*. 1930. Reprint, New York: Harper, 1962, 1–27.

Rollyson, Carl. *Lillian Hellman: Her Legend and Her Legacy*. New York: St. Martins, 1988.

Rooke, Constance, and Bruce Wallis. "Myth and Epiphany in Porter's 'The Grave.'" In *Katherine Anne Porter: Modern Critical Views*, edited by Harold Bloom, 61–68. New York: Chelsea House, 1986.

Rowe, Karen E. "To Spin a Yarn: The Female Voice in Folklore and Fairy Tale." In *Fairy Tales and Society: Illusion, Allusion, and Paradigm*, edited by Ruth Bottigheimer, 53–57. Philadelphia: University of Pennsylvania Press, 1986.

Ruoff, James. "Katherine Anne Porter Comes to Kansas." Reprinted in *Katherine Anne Porter: Conversations*, edited by Givner, 61–68.

Russo, Mary. "Female Grotesques: Carnival and Theory." In *Writing on the Body: Female Embodiment and Feminist Theory*, edited by Katie Conboy, Nadia Medina, and Susan Stanbury, 318–36. New York: Columbia University Press, 1997.

Ruth, Sheila. *Issues in Feminism: An Introduction to Women's Studies*. 3rd ed. Mountain View, Calif.: Mayfield, 1995.

Said, Edward. *Orientalism*. New York: Random House, 1979.

Schwab, Raymond. *The Oriental Renaissance: Europe's Rediscovery of India and the East*. Translated by Gene Patterson Black and Victor Reinking. France, 1950; reprint, New York: Columbia University Press, 1984.

Scott, Bonnie Kime. Introduction to *The Gender of Modernism: A Critical Anthology*, 1–18. Bloomington: Indiana University Press, 1990.

Scott, Shirley. "Origins of Power in the Fiction of Katherine Anne Porter." *Journal of Evolutionary Psychology* 7, nos. 1–2 (1986): 46–56.

Showalter, Elaine. "Piecing and Writing." In *The Poetics of Gender*, edited by Nancy Miller and Carolyn Heilbrun, 222–47. New York: Columbia University Press, 1986.

Simmons, Christina. "Companionate Marriage and the Lesbian Threat." *Frontiers* 4, no. 3 (Fall 1979): 54–59.

———. "Modern Sexuality and the Myth of Victorian Repression." In *Passion and Power: Sexuality in History*, 157–77. Philadelphia: Temple University Press, 1989.

———. "Women's Power in Sex Radical Challenges to Marriage in the Early-Twentieth-Century United States." *Feminist Studies* 29, no. 1 (Spring 2003): 168–99.

Simpson, Lewis P. *The Fable of the Southern Writer.* Baton Rouge: Louisiana State University Press, 1994.

Smith, Stephen. *Gender Thinking.* Philadelphia: Temple University Press, 1992.

Smith-Rosenberg, Carroll. *Disorderly Conduct: Visions of Gender in Victorian America.* New York: Oxford University Press, 1985.

Spence, Jon. "Looking-Glass Reflections: Satirical Elements in *Ship of Fools*." *Sewanee Review* 82, no. 2 (Spring 1974): 316–30; reprinted in *Critical Essays on Katherine Anne Porter*, edited by Unrue, 237–46. New York: G. K. Hall, 1997.

Stout, Janis. *Katherine Anne Porter: A Sense of the Times.* Charlottesville: University Press of Virginia, 1995.

———. "Katherine Anne Porter's 'The Old Order': Writing in the Borderlands." *Studies in Short Fiction* 34, no. 4 (Fall 1997): 493–504.

———. "On Stage at the Great House: Cather, Porter, and the Performance of Southerness." *Southern Studies* 9, no. 4 (Winter 1998): 27–43.

Swann Jones, Steven. *The Fairy Tale: The Magic Mirror of Imagination.* New York: Twayne, 1995.

Tate, Allen. *Collected Poems: 1919–1976.* New York: Farrar, Straus Giroux, 1977.

———. "A New Star." *The Nation* 131 (October 1930): 352–53.

———. "The Profession of Letters in the South." In *Essays of Four Decades*, 517–34. Chicago: Swallow Press, 1968.

Thompson, Barbara. "Interview with Katherine Anne Porter by Barbara Thompson." *Paris Review*, 1963. Reprinted in *Katherine Anne Porter: Conversations*, edited by Givner, 78–98.

Torgovnik, Marianna. *Gone Primitive: Savage Intellects, Modern Lives.* Chicago: University of Chicago Press, 1990.

———. *Primitive Passions: Men, Women, and the Quest for Ecstasy.* New York: Alfred A. Knopf, 1997.

Trimberger, Ellen. "Feminism, Men and Modern Love: Greenwich Village, 1900–1925." In *Powers of Desire: The Politics of Sexuality*, edited by Ann Snitow, Christine Stansell, and Sharon Thompson, 131–52. New York: Monthly Review Press, 1983.

Unrue, Darlene Harbour. "Katherine Anne Porter's Birthdays." In *From Texas to the World and Back: Essays on the Journeys of Katherine Anne Porter*, edited by Mark Busby, 38–53. Fort Worth: Texas Christian University Press, 2001.

———. *Truth and Vision in Katherine Anne Porter's Fiction.* Athens: University of Georgia Press, 1985.

———, ed. *Critical Essays on Katherine Anne Porter.* New York: G. K. Hall, 1997.

Van Leer, David. *The Queening of America: Gay Culture and Straight Society.* New York: Routledge, 1995.

Vickery, John. *The Literary Impact of* The Golden Bough. Princeton: Princeton University Press, 1973.

Waldron, Ann. *Close Connections: Caroline Gordon and the Southern Renaissance.* New York: Putnam, 1987.

Walker, Cheryl. *The Nightingale's Burden: Women Poets and American Culture before 1900.* Bloomington: Indiana University Press, 1982.

Walsh, Thomas. "Braggioni's Songs in 'Flowering Judas.'" *College Literature* 12 (1985): 147–52.

———. *Katherine Anne Porter and Mexico: The Illusion of Eden.* Austin: University of Texas Press, 1992.

Warner, Marina. *From the Beast to the Blonde: On Fairy Tales and Their Tellers.* New York: Farrar, Straus and Giroux, 1995.

Warren, Robert Penn, ed. *Katherine Anne Porter: A Collection of Critical Essays.* Englewood Cliffs, N.J.: Prentice Hall, 1979.

Weiermair, Peter, ed. *George Platt Lynes.* Translated by James Baker. Berlin: Bruno Gmunder, 1989.

Welter, Barbara. "The Cult of True Womanhood: 1820–1860." *American Quarterly* 18, no. 2 (Summer 1966): 151–74.

Wescott, Glenway. *Continual Lessons: The Journals of Glenway Wescott, 1935–1955.* New York: Farrar, Straus Giroux, 1990.

West, Ray B. "Katherine Anne Porter: Symbol and Theme in 'Flowering Judas.'" *Accent* 7 (1947): 182–87; reprinted in *Katherine Anne Porter: A Critical Symposium*, edited by Lodwick Hartley and George Core, 120–28. Athens: University of Georgia Press, 1969.

Wiegman, Robyn. "Object Lessons: Men, Masculinity, and the Sign Women." *Signs* 26, no. 2 (Winter 2001): 355–80.

Willard, T. A. *The City of the Sacred Well.* New York: Grosset and Dunlap, 1926.

Wingrove, Elizabeth. "Interpellating Sex." *Signs* 24, no. 4 (Summer 1999): 869–88.

Yates, Sybille. "An Investigation of the Psychological Factors in Virginity and Ritual Defloration." *The International Journal of Psycho-Analysis* 11 (1930): 167–84.

Young, Thomas Daniel, and John J. Hindle, eds. *The Republic of Letters in America: The Correspondence of John Peale Bishop and Allen Tate.* Lexington: University of Kentucky Press, 1981.

Young, Thomas Daniel, and Elizabeth Sarcone, eds. *The Lytle-Tate Letters.* Jackson: University of Mississippi Press, 1987.

Zipes, Jack. *Fairy Tales and the Art of Subversion: The Classical Genre for Children and the Process of Civilization.* New York: Wildman, 1983.

Zonana, Joyce. "The Sultan and the Slave: Feminist Orientalism and the Structure of Jane Eyre." In *Revising the Word and the World: Essays in Feminist Literary Criticism*, edited by VèVè Clark, Ruth-Ellen Joeres, and Madelon Sprengnether, 165–90. Chicago: University of Chicago Press, 1993.

INDEX

Auden, W. H., 168–69

Auerbach, Nina, 28

authority: female, 28, 40; verbal, 36–39

autobiography: characters in *Ship of Fools* and, 200; fiction and, 180, 185–86; fragments of, 74–78, 209; theory of, 182–83. *See also* Miranda; "Pull Dick—Pull Devil"

Bakhtin, Mikhail, 8, 11, 97–98, 115. *See also* carnival

Barker, Deborah, 7, 50

Barnes, Djuna, 161, 168

Basel, 77, 144

Baton Rouge, 168

Bayley, Isabel, 9

Berger, John, 51

Berlin, 144

Biala, Janice, 79

biological destiny, 17–18, 66

Bishop, John Peale, 189

Bloch, Howard, 19

Bloom, Harold, 188

body: bondage and, 54; control of, 44, 56, 58; as repository of life, 7, 67, 71, 149

Boone family history, 185

Borklund, Elmer, 171

Braidotti, Rosi, 7

Brinkmeyer, Robert, 8, 9, 105, 199

Brontë, Charlotte, 36

burial rites, 81, 87–88

Butler, Judith, 19, 155

Bynum, Caroline Walker, 93

camp, 12, 155, 171, 173, 175. *See also* costume

carnival, 99, 105, 115. *See also* Bakhtin, Mikhail

Carter, Nancy Corson, 84–85

Cather, Willa, 3, 20, 109, 133, 155–57

Catholicism, 42

chastity, female, 130. *See also* virginity

childbirth: as giving legitimacy to women, 6, 14, 48, 122, 147; labor of, 69, 79, 120; as linked with death, 79, 87, 92, 124, 193; Porter's experience with, 11, 121; stillbirth and, 11, 78, 121, 123, 152, 173. *See also* marriage, institution; marriage, Porter's

childlessness, 1, 21, 127, 150–151

"Children of Xochitl," 41, 42, 46

Christian Science Monitor, 41–42

Christian symbols, 57, 59, 93, 126

"Circus, The," 204–5

Clark, Eleanor, 179

clothing. *See* costume

Collected Stories, introduction to, 102

conservatism: Porter's, 12, 132, 155–56, 187, 196; as shown in *Ship of Fools*, 199; and upbringing, 6, 103

costume: gender and, 12, 14, 17, 20, 154–56, 158–61, 166, 187–88; in Lynes's photos, 170–77; as sexual defense, 23, 53; social control and, 18, 164; of Stein, 156; of women artists, 20, 188, 210. *See also* cross-dressing

Cowley, Malcolm, 134, 135, 157, 187

"Cracked Looking Glass, The," 12, 137, 146–151

Crane, Hart, 167

Creation (Rivera mural), 62

creativity: gender and, 3, 39, 40, 50, 112; romantic love and, 136. *See also* artists, female; childbirth

cross-dressing, 5, 12, 166, 171. *See also* costume

Damayanti and Nala, tale of, 29

Dana of the Druids, 41

dancer, 51, 52, 54

dancing, 67, 204; barefoot on broken glass, 58, 67

gender identity: breakdown of, 156, 166; "natural order" and, 18; as performance, 5, 19, 55, 154, 161, 188; war and, 162–164. *See also* artists, female; costume

gender-thinking, Porter's, 8, 10–12, 14, 17, 18, 43, 45, 62, 65, 78, 103, 110, 119, 127, 138, 146, 153, 155, 206, 213; art and, 23, 67, 99; costume and, 158, 161; masculinity and, 163; southern women and, 178, 189. *See also* sexuality

Genesis, 73

gentility. *See* southern gentility, Porter's claim to

German language, 107

"Gerontian," 138

"Gertrude Stein: Three Views," 156

"Gift of Woman, The," 196

Gilbert, Sandra, 7, 8, 21, 109, 110, 154, 188

Gilman, Charlotte, 109

Givner, Joan, 2, 6, 9, 28, 32, 102, 104, 109, 126, 146, 151, 165, 175; mentioned, 79, 120, 166, 185, 196

gluttony, 51, 54, 63, 67

goddess figures. *See* religion: female deities

Goldenweiser, Alexander, 48, 68

Gordon, Caroline, 76, 179, 181, 185, 190, 199, 210–12

grandmother, Porter's. *See* Porter, Catherine Ann Skaggs

grave (burial place), 75, 77–78, 80–82, 85, 195. *See also* death

"Grave, The," 90–95, 118–19, 194; mentioned, 11, 76, 78, 85, 126, 180

Gray, Jane, 173–75

Great Gatsby, The (Fitzgerald), closing echoed, 145

Greenwich Village (New York), 129, 134, 137, 145–46

Guanyin. *See* Kwanyin

Gubar, Susan, 7, 8, 19, 21, 109, 110, 155, 188

H. D., 188

"Hacienda," 158–61; mentioned, 12, 155, 168–69, 173

Hades, 86, 89

handicapped daughter, in "Holiday," 110. *See also* deformity

Harrison, Barbara, 168

Hartley, Lodwick, 194

Hellman, Lillian, 188

Hemingway, Ernest, 135

Herbst, Josephine, 151–52

"Here Is My Home," 74, 80–81, 95–96

heretic, Princess as, 16, 18. *See also* religion

heterosexual relationships, 12, 28, 134; as serving the state, 162; violence in, 62, 202, 205, 208, 211. *See also* dominance, male

Hinkle, Beatrice M., 48–49

Hirsch, Marianne, 8, 84–85

"Holiday": attic in, 108–10, 111; carnival in, 99, 115–116; death of mother in, 113; gender roles and, 106–7, 112–13, 162–63; interpretations of, 100–101, 104, 107, 114; language and, 107–8; Ottilie as narrator's double in, 110, 111–12, 114; writing of, 101–3, 109–10, 117, 120–21; mentioned, 9, 11

Holloway, Gay Porter, 3, 26, 79, 103, 185

Holloway, Mary Alice, 86, 103, 122, 126

Hollywood, 175

homelessness, 28, 35, 54, 73–74, 81, 138, 157, 183. *See also* alienation; exile

homesickness, 34–35, 72–75, 79–80, 95

homophobia, 12, 114, 155–56, 164, 166–68, 175–76

homosexuality, 12; in Porter's literary criticism, 155–56, 166; of Porter's male friends, 166, 168–69, 175, 177; as sign of social disorder, 159–160. *See also* homophobia; gender identity

Horton, Philip, 167

independence, 12, 23, 45, 67, 136, 162. *See also* freedom

Indian Creek, Texas, 2, 69, 79–81, 103, 133, 178, 181–82, 184

influenza, 158, 165

Ingman, Heather, 70–71

interviews with Porter: with Lopez in *Conversations*, 168; in 1969, 196; in *Paris Review* (1963), 80, 165, 188

Iowa Writers' Workshop, 181

Ix-Lol-Nicte, 16

Jane Eyre (Brontë), 36, 109

Johnson, Rhea, 102

Jones, Anne Goodwyn, 107, 180

Jones, Mary Alice. *See* Porter, Mary Alice Jones

Jones, Swann, 31

Joyce, James, 137, 146–47

Juliet, as played by Porter, 175–77

Kaplan, E. Ann, 52, 60

King, Richard, 179

Knowles, J. Hinton, 30

Koontz, Henry, 104

Koontz, John, 103, 133

Kopald, Sylvia, 48

Kristeva, Julia, 77

Kwanyin (Guanyin), 41

Lacan, Jacques, 72

Ladies' Home Journal (1971), 152

lady. *See* southern gentility, Porter's claim to

language: Lacanian theory of, 72; men's controlling, 26, 33, 34, 55, 59–63, 108, 131, 181; 61; misogynist, 36–38; *See also* mother tongue, defined; storytellers

Last Judgment, The (Fra Angelico), 126

laughter, 16, 18, 20, 97–99, 116, 135, 203

Lawrence, D. H., 40, 135

legend and memory, 75–78, 90–91, 95, 182–83, 185–86, 190, 192, 196

Leonardo Da Vinci, 173

lesbians, 5, 114, 159–160, 167, 187. *See also* gay community; homophobia; homosexuality

Life of Saint Rose, The (Storm), 7, 67, 71, 149

"Little Incident in the Rue de l'Odéon, A," 135

loneliness, 27, 73, 99, 136, 198. *See also* alienation

Lopez, Enrique, 168

love, 23, 27, 52, 55, 65, 101, 123–24, 128, 196, 198, 209; death of, in modern world, 137, 141, 143, 145; "Love and Hate," 206–8; romantic, 8, 59–60, 136, 144, 147–148, 177, 195, 206; and woman artist, 22, 118, 129, 131, 136, 143, 213

"Love Song of J. Alfred Prufrock, The" (Eliot), 137–38, 145

"Lovely Legend, The" (unfinished story), 58, 62–65; mentioned, 11, 136, 211

Lyceum Circuit, 3

Lynes, George Platt, 155, 168–77, 187

Lytle, Andrew, 179, 181–82, 190

MacKenzie, Donald A., 29

madness, 2, 16, 21, 22, 108–11, 120–121

"Magic Ear Ring, The," 11, 27, 29, 30–31, 34

Mailer, Norman, 135

Mansfield, Katherine, 135

Nightwood (Barnes), 161, 168
"Noon Wine," 80
"Noon Wine: The Sources," 183
"Notes on Writing," 75

objectification, 51–54, 62–64, 67. *See also* sadomasochism; women, as artist's models
O'Connor, Flannery, 12, 181, 193
Old Mortality, 12, 78, 182, 184, 189–95; mentioned, 4, 6, 35, 119, 171, 197, 209
Old Order, The, 76–78, 85–86, 104; mentioned, 6, 80, 82, 90, 95, 182, 184, 203
Oriental tales, retold, 29, 36–39
Ovid, 25

"Pale Horse, Pale Rider," 11, 122–24, 144–45, 161–66, 171; mentioned, 6, 9, 119, 127–28, 137, 150, 158, 169, 177, 189
Paris, 2, 133, 144, 82, 168, 182, 213
Paris Review interview, 80, 182, 188
patriarchal authority: control of female sexuality by, 18, 49, 59; in "Hacienda," 160; in "Holiday," 101, 105, 110; in Koontz household, 104; men and, 47; in "The Princess," 20; revisions of, 21. *See also* dominance, male
Persephone, Demeter and myth of, 83–86, 89, 127
Pitts, Rebecca, 167
plantation legend, 184
Poe, Edgar Allen, 136, 192–93
poet, 167, 213; male, 24, 26, 56, 57–61, 64–66, 136, 193. *See also individual poets by name*
poetry, Porter's, 9, 11, 81–84, 123, 131–32
Pollock, Griselda, 50–51
Porter, Catherine Ann Skaggs (grandmother), 3, 178, 182–83; mentioned, 69, 74, 81
Porter, Harrison Boone (father), 3, 78–79, 136, 184

Porter, Katherine Anne (born Callie): childhood of 3, 78–80, 133, 179, 183–84, 186; education of, 3, 32–33, 133; as Jenny Brown in *Ship of Fools*, 198; as performer, 3, 6, 9, 20, 172–73, 175, 178, 182, 187–90; photos of, by Lynes, 170–77; relationship of, to family, 3, 35, 75, 80, 86–87, 125, 183, 185; relationships of, with heterosexual men, 12, 66, 120, 130, 134, 136, 145–46, 151; relationships of, with homosexual men, 12, 155, 166–70, 175–77; sexual liberation and, 5–6, 130, 135–37; stillborn child of, 121. *See also* gender-thinking, Porter's; marriage, Porter's; Miranda; southern gentility, Porter's claim to
Porter, Mary Alice Jones (mother), 3, 71, 74, 78–79, 83, 136, 184
Porter, Paul (nephew), 70
Porter's family, 3, 35, 75, 183, 185
"Portrait: Old South," 183
pregnancy, 42, 79, 120, 123. *See also* childbirth; motherhood
Pressly, Eugene, 198
primitivism, 11, 17, 39–42, 45
"Princess, The" (unfinished story): female artist in, 14–16, 19–26; gender roles and sexuality in, 14–15, 17–19, 20–22, 26; madness in, 15–16, 20–21; nature in, 14, 15, 17–18, 107; religion in, 14–18; mentioned, 1, 10, 27, 47, 69, 97, 118, 129, 154, 178, 198
prodigal son, 83–84
proverbs, 37–38
Prown, Katherine Hemple, 181, 195
"Pull Dick—Pull Devil," 3, 78–79, 183–84

quilting, 76–77, 190

racism. *See* white racial supremacy
Ramsay, Allan, 36